'Alexei Navalny's media image is black-and-white: for Kremlin, an arch-enemy of the state. This book fills in the question of whether Navalny is a "nationalist". Spr tions on what draws Russians to his protests and how th ..... repression" to keep them at home. A detailed examination of Russia's most famous opposition activist, politician, and protester—and why the Kremlin wants to silence him.'

Jill Dougherty, Global Fellow at the Kennan Institute, and former CNN Foreign Affairs Correspondent and Moscow Bureau Chief

'Demonised, harassed, poisoned, arrested, imprisoned: Alexei Navalny is not only Putin's most persistent and arguably bravest critic, but as this eye-opening and very readable book demonstrates, he proves the growing hunger for change in today's Russia.'

Mark Galeotti, author of *We Need To Talk About Putin*

'For anyone who wants to know who Alexei Navalny is, what drives him, and what his ultimate goal is, this well-researched and in-depth new biography of Russia's most famous dissident tells the story of the man who has managed to rattle Putin more than any other threat.'

Bianna Golodryga, Senior Global Affairs Analyst, CNN

'Perhaps the only Russian politician shrouded in more myth than Vladimir Putin is Alexei Navalny. Hounded by a range of varyingly dubious descriptors—from "courageous democratiser" to "retrograde chauvinist" and everything in between—the truth of the man who has emerged as the leader of Russia's beleaguered opposition is largely an untold story. Untold, that is, until now. With equal measures of depth, nuance, and flair, Dollbaum, Lallouet, and Noble have produced the definitive political biography of arguably the most consequential figure in Russian politics today. Anyone who cares about the future of Russian politics needs to read this book.'

Samuel Greene, Professor of Russian Politics, King's College London

'This book is a timely and expertly-written biographical and political analysis of Alexei Navalny as the emergent force to be reckoned with in Russian politics—very appropriately produced by three rising stars in European academia and foreign affairs. The authors deploy their formidable collective talents to delve into and explain the specifically Russian context of Navalny's brand of activism. They provide a critical commentary on his personality and popularity, including the reactions he elicits from those who know and work with him, or follow his lead. This is not just a book about Navalny's struggles with the Kremlin, it is the essential primer for anyone outside Russia trying to understand this astonishingly brave and complicated man and the role he plays in contemporary Russia.'

Fiona Hill, Senior Fellow at the Brookings Institution, and former advisor on Europe and Russia, US National Security Council

'A clear, accessible account of one of President Putin's most prominent opponents, Alexei Navalny; a balanced overview to help the general reader make sense of the seething political undercurrents in Russia today.'

Bridget Kendall, Master of Peterhouse, Cambridge, and former BBC Diplomatic Correspondent

'At a moment when Alexei Navalny has emerged as a global figure in his fight from captivity for Russian democracy, Jan Matti Dollbaum, Morvan Lallouet, and Ben Noble have provided the world with a tremendous service by writing the first comprehensive account of the country's most important opposition leader. Filled with facts and devoid of hyperbole, the book offers a complete portrayal of Navalny, as an anti-corruption activist, politician, and protester. *Navalny: Putin's Nemesis, Russia's Future?* is a must read for anyone who wants to learn what Alexei Navalny actually does and believes, and what he might do to shape Russia's future.'

Michael McFaul, author of *From Cold War to Hot Peace: An American Ambassador in Putin's Russia*

'The story of Alexei Navalny is, in part, the unfinished story of David and Goliath: the story of how a bold, creative, and purposeful man repeatedly outplayed the huge state machine. Navalny's fight with a team of like-minded people for the "wonderful Russia of the future" is by definition an optimistic view of the country's development prospects. Rarely does a book written about Russia by Western authors combine a deep and subtle knowledge of developments in the country with such accuracy and timeliness. But that is exactly what this book does. Having provided a complex, multidimensional portrait of Navalny, the authors have also written a comprehensive and essential book on Russian political life—and one not limited to Moscow, but showing the country in its regional diversity, replete with interesting details and presented in very accessible language.'

Nikolay Petrov, Senior Research Fellow of the Russia and Eurasia Programme at Chatham House, and Professor in the Department of Political Science at the Higher School of Economics, Moscow

'A brilliant and highly readable analysis of the most compelling political figure to emerge from Russia in many years. The authors explain who Navalny is, what he stands for, and why he matters. In an era when authoritarianism and strongman politics are advancing all over the world, Navalny is a figure of global significance.'

Gideon Rachman, Chief Foreign Affairs Commentator, *Financial Times*

'Essential reading for anyone interested in the present and future of Russia. This book is less a biography than a primer on the central battle in Russian politics today—the battle, in Navalny's own words, "between good and neutrality". Written in a direct and accessible style by three rising stars of Russian studies, the story is organised around Navalny the anti-corruption activist, the politician, and the protester and uses each of these lenses to draw a sophisticated portrait of the economy, politics, and society in Russia today. While always retaining a sharp and critical eye on its main subject with close readings of the historical record, *Navalny* is nonetheless a story of the personal heroism and political strategies of Alexei Navalny, his team, and the many other brave people taking huge personal risks to fight corruption and promote democracy in Russia today.'

Graeme Robertson, Professor of Political Science, University of North Carolina at Chapel Hill

'A timely and important study of the man, the movement, and the context, based on detailed analysis and balanced judgement. An indispensable contribution to our understanding of contemporary Russian politics.'

Richard Sakwa, Professor of Russian and European Politics, University of Kent, and author of *The Putin Paradox*

'This timely book tells the complex story of Navalny in an accessible conversational style. The trio behind this study—all academics with longstanding Russia expertise—discuss Navalny as an activist, a politician, and a protester and clearly situate him in his wider political and societal context. The book deserves a wide readership, as it furthers a more nuanced understanding of Navalny and contemporary Russia.'

Gwendolyn Sasse, Professor and Director of the
Centre for East European and International Studies (ZOiS), Berlin

'A refreshingly meticulous and detail-filled investigation of a compelling political drama that unfolds across the pages. Readers accustomed to a Putin-centric view of Russian politics—with few actors on stage beyond the president—will likely find a very different take on Russian civil society and the country's political milieu in this book. Even if it does not give a final answer to the "Navalny question"—something that would, anyway, be impossible at this stage—the book has the great merit of presenting to an English-reading public an analytical account of the people and processes that are nothing if not complicated in modern-day Russia.'

Ekaterina Schulmann, Associate Fellow of the Russia and Eurasia Programme at
Chatham House, and Associate Professor at the Moscow School of Social
and Economic Sciences

'A candid and thorough dissection of Alexei Navalny's political views, a Russian politician brave enough to challenge Putin. The book provides a much-needed portrait of this leader of the first grassroots opposition movement in modern Russia.'

Andrei Soldatov and Irina Borogan, authors of *The Compatriots* and *The Red Web*

NAVALNY

JAN MATTI DOLLBAUM
MORVAN LALLOUET
BEN NOBLE

Navalny

Putin's Nemesis, Russia's Future?

OXFORD
UNIVERSITY PRESS

OXFORD
UNIVERSITY PRESS

Oxford University Press is a department of the
University of Oxford. It furthers the University's objective
of excellence in research, scholarship, and education
by publishing worldwide.

Oxford   New York

Auckland   Cape Town   Dar es Salaam   Hong Kong   Karachi
Kuala Lumpur   Madrid   Melbourne   Mexico City   Nairobi
New Delhi   Shanghai   Taipei   Toronto

With offices in

Argentina   Austria   Brazil   Chile   Czech Republic   France   Greece
Guatemala   Hungary   Italy   Japan   Poland   Portugal   Singapore
South Korea   Switzerland   Thailand   Turkey   Ukraine   Vietnam

Oxford is a registered trade mark of Oxford University Press
in the UK and certain other countries.

Published in the United States of America by
Oxford University Press
198 Madison Avenue, New York, NY 10016

Library of Congress Cataloging-in-Publication Data is available
Jan Matti Dollbaum, Morvan Lallouet and Ben Noble.
Navalny: Putin's Nemesis, Russia's Future?
ISBN: 9780197680667

Printed in the United Kingdom on acid-free paper
by Bell and Bain Ltd, Glasgow

CONTENTS

ACKNOWLEDGEMENTS

'Can you recommend an English-language book on Alexei Navalny?' With his return to Russia in 2021, there was clear demand for more information about Navalny and the movement he has built. But the answer to the question was clear: 'No—because nobody's written that book yet.' This is our attempt to fill the gap.

We thank everybody who has helped create this book—whether they know it or not—by giving general guidance on the publishing process, providing invaluable contacts or background information, commenting on different drafts of the manuscript, or by providing indispensable material and moral support: Laure Assumpçao, Golineh Atai, Anatole Barde, Vsevolod Bederson, Reinhard Beule, Barbara Brown, Biggi Dollbaum, Brigitte Evano, Clara Ferreira Marques, Seán Hanley, Acika Kaurin, Irina Kozlova, Fyodor Krasheninnikov, Yuri Kuzminykh, François Lallouet, Masha Lipman, Edward Morgan-Jones, Catherine Noble, Christopher Noble, Nikolay Petrov, Heiko Pleines, Graeme Robertson, David Roth-Ey, Kristin Roth-Ey, Richard Sakwa, Masha Sibiryakova, Regina Smyth, Cloé Tralci, and Sarah Ulysse.

There isn't space here to list and personally thank the many, many journalists in Russia—and abroad—on whose reporting we draw. But, at a time when independent journalism faces increas-

ACKNOWLEDGEMENTS

ing pressure in Russia, we can say confidently that this book would not exist without their work.

The book also wouldn't have been possible without our agent, Euan Thorneycroft of A M Heath; Erik Riemenschneider of Hoffmann und Campe, with whom we secured the first publishing deal; and, last but not least, Michael Dwyer of Hurst Publishers. We can't thank them and their teams enough for helping turn this project from an idea hatched at the end of January 2021 into a finished book: Alison Alexanian, Vickie Dillon, Alex Elam, Mairi Friesen-Escandell, Gosia Jezierska, Jessica Lee, Daisy Leitch, Kathleen May, Alexandra McNicoll, Tim Page, and Prema Raj.

We are also grateful to various institutions for support. Jan Matti Dollbaum's field research was part of the research project 'Comparing Protest Actions in Soviet and Post-Soviet Spaces', organised by the Research Centre for East European Studies at the University of Bremen with financial support from the Volkswagen Foundation. It has also been funded by the German Academic Exchange Service and grants from the University of Bremen.

Morvan Lallouet thanks the University of Kent and the Economic and Social Research Council (ESRC) for supporting and funding the research that appears in this book.

Ben Noble thanks staff and students at the UCL School of Slavonic and East European Studies (SSEES) for their support and patience during the time the book was written. He also gratefully acknowledges support from the Basic Research Programme of the National Research University Higher School of Economics, Moscow.

It goes without saying that none of the people listed above—who have helped the authors in various ways—bear responsibility for any problems with the content of the book. However, each of the three authors blames the other two for any errors remaining!

WHO IS ALEXEI NAVALNY?

'Aren't you afraid?'

Alexei Navalny faces this question as he boards Pobeda ('Victory') Airlines flight DP936 at Berlin Brandenburg Airport. It's Sunday, 17 January 2021.[1]

The plane is packed with journalists eager to accompany Navalny—the forty-four-year-old anti-corruption activist and opposition politician—on his journey home. Entering the cabin with his wife, lawyer, and press secretary, he encounters a sea of smartphones held up to capture and livestream the moment. The world is watching.

Navalny is upbeat and optimistic. But he clearly has reasons to be afraid. Russian law enforcement had earlier warned he would be detained upon his return to Russia, accusing him of violating parole conditions for a 2014 fraud conviction. He faced years in prison.

That Navalny was able to walk on to a plane at all was a miracle. The last time he'd boarded a flight on his own was in Tomsk, Siberia, on 20 August 2020, for what should have been a routine trip back to Moscow. He'd been working on an investigation into the business activities of officials and municipal politicians in Tomsk.[2] He'd also been campaigning with opposition forces in the run-up to regional and local elections on 13 September—polls in which he hoped to secure victories against candidates backed by the authorities.

But things started to go wrong during the flight. Navalny became ill, eventually howling with what appeared to be agonising pain.[3] According to one passenger, Navalny 'wasn't saying any words—he was just screaming'.[4] A flight attendant asked if there were any medical professionals on board. A nurse came forward. Along with the cabin crew, she administered first aid—and tried to keep Navalny conscious.

The pilot decided to make an emergency landing in Omsk—around 750 kilometres west of Tomsk, but still in Siberia—despite a mysterious bomb scare at the airport.[5] Navalny was stretchered off the plane and taken by ambulance to an emergency hospital.

Navalny's press secretary, Kira Yarmysh, said that the only thing Navalny had eaten or drunk that day was black tea from a plastic cup at the airport before his flight—and that this might have been laced with poison.[6] Navalny was, it seemed, a fit man with no known health problems, who didn't smoke and drank little—not the profile of somebody likely to become suddenly unwell.

Yarmysh's fear was worryingly familiar to those following Russian politics. In previous years, personalities critical of the Kremlin had fallen ill—and suspicions were rife that they had been poisoned.[7] At the same time, Navalny had made many enemies with his investigations into elite corruption—businesspeople, local politicians, high officials.[8] The list of potential suspects was long.

On arrival at hospital, it was reported that Navalny received a preliminary diagnosis of 'acute psychodysleptic poisoning'.[9] He was put on a ventilator, placed into a medically induced coma, and administered atropine.[10] His condition was described as 'serious but stable'.[11] Normal medical processes were taking their course.

But then things took an odd turn.

The hospital began to fill with law enforcement personnel, some in plain clothes.[12] And they started confiscating Navalny's personal belongings, Yarmysh said.[13]

When the plane Navalny had been on finally reached Moscow, law enforcement officials were waiting to board the aircraft. They instructed passengers who had been sitting closest to Navalny to stay put while others disembarked. This struck one passenger as puzzling: 'At that point, the case did not look criminal ... [and yet] security officials clearly thought the incident to be criminal all the same.'[14]

Back in Omsk, Navalny's wife, Yulia, faced difficulties in getting to her husband—because, the hospital authorities said, he had not explicitly consented to her visit.[15] And doctors became less forthcoming about Navalny's condition with his team, who wanted to move him to Germany for treatment. On 21 August—that is, a day after Navalny was hospitalised—a plane ready to transport him to Berlin's Charité Hospital landed in Omsk.

A strange incident was also reported by Ivan Zhdanov—a close associate of Navalny—and Yulia Navalnaya. They claimed that, during a conversation with the head of the hospital, a police-woman said that a substance dangerous both to Navalny and others around him 'had been found'.[16] But she declined to name it, as it was an 'investigative secret'.[17]

On the same day, a national Russian newspaper published a sensational story. Citing anonymous sources, it claimed that law enforcement personnel had been trailing Navalny in Tomsk. Had he been poisoned? The sources reported that 'no unnecessary or suspicious contacts that could be linked with poisoning' had been seen.[18] The story was widely interpreted to be a controlled leak from Russia's Federal Security Service (FSB) to distance itself from the incident.[19]

Meanwhile, doctors in Omsk revised their initial diagnosis.[20] They now said that Navalny was experiencing the effects of a serious metabolic disorder, not the effects of poisoning. The hospital's chief physician said this 'may have been caused by a sharp drop in blood sugar in the plane, which led to the loss of consciousness'.[21] Doctors also now said that the substance found in samples from Navalny's hands and hair was a common industrial component and could have come from a plastic cup.[22] And yet, they now thought that Navalny's condition was 'unstable', and it would be inappropriate to fly him to Germany.

Navalny's personal doctor saw a clear motive: '[T]hey are waiting three days so that there are no traces of poison left in the body.'[23] Yulia Navalnaya appealed directly to Vladimir Putin for permission to fly her husband abroad.[24]

After facing initial resistance, German medics were allowed access to Navalny—and said he was in a suitable state to be flown to Berlin. And Russian doctors gave their consent, too, saying that his condition had 'stabilised'. The plane took off from Omsk with Navalny on 22 August.

Two days after arriving in Berlin, German doctors said that they believed Navalny had been poisoned with a cholinesterase inhibitor—a substance that interferes with the nervous system.[25] The source could have been an everyday pesticide—or a weapons-grade nerve agent. This news, therefore, increased suspicions relating to the Russian state.[26]

But Russian officials pushed back against the increasing number of fingers pointing at them. 'WHY would we do it? And in such a clumsy inconclusive way?'—so tweeted one of Russia's top diplomats at the UN on 24 August.[27] In early September, the speaker of the State Duma—the lower chamber of the Russian parliament—claimed the reaction of the West to the 'alleged' poisoning was a 'planned action against Russia in order to impose new sanctions and to try to hold back the development of our country'.[28]

Meanwhile, police authorities in Russia seemed in no hurry to investigate the incident. The regional transport police—far from a top law enforcement body—carried out a 'preliminary investigation'.[29] The hotel where Navalny had stayed in Tomsk was inspected by police and FSB officers, but the local press mentioned this lasted only a 'couple of days'. To Navalny's associates who were questioned by the police, everything pointed to inaction—or worse, a cover-up.[30]

On 2 September, German Chancellor Angela Merkel asserted it was 'beyond doubt' that Navalny had been poisoned with a nerve agent of the Novichok group—a finding later confirmed by the Organisation for the Prohibition of Chemical Weapons.[31] This was the same type of nerve agent used against Sergei and Yulia Skripal in Salisbury, England, in March 2018—an attack the British government said was 'overwhelmingly likely' to have been ordered by President Putin.[32]

As with this earlier poisoning episode, the international reaction to Navalny's case became increasingly loud and critical of the Russian state. Merkel claimed the poisoning raised 'very serious questions that only the Russian government can answer—and must answer'.[33] In response, the Russian authorities said that the alleged proof of the poisoning had been found in Germany—and it was, therefore, for the German authorities to cooperate with Russia and produce the corroborating evidence.[34]

In addition, a number of narratives emerged on state-aligned Russian media to contest the international accusations. Some questioned whether there was any poisoning at all—one Russian journalist wrote a whole book on the topic.[35] Others said that, while Navalny might have been poisoned, Novichok was not used. So claimed the chemist Leonid Rink, who had worked on the Novichok programme himself—and had even, according to his own testimony, sold doses of the substance to criminal groups in the 1990s.[36] Navalny couldn't have been poisoned by the nerve agent because, if he had, Rink argued, Navalny would be dead.[37] However, another chemist who had participated in the creation of Novichok found the symptoms Navalny experienced to be consistent with poisoning by the nerve agent.[38]

Yet another theory was that, although Novichok might have been used, it was not administered in Russia but in Germany. This version was voiced by Andrei Lugovoy—a member of the Russian parliament and a prime suspect in the 2006 assassination of a former FSB agent, Alexander Litvinenko, with polonium-210 in London.[39]

By 7 September, Navalny was out of a coma, making an incredibly speedy recovery. He was discharged from hospital on 23 September and then spent time rehabilitating in the Black Forest.[40]

Months passed. Navalny built up his strength, one push-up at a time. Elsewhere, others were busy investigating his poisoning. How was it carried out—and by whom?

On 14 December, Bellingcat—an online investigative journalism collective—released the findings of its investigation carried out with a Russian partner, The Insider, and in collaboration with CNN and *Der Spiegel*.[41] Navalny, it claimed, had been poisoned by an FSB assassination team—a 'clandestine unit specialized in working with poisonous substances'—which had been tracking him for years, and had possibly tried to poison him previously.

Drawing on leaked phone records and flight manifests, the investigation tracked the movement of these FSB operatives—which often mapped uncannily onto the movements of Navalny himself.

If things had been sensational up to this point, they soon became surreal. On 21 December, Navalny released a video of a phone call that took place just before the Bellingcat investigation was released.[42] In it, Navalny spoke to somebody the investigation claimed was involved in the attempt on his life with Novichok—Konstantin Kudryavtsev. Pretending to be an assistant of the former head of the FSB, Navalny managed to get Kudryavtsev to reveal operational details. 'The underpants ... the inner side ... where the groin is'—that's where the the concentration of the substance was highest, said Kudryavtsev.[43]

Even more fingers now pointed to the Kremlin. In response, Putin quipped on 17 December that, if the FSB had wanted to kill Navalny, 'they would have got the job done'.[44] While for some this did not look at all like a full rejection of the accusation, Russian authorities denied their involvement vehemently. But they showed little interest in finding out who was responsible. No criminal case was launched.

According to one of Navalny's long-time collaborators, Navalny 'became more and more convinced of the involvement of Putin in his poisoning', and, therefore, 'more and more focused on trying to expose' the president.[45] In addition to the phone call with one of his alleged poisoners, this also meant digging deeper into allegations of Putin's own corruption—of his alleged hidden wealth. And this was a clear shift on Navalny's part: according to a close associate, 'Alexei used to say that when we write about Putin, it will be our last investigation'—it would cross a red line and incur the wrath of the president.[46]

Navalny announced his plan to return to Russia on 13 January 2021.[47] He said he never questioned whether he would return: he hadn't decided to leave Russia, but ended up in Germany following an attempt on his life. He was not returning from exile, but simply finishing his interrupted journey to Moscow, begun all the way back on 20 August 2020 in Tomsk.

* * *

After making his way past the throng of journalists on the Pobeda Airlines flight on 17 January, Navalny takes his seat, with his wife next to him. As the plane flies eastwards to Moscow, the couple pass the time by watching *Rick and Morty*—a US animated comedy series. The contrast with the weight of the moment could hardly be starker.

Who is Alexei Navalny?

Navalny's return to Russia in January 2021 saw much Manichean commentary—of white versus black, good versus evil, Navalny versus Putin. This pared-down script is commonplace in Western commentary on Russia—a possible hangover from the Cold War's binary political logic. Or it forms part of a longer tradition, 'othering' Russia as a dark and mysterious foreign land where dictators rule over enslaved masses—a view shaped by ideology, but also ignorance.

This simple narrative quickly ran into trouble, however. In January, Amnesty International declared Navalny a 'prisoner of conscience'.[48] But, a few weeks later, the human rights NGO decided to revoke its decision—something that confused people who had thought of Navalny as an unblemished hero, willing to take on Putin. Amnesty's decision related to past comments by Navalny, which the organisation concluded 'amounted to advocacy of hatred that constitutes incitement to discrimination, violence or hostility'.[49]

Beyond these general moral evaluations, Navalny was also being compared to historical figures. Media coverage was peppered with attempts to compare Navalny to people, both from Russia and beyond. Is he the Nelson Mandela or the Aleksandr Solzhenitsyn of modern-day Russia? But these comparisons obscure more than they reveal. Navalny is Navalny. And the urge to find parallels might, in fact, reveal the paucity of knowledge about him outside Russia.

In order to understand him, we need to go—briefly—to the very beginning.

WHO IS ALEXEI NAVALNY?

Navalny before Navalny

Alexei Navalny was born on 4 June 1976 in Butyn—a village to the west of Moscow. His father was an officer in the Soviet Army, his mother an accountant. In his youth, Navalny's family would follow the frequent moves of his father, from one military town to the next.

Not everyone in Navalny's family supported the Soviet system wholeheartedly. His father listened to Voice of America; his grandmother passionately hated Lenin.[50] And Navalny's family had the opportunity to see first hand one of the major failings of the system: his father came from Ukraine, and the young Navalny spent most of his summers at his grandmother's house in a village near Chernobyl. He stopped going there when the region became uninhabitable in 1986.[51]

When the Soviet Union collapsed in 1991, Navalny was fifteen. The USSR didn't leave him with many good memories: when talking about it, he recalled mostly the queues for basic products. He also remembered the hypocrisy of card-carrying communists: they praised the system the loudest but were also those who looked to the West with the most envy. Beneath the ideals, the Soviet Union that Navalny knew was, he thought, just hypocrisy—just 'games and tricks'.[52]

Navalny, then, had no illusions about communism. He was a fan of rock music and watched popular television programmes that were critical of the Soviet system. All this, Navalny claims, gave him his first political identity. 'At seventeen it seemed to me that my political views were formed. And I proudly proclaimed them to everyone.'[53] Navalny was a liberal.

The word 'liberal' means different things in different contexts—its use in the United States, for example, varies markedly from its meaning in the United Kingdom. In the Russia of the 1990s, it designated those who sought to transform the country into a free-market economy and a rule-of-law democracy along Western lines. Liberals, whatever their disagreements, shared this basic goal—and all were staunchly anti-Soviet.

The specifics were then more complicated. Some liberals were in power, others in the opposition. Some called themselves 'liberals', others 'democrats'. Some were technocrats, others intellectuals or grassroots activists. Some favoured a gradual transition to capitalism, others a radical 'shock therapy'. Some were principled democrats, others thought that Russia needed a strong hand to achieve its transition to liberal democracy and capitalism.

In his youth, Navalny supported the radical kind of liberalism. He backed Boris Yeltsin—the first president of Russia—and his team of reformers. By Navalny's own admission, he loudly approved of Yeltsin's economic reforms despite all the suffering they inflicted on the most vulnerable in society. And he had few issues with the authoritarian tendencies of the Yeltsin administration. But he would later regret this support—and acknowledge that reformers had sown the seeds of Putin's authoritarian rule.[54]

In 1993, immediately after finishing school, Navalny entered the Peoples' Friendship University of Russia (RUDN) in Moscow, just missing out on admission to the most prestigious university in the country, Moscow State University. He studied law, and then got another degree—in securities and stocks trading. At RUDN, Navalny claims he began harbouring doubts about liberalism—and veering towards nationalism.

Liberal parties in Russia were at that point already in decline. And it seemed to Navalny that the 'liberal project' didn't appeal to people anymore. Why? Because Russian-style liberals were, for him, even more socially liberal than their European counterparts—especially on the issue of immigration.[55]

Even though Navalny held strong political views and followed the news, he was not an activist at this point. At university, he thought his priorities were to 'get an education, find a job, and get rich quick'.[56] He started working young, while he was still studying. His first job was at Aeroflot Bank; he then moved to a real estate development company.[57] 'Working there taught me how things are done on the inside, how intermediary companies are built, how money is shuttled around', he told journalist Julia Ioffe in 2011.[58]

At the turn of the 1990s and the 2000s, Navalny worked as a lawyer, invested in stocks, and created several businesses. This work allowed him to earn sums unheard of by most Russians. In 'good months', he could make between US$4,000 and $5,000.[59] And Navalny's parents also joined the ranks of the new middle class of the 1990s, becoming owners of a wicker factory in the Moscow Region.

Navalny is well educated and well read. But, as pointed out by writer Keith Gessen, he 'is not from the intelligentsia'. For a start, military career officers—like Navalny's father—are not counted as such in Russia. But Navalny's style also sets him apart:

> Navalny is extremely intelligent, articulate, and even a very good writer ... but he doesn't have that particular form of politeness, circumlocution, over-thoughtfulness [that is associated with the intelligentsia] ... There is no hidden depth, no internal dialogue that Navalny, when he speaks, is trying to distill. What he says is what he thinks; what you see is what you get.[60]

At the same time, Navalny appears to be imbued with a deep feeling of moral certainty. And many of his slogans testify to this. The subtitle of his blog was once 'the final battle between good and neutrality', and he usually concludes his YouTube videos with the line 'Subscribe to our channel. Here we tell the truth.' After his poisoning in 2020, Navalny was asked 'where does power lie?'—a cult line from a 1990s Russian movie. And he answered, without a flicker of hesitation, as the hero of the film had answered: 'Power lies, of course, in truth. Excuse me that this is so trivial, but power lies in truth, and in self-belief.'[61]

Navalny is a politician. He has, over the years, cultivated a public persona—one reminiscent of democratic, centre-right politicians in the West.

He's a family man—and quite a traditional one at that. Though not a church-goer, Navalny is an Orthodox Christian. He has, since 2000, been married to Yulia Navalnaya (née Abrosimova); they met a few years earlier while on holiday in Turkey. Yulia studied international economics, but worked only for a short time, opting to take care of life at home with their two children, Daria (born 2001) and Zakhar (born 2008).[62] She considers herself to be 'the wife of a politician'—and has never hinted at any public ambitions of her own.[63]

In spite of this traditional family portrait—and his self-professed conservatism—Navalny holds some progressive views that are far from the majority position. For instance, he supports same-sex marriage—quite an unpopular measure in Russia.[64]

Navalny is no-nonsense and business-like. Pro-Kremlin tabloids relish pointing out that he wears expensive clothing brands and that he holidays abroad. But they haven't uncovered much else. His lifestyle is much above that of the average Russian—which he is conscious of.[65] But it is far from that of the many government officials he investigates.

Navalny is quick-witted, engaging, and funny. But also quick-tempered. Quite often, he is direct to the point of being blunt. He's got into numerous public spats with journalists, former allies, and politicians. In the world of Moscow liberal politics and media, but also far beyond, he divides opinion.

A complex figure

Navalny is different things to different people. To some, he is a democratic hero—a figure willing to stand up to Putin's authoritarianism. Some even call him the leader of the opposition. To others, he is a traitor—a CIA-paid agent of the West who is betraying the Motherland. To others still, he is a nationalist or a xenophobe.

Even a quick glance at Navalny's words and deeds makes clear why people might be confused. He is a liberal who has made nationalist—even racist—statements. He is an anti-corruption activist who himself has been convicted of embezzlement. He is a Russian patriot who calls for sanctions against Russian authorities. He is an avowed democrat who leads his movement with a strong hand. Navalny wants Russia to be 'happy' but attacks opponents with scathing comments and rarely backs down.

Because Navalny is both an inspiring and complex personality, people of all stripes project their hopes, frustrations, and suspicions onto him. For those who see him as the future of Russia, the sheer weight of expectation is bound to lead to disappointment. And this problem is compounded by the absence of other figures quite like him—a well-known, charismatic, media-savvy opposition politician in a regime that doesn't deal well with dissent.

Three dimensions of Navalny

How to make sense of this complexity? We tell Alexei Navalny's story by tracing three distinct paths: Navalny the anti-corruption activist; Navalny the politician; and Navalny the protester. These are the most important dimensions of Navalny's career when evaluating his place in modern Russian politics. But we also look further and discuss his contentious relationship with the Kremlin. We explain how it is not only the Russian political leadership that has impacted Navalny, but that Navalny has, in turn, shaped the Kremlin.

This confrontation has forced many people in Russia to pick sides—and to prioritise. Arguing about Navalny's controversial statements, for example, has to wait, some argue. The overriding goal now is taking down Putin. As Yevgenia Albats—a leading Russian journalist and a close friend of Navalny—has put it: 'We are back in black and white politics. There is an evil empire, and there are people who are fighting for their basic rights. Navalny is the leader of the latter. On the other side, there are Putin's enablers in the West and Putin's collaborators inside Russia.'[66]

Given the current state of Russian politics, the very act of acknowledging complexity can be interpreted politically—that is, as an attempt to weaken support for Navalny. And this is a charge levelled by Navalny's supporters against Russian state media outlets when they have pointed to the darker pages of his story.

Whatever our sympathies or our antipathies for this or that aspect of Navalny's political ideas and career, we are not on the battlefield of Russian politics. Drawing on our research on Russian politics—on our work as non-Russian academics—we will analyse shades of grey, but without implying that this debate about complexity is the most important task on the ground in Russia.

Why focus on Navalny?

Some analysts of Russia have argued that you don't need to understand Navalny at all. That what matters are structural conditions and that Navalny is just a product of them.

Indeed, a number of features have played a strong role in making Navalny Navalny. The main factor is corruption. Power and money attract each other everywhere. In Russia, though, elite corruption is central to how Putin holds on to power. The 'oligarchs' of the 1990s—the well-connected super-rich who used to dominate the Russian state—have not disappeared. They have simply been turned from threats to stabilisers of power.[67] More generally, the pervasiveness of corruption puts people like

Navalny—who know both law and finance and are able to trace complex ownership structures—in a privileged position to challenge the authorities.

Russia is rich in resources and has a highly educated population, but it is a very unequal society economically. Boosted by rising oil prices, living standards significantly improved in Putin's first two terms as president, but stagnated from the mid-2010s. And yet, Russia has over 250,000 dollar millionaires, while tens of millions live in poverty.[68] Exposing blatant corruption—and the luxuries that many officials indulge in—is especially effective when many citizens cannot afford a decent life. But there are limits to the extent to which people can rock the boat.

For one thing, Russia has an authoritarian political system. Opposition is not banned outright; the parties of the so-called 'systemic opposition' can take part in elections alongside Putin's party, United Russia. These 'opposition' parties criticise the government and they attract disaffected voters. But they do not challenge the president's power—and, if they become too oppositional, they face the same barriers and manipulations that the authorities use against any other potential challengers.

To make matters worse for someone like Navalny, many Russians are distrustful of politics as such—even more so than people in many Western countries. This is, in part, a consequence of the 1990s in Russia. Political competition then was often aggressive and unconstructive. Parties and politicians seemed to represent powerful private interests—including criminal ones—more than the people. Politics has, thus, come to be a dirty word for many. So, in the unlikely case that somebody can overcome all the hurdles that the Kremlin places before them, it is still difficult to gain voters' trust, even if many think that change is badly needed.

Rather than a book on Navalny, then, shouldn't this be a book about corruption, inequality, and authoritarianism? In a way, it is.

Tracing Navalny's career as a politician and an activist allows us to understand all of this—the things that make today's Russia what it is. But even though Navalny wouldn't be Navalny in any other time and place, he is not just a product of his country's history. To become a serious challenger in this environment, it takes courage, creativity, and wit. Navalny has all of these qualities—and that's why he stands out. The Kremlin knows that, too—and has adapted to Navalny as a result.

Terms we use like 'the Kremlin' or 'the authorities' are, of course, quite general—and can gloss over the complexity of political institutions in Russia. As researchers, we are conscious of the problems with using blanket terms that hide important nuances. And yet, these terms can sometimes provide a useful shorthand, particularly in cases when the details they smooth over are not important to the particular subject in question.

Who supports Navalny?

Kremlin-friendly media have, for a long time, argued that Navalny's significance is overblown in the West—that in Russia itself, he really isn't that important. How does this square with the numbers?[69]

After Navalny's return to Russia in early 2021, his approval rating stood at about 20 per cent, with a solid 50 per cent disapproving of his activities. But these are averages for Russian society as a whole. People between eighteen and twenty-four have a more favourable picture of him—more than a third approve of his activities.

In contrast to age, a person's education plays almost no role. Navalny's support among people with a university degree is not much higher than among those without. And there is virtually no difference between residents of large cities and those in rural areas. What population surveys clearly show, therefore, is that Navalny is not just a phenomenon of urban centres in Russia.

But these figures change when considering people's primary information source. Among users of the messaging and social media app Telegram, those who support Navalny's activities outnumber those who don't, while of those who mainly watch state-controlled television, a full two thirds disapprove of him.

Many critics of Putin's political system claim this is just the effect of propaganda. People are simply brainwashed by state television, they argue. To be sure, there is much propaganda. But there is also widespread, genuine readiness to support Putin—and a deep distrust towards those who challenge him and challenge the status-quo. This relationship between Putin and his supporters is as much based on emotions as it is on the—still palpable—improvement of living standards that coincided with the first decade of Putin's reign. Precisely because it is not the result of mere propaganda, this relationship is difficult for any challenger to break.

And yet, that is exactly what Navalny has sought to do—by focusing on corruption as the cause that could undermine Putin's support and building the widest coalition possible against him. This is a simple message—but merely one dimension of a complex political figure.

* * *

A plane above Moscow

Flight DP936 starts its descent into Moscow's Vnukovo Airport. Navalny's supporters have gathered in their thousands—but the riot police are there, too.[70]

The pilot makes an announcement: the plane cannot land at Vnukovo as scheduled due to 'technical difficulties'. Instead, the aircraft will touch down at Sheremetyevo Airport 'where the weather is great!', he adds with amusement.[71]

The cameras stay trained on Navalny as he disembarks the plane and heads to the terminal. After authorities had accused him of violating his parole, what follows next seems inevitable. At passport control, Navalny is detained.

He is taken to a prison in the north of Moscow. The next day, an improvised court hearing is set up in a police station. Navalny's lawyer receives notice just two hours before. Navalny calls the whole process 'an amazing absurdity'.[72]

The court places him in pre-trial detention before a hearing set for 2 February. On that date, a judge would decide whether the suspended sentence for his 2014 fraud conviction—in what was referred to as the Yves Rocher case—should be converted into real time behind bars.

'I am not afraid'

Navalny was now at the mercy of the Russian state.

Before reaching passport control and his subsequent detention, he stopped and spoke in front of the ideal backdrop: a huge poster of the Kremlin and the Russian flag.

He was still optimistic—and he was back in Russia. 'This is my home', it was 'my choice' to return: 'This is the best day of the past five months for me ... I am not afraid ... and I urge you not to be afraid either.'[73]

2

THE ANTI-CORRUPTION ACTIVIST

Krasnodar Krai, near the resort town of Gelendzhik—a five-hour drive north-west of Sochi, the location of the 2014 Winter Olympics.

A drone with a camera flies above the Black Sea, edging closer to the shore. In front, tree-covered coast—and an enormous building. At 17,691 square metres, it is the 'largest private residential building in Russia', set in land equivalent to '39 principalities of Monaco'.[1]

An underground ice hockey rink. An arboretum. Helipads. An 'aqua-disco'. Vineyards. A private casino. An amphitheatre. A secret tunnel to the beach. Is it a Bond villain's lair?

No. This is 'Putin's Palace'—according to an investigation by Navalny's 'Anti-Corruption Foundation' (FBK).[2] It is the 'most secret and guarded facility in Russia, without exaggeration. This is not a country house, not a dacha, not a residence—this is a whole city, or, rather, a kingdom.'

Published on YouTube on 19 January 2021, the feature-length investigative film is an instant hit. By 28 January, it has racked up a staggering 100 million views.[3] By the beginning of February, more than one quarter of the entire adult population of Russia has seen it.[4]

The video catalogues the mind-boggling luxury of the palace and its surrounding grounds. It also presents a complex web of financial relationships meant, the FBK claims, to conceal the ultimate beneficiary of it all—the president of Russia himself. This is, Navalny and his team argue, the 'world's largest bribe'.[5]

One detail included in Navalny's investigation—of a single Italian toilet brush worth €700—becomes a symbol of subsequent protests. According to Navalny's team, however, the brush wasn't even meant for the palace itself: it was bought for a vineyard nearby—separate from, but part of, the main estate.

Vladimir Putin dismissed the accusations: 'Nothing that has been shown as my property ... has ever belonged to me or my close relatives. Ever.'[6] The Russian billionaire Arkady Rotenberg told the press that he was the actual owner of the property—it was, he said, 'a real find in a gorgeous place'. And he planned to turn it into a hotel—it 'has quite a lot of rooms'.[7]

'Putin's Palace' is by far the most well known of the FBK's investigations. But Navalny's anti-corruption work goes back a long way. In fact, Navalny first achieved national and international recognition for his anti-corruption activism.

We tell this story—the story of how Navalny turned from a small-time blogger and minority shareholder activist into one of the most famous anti-corruption crusaders in the world. We introduce some of the key characters who have joined him along the way—and chart the many difficulties they faced, from harassment by law enforcement officials to physical attacks by unidentified thugs. And we discuss the accusations made against Navalny himself—including that he is a paid proxy for corporate interests or somebody selfishly seeking a cause to help launch his political career.

THE ANTI-CORRUPTION ACTIVIST

'Who owns Surgutneftegaz?'

Surgut—a city in western Siberia, three hours by plane northeast of Moscow.

It's 30 April 2008—and the annual shareholders' meeting of the oil company Surgutneftegaz is taking place. The business daily *Vedomosti* refers to it as 'one of the most closed oil companies in the country'.[8] Around 350 people are present.[9]

Once CEO Vladimir Bogdanov has finished reporting on the company's results from the past year, he asks if there are any questions from the audience. One figure takes to the stage. It is Alexei Navalny.

'Who owns Surgutneftegaz?'

The company's management are stunned. They're not used to facing such a probing question in public—something that confronts directly the lack of transparency in the company's ownership structure.

Navalny asks two more questions. Why is the company's dividend yield so low? And why is it so difficult to access information, including the company's annual report, which can only be read before the meeting in remote Surgut itself?

There is an awkward silence. Then, out of nowhere, applause. An isolated group of shareholders in the back of the hall show their support for Navalny's critical questioning.

This is Navalny as a minority shareholder activist—something he begins in 2007. By buying shares in Russian companies, some of which are majority state-owned, Navalny gets at least two things: access to information on these companies' activities and opportunities to ask awkward questions, such as in Surgut. He can also use the information to take companies to court, either with a view to getting more information or trying to hold them directly accountable.[10] His education in law and financial markets helps him navigate this world.

But the next step is no less important: Navalny makes the information public on his LiveJournal blog—a vital platform. 'My blog exists only because there is censorship in the media', he told a magazine in 2011.[11] He starts the blog in March 2006 simply to post the transcripts of a weekly show he hosts on the radio station Ekho Moskvy ('Echo of Moscow'). Over time, however, it becomes something much more.

Blogs work

The blog allows Navalny to spread awareness of issues not readily covered in the Russian media, including his shareholder activism. As an early form of social media, the blog also allows him to build a community—of those interested in uncovering shady corporate activities, but also of those willing to help:

> Basically, blogs work. A blog is your own media, only interactive. If I write 'Guys, I need to find a specialist in the field of building design to analyse some corrupt thing that is happening in construction', I'll find such specialists through the blog. If needed, I can call on everybody through the blog to write appeals to the [Federal] Anti-Monopoly Service and thousands will write. A blog is a universal tool ... Online and offline are united through a blog.[12]

In one of Navalny's campaigns against the energy giant Gazprom, he claimed that more than 500 people were involved in the investigation.[13] And, in another example of community building, Navalny set up the 'Union of Minority Shareholders' to pool know-how and coordinate activities.[14]

His blog posts make a splash. And it's possible to track their growing impact over time. An August 2008 post gets 235 comments.[15] A December 2008 post gets 832 comments.[16] A November 2009 blog entry receives 1,394 comments.[17] But a November 2010 post blows all of these out of the water, receiving 8,965 comments.[18] Yes, this is a crude measure. But the basic metric shows Navalny's growing visibility and impact over time: by the end of 2011, his blog was being read by 55,000 people daily.[19]

Navalny picked cases that he knew would anger readers—and it worked: 'The topic should resonate. When I wrote on my blog [in 2008] about the lawsuit against [the Russian oil pipeline monopoly] Transneft—which did not disclose for which charitable purposes it directed half a billion dollars over two years—there were hundreds of responses. It upsets people.'[20]

In a separate 2010 investigation into Transneft, Navalny claimed that no less than US$4 billion was stolen during construction of the Eastern Siberia–Pacific Ocean pipeline—a vital piece of infrastructure for the export of Russian oil to Asia-Pacific markets. The source of Navalny's information? Leaked documents from a 2008 audit carried out by the Audit Chamber—a state body tasked with monitoring the use of budget funds and public resources. Transneft itself dismissed the investigation as part of a campaign against the investment project.[21]

Navalny's claims caused such a stir that Vladimir Putin—then prime minister—commented publicly, calling for the Procuracy—the Russian public prosecution body—to investigate.[22] This never happened, however. And, by September 2011, Putin's tune had changed markedly: he suggested that Transneft management did not steal funds, but, rather, used them for a different purpose than originally intended.[23]

Nevertheless, in February 2011, a Moscow court did order Transneft to release more information relating to the case—to the protestations of the company's management.[24] Navalny reacted to the decision almost immediately on his blog: 'yabada-badoo!'—a 'big victory'.[25]

Overall, however, Navalny's attempts to hold companies and individuals accountable through the courts were rarely successful. But he took that with a shrug: 'We're realists, and perfectly well understand it's unlikely that in today's Russia we'll win in court' against the highest authorities.[26]

A topic for everyone

Russians worry about corruption. Over the past twenty years, polls show that it is one of the topics they worry about the most—after rising prices, unemployment, and poverty.[27] And corruption concerns everybody, regardless of their level of skill, income, or education. Being against corruption, therefore, seems like a winning strategy for somebody looking to broaden their visibility and appeal.

In addition to appealing to virtually all social groups, an anti-corruption agenda has one more decisive advantage: it's possible to defend it from both the political left and right. In contrast to other demands that Navalny has put forward at various points, fighting corruption cannot easily be assigned to a liberal, left-wing, or nationalist agenda.

Certainly, anti-corruption reforms are often advocated by the World Bank and the International Monetary Fund as part of a liberal economic programme. Favouritism and bribe-paying, the argument goes, undermine the healthy competition of market forces.

But an anti-corruption agenda can equally be justified from a left-wing platform of social justice. Embezzlement, rigged procurement contracts, and funnelling taxable wealth into offshores takes money from the state's budget—money that could be used for the public good.

Despite an economic boom in the 2000s—partly driven by a rise in world oil prices—income inequality remains very high in Russia.[28] Seeing political elites indulge in luxuries paid for with taxpayers' money is always infuriating. But it is especially angering when inequality is high, public services are of poor quality, and living standards are low. And all of this makes corruption a question of social justice.

THE ANTI-CORRUPTION ACTIVIST

It's personal

When speaking to those who ended up joining Navalny's movement, it's striking to see that everybody has their own personal experience with corruption, their own idea of why it needs to be fought—no matter where they stand politically.[29]

Before devoting himself full time to supporting Navalny's cause, Viktor, thirty-nine, worked as a retail manager. When businesses need to pay bribes, he says—for instance, to avoid excessive pressure from tax authorities or health and safety inspectors—then that will drive up prices. 'If, as a businessman, I have corruption-related expenses, of course I will add that to the price of my product. Everybody will pay that price. But only very few officials benefit.'

Katerina—another Navalny activist and a lawyer by training—has a different story: 'I have this fear',

> it's a little irrational, but I have it nonetheless. They recently opened a two-level motorway intersection here. And I'm really afraid that sooner or later it's just going to collapse. You know how corruption works, right? The state signs a contract for, let's say, 100 roubles. But to build the actual infrastructure, they use only 25 or 30 roubles.

The rest, Katerina continues, is pocketed by various people along the way. 'That's the way it is, I know it from people in the system. And naturally, when building the intersection, that means they save on every component, the quality is horrible, and one day it will collapse.'

These stories show that corruption is part of people's everyday lives. Without corruption, they can easily imagine their lives would instantly be better, safer, and wealthier. And it's not just their own lives that corruption affects, but social well-being more broadly. Echoing Navalny's arguments, Polina, twenty-six, says that corruption is theft, because it is usually the state budget—the taxpayers' money—that is embezzled: 'If someone steals our wallet, we will consider that person the worst in the city. But when people steal from us at the government level, we're like, "well, all officials steal". But no, not on this scale. We just cannot tolerate that.'

Because everybody experiences corruption, the topic makes it easy to build a personal connection to Navalny's cause.

With posts like the investigation into Transneft that made an emotional connection with readers, Navalny soon became 'Russia's best-known blogger'.[30] And he sought to capitalise on his growing blog following in December 2009 by setting up—in collaboration with the Russian edition of *Forbes*—a 'Centre for the Protection of Shareholders', which would help coordinate the activities of minority shareholders.[31] *Vedomosti* named Navalny one of its 'People of the Year' in 2009.[32]

'Have you noticed anybody following you?'[33]

Navalny's awkward questioning and litigiousness make him enemies—lots of them. And that leads to concerns about his safety:

> I haven't received direct threats, but friends who are involved with the oil industry ask, Why does Navalny need all of this trouble and who is pulling the strings? I haven't given anyone a serious headache, but there is anxiety. At a meeting of Rosneft shareholders, [the CEO Igor] Sechin tried for a long time not to give me the floor. I passed note after note [requesting to speak], but Sechin said from the rostrum: 'No more requests to speak have been received.' Then I stood up and yelled [to Sechin]: 'I wrote five notes to you', and only then was I given the floor.[34]

There is a reason, perhaps, why Navalny raised the particular example of Igor Sechin. In a profile of the head of Rosneft, the *Financial Times* journalist Henry Foy noted that the CEO is '[f]eared by fellow businessmen and politicians alike', known for the 'brutal way he has dispatched those who cross him'.[35] Navalny ran the distinct risk of making powerful foes.

When asked whether he had noticed being followed by anybody, Navalny responded nonchalantly. He said he'd noticed a car a few times—but that he didn't pay attention to it: 'What will they find out about me? I write about everything that I do on the blog.'[36]

Around this time, another individual was investigating corruption—and would lose his life in the process. Sergei Magnitsky was a tax specialist employed by a Moscow-based law and accounting firm. Among the firm's clients were subsidiaries of the Hermitage Fund—'at the time the largest foreign investment fund in Russia'[37]—and its chief advisor was Bill Browder, a leading financier who had made his fortune in post-Soviet Russia.[38]

While investigating the changed ownership of three subsidiaries of the Hermitage Fund, Magnitsky alleged that they had been stolen by officials, who then used them illegally to arrange a tax refund of US$230 million from the Russian state.[39]

But it was Magnitsky himself who was arrested in November 2008, accused of taking part in tax evasion.[40]

The details of the accusations against Magnitsky continue to be disputed.[41] What is much clearer, however, is his appalling treatment during pre-trial detention. Sergei Magnitsky died on 16 November 2009 of toxic shock and heart failure as a result of diagnosed, but untreated, pancreatitis.[42]

Investigating corruption allegations was a perilous activity.

The system bites back?

Soon after Navalny posted his 2010 allegations of embezzlement at Transneft, he was himself facing serious accusations: a criminal case was initiated against him in May 2011. In order to understand why, we need to rewind a bit—and head to the Kirov Region, a one-and-a-half-hour flight north-east of Moscow.[43]

In 2009, Nikita Belykh—then a leading liberal politician—became the governor of the region and invited Navalny to advise him on a voluntary basis. As an advisor, Navalny soon got involved with Kirovles—a timber company belonging to the regional government and headed by Vyacheslav Opalev.

Kirovles was losing money. Navalny said he wanted to improve the company's transparency and make it profitable again. As part of this project, a contract was signed between Kirovles and another company, VLK, founded by a man named Piotr Ofitserov—an acquaintance of Navalny. According to this contract, VLK would buy timber from Kirovles and sell it on to third parties for a commission.

Introducing a trading company as an intermediary would, Navalny said, bring in additional customers and would put an end to the practice of off-the-books cash payments for timber. Between April and September 2009, Kirovles supplied VLK with timber worth around sixteen million roubles (about £300,000 at the time).

By autumn 2009, however, Governor Belykh dismissed Opalev, claiming he had mismanaged Kirovles—and the contract between VLK and Kirovles was terminated.

Opalev wasn't happy. He claimed that he'd been pressured by Navalny and Ofitserov into a loss-making agreement. After looking into Opalev's accusation, however, the Investigative Department of the Kirov Region decided in January 2011 not to open a criminal investigation as they could not establish that an offence had been committed.[44] But things were about to get complicated.

The regional decision from January was overruled in February by federal-level investigators—specifically, the Central Office of the Investigative Committee in Moscow.[45] The Office re-assigned the case to other investigators in order to prevent 'possible pressure' from regional actors.

And yet, in March 2011, the newly appointed investigators also refused to initiate a case.[46]

Moscow was still not happy, however. A criminal case was initiated in May 2011 by the central Investigative Committee. Investigators declared that Navalny and Ofitserov had caused material damage to Kirovles by deception or breaching the trust of Opalev.[47]

If heads weren't dizzy by this stage with U-turn after U-turn, they soon would be. On 10 April 2012—that is, after eleven months of digging around—investigators closed the criminal case, stating that there was no evidence of criminal wrongdoing.[48]

Navalny posted the good news on his blog on 28 May: 'All's OK'.[49]

It wasn't. The federal-level Investigative Committee overturned the April decision to terminate the case.[50] The rollercoaster ride was far from over.

Headed by Aleksandr Bastrykin, the Investigative Committee had shown a determination to pursue Navalny, rejecting the conclusions of lower-level officials. Speaking at a general meeting of the Investigative Committee, Bastrykin said: 'You had a criminal file against this man, and you have quietly closed it. I am warning you, there will be no mercy, no forgiveness if such things happen again.'[51]

A new criminal case was subsequently opened—but, this time, for embezzlement. In other words, Navalny was accused of being as corrupt as the officials he was famous for calling out. He was now charged with 'stealing a forest', so the joke went.[52] But he also faced ten years in prison.

Many other cases would be brought against him during his career in politics. The most fateful involved a French cosmetics company, Yves Rocher—the case that resulted in Navalny going to prison in 2021.

Why bother?

How did Navalny end up as a minority shareholder activist—an activity that appeared to set him on such a dangerous path? According to Navalny himself, it was almost by accident. He started off as a simple investor—not somebody with a broader goal:

> I made nearly all of these investments with a view to capital allocation [i.e., to making money]; there was no goal of buying shares in order to sue ... Having bought shares, I began to read the companies' reports regularly, to follow what was written about them in the press, and I was horrified. At that time, there was still no [global financial] crisis, oil prices were breaking all records, and the companies in which I held shares were 'chocolate-covered', but the companies' reports said: There will be no dividends. As a shareholder, that didn't suit me, and I decided to figure out where the companies' profits go and why they don't share them with me.[53]

He was, in short, turned into an activist by peering behind the curtain of Russian companies—and that was enough: 'At some point, it became a matter of principle.'[54]

During this time, Navalny was still working as a lawyer in Moscow, using the money he made from clients to subsidise his anti-corruption activities.[55] He says that he worked 20 per cent of the time on his conventional legal work and the remainder—the vast majority—on activism.[56]

And yet, Navalny has been dogged from the very start by claims regarding the *real* reasons for his anti-corruption activities. Navalny has said that this was 'the most common question' put to him, with conspiracy theories abounding.[57]

Speculations have ranged from Navalny extorting money from the companies he investigates, to knowingly being in the pocket of these same companies' competitors.[58] The CEO of Transneft, Nikolai Tokarev, claimed, for example, that Navalny was serving the interests of the company's opponents in constructing the Eastern Siberia–Pacific Ocean pipeline.[59] Navalny has also been accused of being an unwitting pawn in domestic elite battles[60] and geopolitical conflicts: a United Russia deputy in the State Duma implied during a debate with Navalny that the anti-corruption activist was being paid by the CIA or the US State Department.[61] Navalny has denied all of these allegations.[62]

Corruption: threatening power

Russia is sometimes called a 'kleptocracy'—a system set up so that officials can steal.[63] But does this fully capture the role corruption actually plays in Russian politics?

Corruption has been central to political life in post-Soviet Russia. And it has been significant in different ways. The privatisation of the Soviet economy was carried out in a way that favoured the politically well connected. Soviet factory directors took control of their businesses during the collapse of the USSR—and then made them their personal property with the help of the authorities. Ambitious individuals were able to build enormous corporate empires through all kinds of schemes.

In the 1990s, this was threatening the integrity of the state: oligarchs blackmailed the weak—and poor—Russian state into selling national property far below market value in exchange for much-needed credit. This way, they effectively controlled many important political decisions—a process known as 'state capture'.[64]

When Putin came to power, he showed his determination to re-establish central state control by moving against these oligarchs. And many Russians liked it.

One crucial moment in this process came in February 2003, when President Putin met with business elites for a tele-vised exchange in the Kremlin.[65] Among them was Mikhail

Khodorkovsky, co-owner of Yukos—then Russia's largest oil company. With trademark audacity, Khodorkovsky put Putin on the spot: was it not strange, Khodorkovsky asked, that officially low-paid work for tax agencies was so much more attractive for young graduates than jobs in the private sector? He was openly accusing Putin of presiding over a corrupt system.

As Putin turned to Khodorkovsky, you could hear a pin drop. Putin brushed off the charge and counter-attacked: was it not Yukos that had recently had problems with paying its taxes? Perhaps this was when Khodorkovsky realised that things had changed. He was arrested on 25 October 2003 and charged with tax fraud.

Khodorkovsky had acquired Yukos in a controversial auction in 1995, benefitting from his connections to Yeltsin and his past role as deputy minister of energy.[66] In fact, he said himself that, in the 1990s, 'everyone in Russia was engaged in the primary accumulation of capital. Even when laws existed, they were not very rigorously followed. Therefore, if you conducted yourself too much in a Western manner, you were simply torn to pieces and forgotten.'[67]

But no matter Khodorkovsky's possible wrongdoings, the case against him was clearly political. Khodorkovsky's political ambitions, as well as his financing of opposition groups and independent media, crossed a line. So did the way he ran Yukos—as a privately owned oil major, independent from the state and ready to accept foreign investors. Yukos was dismantled, with the bulk of its assets snapped up by the state company Rosneft.

Khodorkovsky spent a decade behind bars. The Kremlin had issued a warning.

Corruption: stabilising power

Corruption did not disappear under Putin, however. It merely turned from something that undermined central state control to something that stabilised it.

In this paradigm shift, oligarchs needed to adapt to a new reality. Khodorkovsky was imprisoned, others were driven into exile, and some of their assets ended up in state corporations. Other wealthy business leaders, meanwhile, were allowed to thrive. Under Putin, the number of dollar billionaires has risen sharply. This followed a global trend, but analyses show that Russia has many more billionaires than one would expect given its relatively weak economy.[68]

This is standard practice in authoritarian politics: an incoming leader makes sure that leading businesspeople don't get any wrong ideas by punishing a few—but allows many others to get extremely rich.[69] This is a form of social contract with elites: you may enrich yourselves, sometimes at the cost of the state, as long as you do not use your money and influence to challenge political rule. And most of the economic elite are fine with this arrangement.

One of Navalny's most well-known slogans—first used in early 2011—frames United Russia as the 'party of crooks and thieves'.[70] This phrase directly addresses the idea that politicians—especially those in the 'party of power'—are far from honest public servants. But it also says something deeper about the nature of power and corruption in the country: officials offer loyalty in exchange for opportunities to satisfy their avarice. Corruption can, therefore, be an instrument to secure Putin's rule, rather than something that undermines it.

But corruption has a second function to keep Putin's rule afloat: it's not just a carrot, it's also a stick.

The government has taken several public steps against corruption, such as requiring officials to publicly report their income and assets, and—sometimes—fining them if discrepancies are found between formal declarations and actual wealth.[71] Each year, thousands of cases of bribe-paying, favouritism, and embezzlement come before Russian courts, and the judicial system hands down hundreds of prison sentences.[72]

Not all of these cases are politicised. But because corruption is so widespread, a charge of it is very plausible. This makes it an ideal tool to 'discipline elites'.[73] Through the media, the courts, and the security services, the Kremlin and lower-level authorities can use the accusation of corruption to blackmail or destroy opposition members and elite opponents.

For instance, several of the very few oppositional mayors who have managed to get elected in Russia since 2000 have faced corruption charges shortly after taking office. In 2021, when a popular Communist Party deputy from Saratov, a city on the Volga, publicly supported protests for the release of Navalny, the Procuracy opened a corruption case against him—an ominous move.[74] And even top members of the government are not immune. In 2016, Minister of Economic Development Alexei Ulyukayev was detained, charged with soliciting a bribe of US$2 million from Igor Sechin, and eventually sentenced to eight years in a labour colony.[75]

Both functions—allowing elites to enrich themselves and disciplining them when necessary—work hand in hand to stabilise Putin's rule. The idea of Russia being a kleptocracy is, therefore, too simplistic. Politics attracts many people who are in it only for the money. But, instead of organising power to be able to steal, stealing is organised to buttress power.

Russian politics at the highest level is often driven by the intention to achieve goals that Russians generally approve of: strengthening the state, projecting the country's might internationally, and improving the welfare of citizens. To be able to do all that, in Putin's view, he must remain in power. And corruption serves this goal and is managed in its service. It is a tool rather than the system's *raison d'être*.

Anti-corruption activism or politics—or both?

In December 2009, Navalny was asked whether his anti-corruption activism was simply a springboard into mainstream politics:

No, of course it's not a springboard. I've always been involved with political activities. What's in the foreground—the defence of minority shareholders or politics—that's the question. For example, I consider my battle against the strange company Gunvor, which controls more than half of all oil exports from Russia, probably to be, one way or the other, a political battle. It's quite difficult to separate these things now.[76]

One reading of Navalny's activism is that these are the actions of a frustrated politician. That interpretation is supported by Sergei Guriev, once rector of the New Economic School—a leading economics and finance university in Moscow: 'His generation of opposition politicians has been denied a career in politics ... They may have to wait twenty years. So he has taken what looks like a smart, reasonable path.'[77]

This path might not have been a conscious decision at the start. But, as Navalny's profile grew, it became a strategy. According to the *New York Times* journalist Andrew Kramer, Navalny began to refer to himself as 'an advocate of the rights of members of the Russian middle class—people who have invested in the stock market and who he says are losing money to corruption and mismanagement'.[78]

In Russia's system of state capitalism—where capital and state power are tightly interwoven—needling company managers has been a way to attempt to hold the powerful to account. In the words of journalist Carl Schreck, writing for *Time* magazine, Navalny was 'demonstrating that there may be a tool more effective than the ballot box in keeping Russia's ruling class in check: stock'.[79] And Navalny himself was explicit at the time about the political nature of his shareholder activism: 'All of this litigation, if you will, is a little, personal "march of dissenters". Some go onto the streets, and I go to the courts.'[80]

But Navalny was joined by an ever-growing number of people on this march to the courts. And this posed logistical challenges.

How was he meant to handle the volume of information and respond to all the comments he received on his blog? 'We need a website', Navalny announced in June 2010. 'Roughly speaking, to coordinate the civil movement against corruption and all that stuff. Purely utilitarian in nature. No articles, manifestos or other crap.'[81]

Branching out—RosPil

December 2010 saw the launch of one such website: RosPil. This time, instead of exposing corporate malfeasance, the goal was to sniff out the embezzlement of state budget funds by investigating corruption in the state procurement system. At the time, the Presidential Administration claimed that around one trillion roubles (£20 billion at the time) were embezzled each year during the state procurement process.[82]

The name itself—RosPil—is a play on words. The Russian word 'raspil'—literally, a 'saw cut'—is slang for a variety of corrupt practices, as in 'cutting off' budget funds.[83] The prefix 'Ros' is commonly used in the names of Russian state organisations. Indeed, at first sight, RosPil's logo—featuring a golden double-headed eagle—looks like many other symbols for Russian state bodies. Except the eagle is holding two wood saws.

This is humour, Navalny style—and it's a conscious choice: 'I'm trying to do this in an entertaining format. I'm trying to prove to everyone that the fight against the regime is fun.'[84]

RosPil's purpose is to crowd-source online investigations into state contracts. And this is possible because of at least three factors. First, information on state procurement has been made available online in Russia since the mid-2000s.[85] Second, Navalny's growing online following—along with the possibilities provided by the internet for coordinated, remote working—provided a pool of keen volunteers. But there were still costs involved. The third feature dealt with that: RosPil was to be funded through donations.

In under four months of going live, RosPil had—according to its own records—achieved the cancellation of nearly US$7 million worth of tenders.[86]

Politicising potholes

RosPil is not the only new initiative at the time. Other projects include RosVybory—an election monitoring project[87]—and RosYama.[88] Launched in May 2011, the approach of RosYama—like RosPil—is to crowd-source activities, but this time focusing on potholes in Russia's roads rather than state procurement. This is how Navalny presented it:

> The Code of Administrative Violations states that, if there is a pothole in a road with a depth of more than 50 centimetres and a length of more than 80 [centimetres], then that means that this hole must (a) be filled in urgently and (b) the particular official who is responsible for the road—and each road has its own official responsible for it—should be fined for not doing anything. Therefore, we will try to use this simple article 12.34 of the Administrative Code to organise activists for a very simple thing—to fill in the potholes in front of your home and punish the official who is responsible.[89]

This was another expression of the drive to hold state actors accountable—but at the other end of the spectrum compared to suing state corporations. And, like many Navalny projects, it started with a simple problem, a simple idea to tackle it—and little money. To start the project, Navalny spent, by his own account, 100,000 roubles (about £2,200 at the time).[90]

Other initiatives sprang up around this time that were not led by Navalny but that have a family resemblance. Co-founded by Andrei Zayakin, Dissernet is a project tackling plagiarism in university dissertations—particularly the dissertations of senior officials.[91] Navalny did not, therefore, have a monopoly over internet-based, crowd-sourced projects to highlight official wrongdoing. But he was a key figure in this world.

For Navalny, though, the actual focus of the respective projects was no more important than what else they could do: 'We will once again identify activists ... and we will try to attract them to future projects.'[92] A clear goal was, therefore, to recruit talent.

Navalny assembles his team

In February 2011, Navalny posted a job advert on his LiveJournal blog: he was looking to hire lawyers. The most important condition to get the job: 'You need to WANT to fight against crooks. You need to think about it day and night.' The pay was 60,000 roubles a month (about £1,300 at the time). To be hired, you needed to submit a CV and a cover letter. But also something more original: a 'trophy for RosPil'. Applicants had to find a 'corrupt state procurement contract at the stage of tendering'. They could do this by whatever means necessary—'monitoring of procurement websites, media, insider info'. Applicants should then submit a link to the procurement, the text of their complaint, and a plan to work the case.[93]

A few weeks later, Navalny announced that he had found the first lawyer: Lyubov Fedenyova—soon known by her first husband's name, Sobol.[94] Navalny lauded her professional accomplishments—at twenty-three, she had already worked a year in court. He described the soon-to-be graduate from Moscow State University as 'purposeful, ambitious, intelligent'.

And she was a good fit. She had, in her own words, 'personal hatred for the system'. On her own LiveJournal blog, Sobol claimed not to be afraid—and that 'if you break the law, I'll use all my energy to prosecute you ... Get ready, gentlemen.'[95]

Navalny claimed his disillusionment with the 'system' had come partly from his experience as a minority shareholder. Sobol claimed her own realisation came during work in the Moscow court system.

Her father was an auditor and her mother was an engineer working at Sheremetyevo Airport.[96] Sobol dreamt of becoming a lawyer and read 'the works of pre-revolutionary lawyers and prosecutors'. But, with experience of court proceedings in Moscow, she understood that she wanted to become neither— not even a judge: 'All of them, to varying degrees, are power-less and tied up with corruption. It's impossible for citizens to defend their rights. In the offices next to mine, hundreds of cases against the Russian state were adjudicated, and not a single citizen won.'[97]

Sobol came to the conclusion that, in the justice system, 'an honest person cannot thrive. You need to make compromises with your conscience and turn a blind eye to many things.'[98]

After being appointed the first lawyer in Navalny's team, Sobol would become one of Navalny's most prominent allies—and the most prominent woman in a team whose leadership is mostly made up of men. In 2017, Navalny was interviewed by the rising star of Russian online journalism—thirty-year-old Yuri Dud— who accused Navalny of not advancing other politicians. The first name Navalny came up with was Sobol, to which the journalist replied that she was 'well dressed' and 'pretty'—but 'not a man'. Navalny retorted that she 'knew her own business better than any man' and would make a better legislator than the '450 boneheads' sitting in the State Duma.[99]

Navalny's team took shape during 2011. RosPil recruited a coordinator, Konstantin Kalmykov. Then twenty-eight years old and a political science graduate, he had volunteered with Navalny, helping him with his work on state procurement. By the end of 2011, two other young lawyers had joined the team.[100]

Beyond Navalny

Navalny wasn't a sole crusader. He had his team, as well as an army of supporters and voluntary workers linked to initiatives like RosPil and his blog. But he also formed part of a broader eco-system of anti-corruption activism in Russia.

Part of the anti-corruption landscape consisted of politicians. Boris Nemtsov—a leading politician in the 1990s—and Vladimir Milov—a former deputy energy minister—published a number of reports centring on corruption. Along with other former members of the Russian government, they created the 'People's Freedom Party "For Russia without Lawlessness and Corruption"' in 2010.

There was one problem, though. These politicians were, in a sense, compromised. Having been high-level insiders themselves, it was easy for people to dismiss them as criticising a system they had helped construct and sustain.[101]

Others working on anti-corruption were not politicians. One such person was Ivan Begtin, who was active at the same time as Navalny, carrying out careful work on state procurements. In fact, Begtin was critical of Navalny's approach, which he claimed was 'harmful to Russian society', as Navalny talked about 'aspects of state purchases of which he has only partial knowledge'.[102]

And yet, Navalny's approach brought corruption to the attention of many more people than Begtin's work. According to journalist Mikhail Loginov, 'Begtin's anti-corruption work resembles a scholarly study of interest only to a select group of experts ... [But a]nyone with a university degree will find ... [Navalny's] investigations accessible. Navalny is something of a science populariser for whom the audience is just as important as the science.'[103]

The Anti-Corruption Foundation

In February 2012, *Vedomosti* revealed that Navalny was planning to merge his multiple projects under a single umbrella structure, the 'Anti-Corruption Foundation' (FBK).[104]

Vedomosti obtained the names of two prominent sponsors of the Foundation, Boris Zimin and Vladimir Ashurkov. And Navalny told journalists that 'everything will be clean and without [off-the-books] cash. The names of all the people who give us money and the amounts will be public, as will be our expenses.'[105]

Until then, Navalny's project had been crowdfunded and managed by himself and his small team.[106] But, with the FBK, Navalny announced a change in scale, with a bigger budget—the Foundation would need US$300,000 a year.[107]

Meaning business

With a bigger budget came Vladimir Ashurkov, a manager hailing from the world of finance—another background altogether to the lawyers and political science graduates who had until then worked with Navalny. Ashurkov was to play a major role in the administration of the FBK as its executive director. And when he was mentioned in the media in 2012, the Russian press presented the forty-year-old investment banker as a *wunderkind* with a biography full of superlatives.

Born in 1972 to a family of the Soviet intelligentsia—his parents were Solzhenitsyn-reading engineers in the military-industrial complex—he went to one of the best schools in Moscow, learning English and German. He proceeded to one of the best universities in Russia, the Moscow Institute of Physics and Technology—home to several Nobel Prize-winning scholars. And, finally, he progressed to the Wharton Business School, where he received an MBA in 1996.

Ashurkov worked in finance for Renaissance Capital, the Port of St Petersburg, and, finally, Alfa Group, where he was director of group portfolio management, making about US$1 million a year.[108] One of Russia's largest investment groups, Alfa Group is owned by oligarch Mikhail Fridman. In 2012, the Russian edition of *Forbes* named him the sixth richest businessman in Russia, with a net worth of more than US$13 billion.[109]

Ashurkov told journalists that, while he had always been interested in politics and felt close to liberal parties, he had never really wanted to enter politics. But that changed when he started reading Navalny's blog. Ashurkov offered Navalny his services—his expertise in finance and corporate management.[110]

Before getting closer to the liberal opposition, Ashurkov had voted for Putin in the 2004 presidential election. But Ashurkov was disappointed by the lack of state investment in infrastructure—and by 'corruption as a form of state governance'. The final frustration came with the 2008 financial crisis, when, as Ashurkov viewed it, 'manual control' by the authorities replaced 'economic mechanisms'.[111]

Navalny described Ashurkov as representing a group he thought would be crucial in the future. They were successful businesspeople who could live abroad if they so wished, but they wanted 'to make it possible to live normally and comfortably in Russia'. People like Ashurkov, Navalny thought,

> don't agree with the actual ideology of the crooks in the Kremlin and United Russia: that Russia is a grey zone to make money ... while the place to spend your time comfortably and safely is Europe, where you send your kids to save them from trashy Russians ... It's just that he's one of the first to say that aloud in public and not in office corridors. That's why he's a great guy.[112]

Fridman, Ashurkov's boss, thought otherwise: Ashurkov had to choose between politics and business.[113] Such was the reality of Russia, where opposition was often incompatible with business.[114] Ashurkov left his job at Alfa—apparently without any grudges.

The dash for cash

One of the most pressing tasks for Ashurkov at the Anti-Corruption Foundation was to raise money. At the end of May

2012, Navalny claimed that the goal of $300,000 had almost been reached. He published a list of sixteen 'brave people' on his blog who publicly declared that they were donating money to the FBK—all of them giving at least 300,000 roubles (around £6,000 at the time).[115]

Some of these public donors were leading members of the intelligentsia already known to be close to Navalny: writers, journalists, economists.[116] The rest of the list consisted of businesspeople.

Ashurkov told Reuters that the FBK's strategy was 'to gather a critical mass of supporters who would not be afraid to say, "Yes, I have supported this foundation."' He added, cautiously: 'But of course this is also a test of what is possible and what's not possible in Russia. We'll find out.'[117] This was a bold move indeed. The Khodorkovsky case had taught oligarchs they should steer clear of independent political activity. Navalny's funders were not oligarchs, but some were businesspeople getting directly involved in opposition politics.

The test was failed by Ashurkov himself. In 2014, the Russian authorities charged him with embezzling funds from Navalny's own pocket—an allegation that Navalny dismissed as pure fantasy.[118] Ashurkov remained the executive director of the FBK, but he would now work from London, where he had been granted political asylum.[119]

The team grows

The Foundation grew quickly—both in revenue and staff. In February 2012, Navalny sought to hire a press secretary who would 'hate crooks and thieves', could speak English, and knew what anti-corruption activism was all about. Navalny presented the process as business-like and 'meritocratic': an HR-specialist would do the selection, not himself.[120]

Anna Veduta, a twenty-two-year-old graduate in political science from Moscow State University, matched the job description.

During her first months working with Navalny, Veduta was offered a scholarship at Oxford, but stayed at the Foundation. She thought she would get other university offers in the future—to which Navalny responded that, 'one day', she 'would go to Harvard'.[121]

The team at RosPil was also growing. According to a report published by the organisation, seven people were on the payroll by the end of 2012.[122] And, for the first time, investigators started working at the FBK. One of these investigators in particular would play a major role in the Foundation's development and become one of Navalny's closest associates: Georgy Alburov. Born in 1989 in the Volga region, Alburov moved to Moscow to study political science. It was there, he says, that he started to 'read *Novaya Gazeta* and listen to Ekho Moskvy'—two major outlets for the Russian opposition. 'Demonstrations, pickets ... I tried to participate in all protests in Moscow.'[123]

Alburov met Navalny at a trial in 2011 and started working with him the next year. He was drawn to Navalny by his concrete approach to politics—and his humour. One of Alburov's first targets was the illegal enrichment of public officials. He had learned from Zayakin—the anti-plagiarism activist and co-founder of Dissernet—about real estate registers abroad.[124] So he started poring over them, from the Czech Republic to the United States by way of the French Riviera, checking whether prominent Russian officials featured.[125] Alburov found luxury property belonging to Vladimir Pekhtin—a United Russia official—in Miami. He wrote a blog post on the story—and it was a hit, attracting a record number of views for his blog at the time. Pekhtin resigned—a rare win for the FBK, it seemed.[126]

In 2013, Alburov came to Navalny with an idea: 'What if, instead of showing the estates of officials on satellite maps, we take footage of them ourselves? We just need a drone. Is there money for this?' Navalny gave the green light and Alburov bought a cheap drone, to which he taped a GoPro camera. And, just like that, the FBK now had its first 'flying squad', Alburov joked.[127] They flew it over a senior government minister's dacha—the value of which was inconsistent with his declared assets, the FBK alleged. 'I can see everything from above, just so you know', the title of Navalny's investigation triumphantly proclaimed.[128]

The FBK proceeded to investigate an impressive list of officials. Targets included senior members of United Russia, members of the national parliament, Moscow's Mayor Sobyanin, oligarchs, the head of the Russian National Guard, members of the federal government, members of Moscow City Council, and officials in the Central Electoral Commission.

Navalny, the social media mogul

These investigations initially took the form of blog posts. The pro-Kremlin media is, indeed, fond of dismissing Navalny as just another blogger. He definitely is a blogger—but a blogger with an organisation and with what Russian journalists have called his own 'media empire'.[129] That empire was started on the LiveJournal platform, but it soon expanded to all social media.

Navalny had always been an extremely online person—and always keen to solicit the advice of some of the pioneers of the Russian internet.[130] He was an early, avid Twitter user. He's also been an enthusiastic Instagrammer, posting political content, but also numerous selfies with his family. And he has built a large audience on YouTube.

This social media strategy took a step ahead in 2012–13. To spread his message further, Navalny hired a press secretary, Anna Veduta. When he launched his first major electoral campaign—in the 2013 Moscow mayoral election—he developed a full media plan with Veduta. No fewer than three posts a day on his blog, the most important at around midday. And he ceased being the sole writer of his blog. In 2014, when asked who wrote his blog, he answered 'the collective Navalny'.[131] Even though he was still involved in the writing process, his associates had now mastered his style—'sharp, [with] no self-censorship'.

This proved helpful when Navalny found himself in jail—as happened quite often. Blog posts would continue appearing. And, when needed, Navalny asked Veduta's successor as press secretary, Kira Yarmysh—a young graduate from a prestigious international affairs institute in Moscow—to sound 'neutral and respectable'.[132]

YouTube would be his own television: the one he could access while being banned from regular channels in Russia. Although Navalny had created a YouTube channel in 2007—and had tried his hand at creating videos for investigations—he didn't initially invest much in this medium.

At first, the FBK's videos summarising its investigations looked rather amateurish. But everybody at the FBK was convinced that YouTube was the future, and that professionals were needed to make it work. Navalny himself saw the full potential of YouTube when, in 2015 and 2016, videos started getting millions of views.[133] Dozens more videos would follow. And not only videos, but livestreams, too.

By 2016, livestreaming was on the rise in Russia. The FBK hired a producer with a background in the Russian glossy press to design a livestream channel—Navalny LIVE. They started with a morning show, and the result was slick and stylish—something that became a trademark of the FBK's approach. In 2017, *Navalny at 20:18* was launched—a daily show where Navalny would comment on the news, answer questions from viewers, and explain his political strategy. In the year the show started, each episode got 400,000 views, on average.[134] Navalny had found another audience.

Engaging investigations

The Foundation made a particular impact, therefore, with professional YouTube videos summarising its investigations. With high production values and an engaging style, the videos have caught the imagination of Russians on a topic that can arouse strong emotions—but the details of which can quickly become complex, confusing, and boring.

And with engagement came money. One of Navalny's first investigative films—on the family of the Prosecutor General Yuri Chaika and released in December 2015—cost 250,000 roubles to produce (about £2,500 at the time). But it also featured a direct link to donate money to the FBK. It raised 3,075,000 roubles in single donations (then around £29,000).[135]

The FBK's next major investigative film cost 415,000 roubles (about £5,800 at the time).[136] The subject this time was the sitting Russian prime minister—and it caused a real stir.

'Don't Call Him "Dimon"'

> You would never take this man for some kind of a villain or an underground billionaire. He's a smartphone and gadget enthusiast, a ridiculous simpleton, who falls asleep during important events … he's one of our country's richest people and one of its most corrupt officials.[137]

So says Navalny at the start of a video published on 2 March 2017 on YouTube. The subject is the then prime minister, Dmitry Medvedev—with 'Dimon' being a diminutive of his first name.

When president, some asked whether Medvedev would be a 'second Gorbachev'—a person capable of bringing about 'something not dissimilar to a second perestroika'.[138] But the 'Dimon' investigation painted a different picture.

Yachts. A villa in Tuscany. A mansion in Moscow's most exclusive residential neighbourhood. Vineyards. A mountain residence. An ancestral home in the Kursk Region. A palace in St Petersburg. The FBK investigation claimed all of these formed Medvedev's own property empire, established via a complex web of financial ties, much like the allegations in 'Putin's Palace'.[139] And, once again, drone footage was used in the investigation to overcome obstacles (like 6-metre fences)—and, in the resulting YouTube video, to bring the content to life.

Medvedev dismissed the investigation as politically motivated—an attempt to get people out on to the streets:

> They take all sorts of stuff there [in the investigation], collect all sorts of nonsense about me, if it concerns me, about people I know, and about people I've absolutely never heard of. About some places I've been. About some places I've also never heard of. They collect there [in the investigation] some pieces of paper, photographs, clothes. Then, they create a product and present it.[140]

The investigation had more than nine million views on YouTube a week after its release—and, as of April 2021, had more than forty-three million views.[141] But Navalny bemoaned the lack of response from the authorities: no official appeared to face the consequences.[142] More pressure on the authorities was needed—and so Navalny called for demonstrations on 26 March 2017. They gathered tens of thousands of people across Russia.[143]

How does an activist put food on the table?

Navalny has always said that he does not receive any money from the FBK. How was he supposed to make a living? To answer that, we need to turn to Boris Zimin. Born in 1968, he is the son of a prominent businessman, Dmitry Zimin, who founded VimpelCom, one of the top Russian telecommunications groups—better known in Russia as Beeline. In 2006—the last time he figured in the *Forbes* annual list of the richest Russian businesspeople—Dmitry Zimin's net worth was estimated at

US$550 million.[144] Zimin Senior was also one of the most generous Russian philanthropists, funding science through the Dynasty Foundation. His son Boris continued this work and supported liberal publications such as *The New Times* and *Meduza*, as well as human rights and other organisations such as Memorial and the Sakharov Center.[145]

And the FBK. Since its creation, Zimin has donated 300,000 roubles a month (about £2,900 as of April 2021) to the Foundation.[146]

Since 2019, Zimin has also been Navalny's personal sponsor—his main source of income. In a 2017 interview with Yuri Dud, Navalny stated that he earned more than five million roubles the previous year (about £67,000 at the time), and that most of his income came from providing legal services.[147] Two years later, in 2019, Navalny revealed that Zimin was his main sponsor, starting 'a few months before'.[148] Navalny did not name the amount, but it appeared in his next declaration of income: in July 2020, he declared he had earned 5,440,000 roubles in 2019 (then about £67,000). He named Zimin again as his main sponsor, praising the 'transparency' of his earnings and the good works of the Dynasty Foundation.[149]

The money Navalny receives from Zimin corresponds, in Navalny's own words, to 'some work' he has done, including legal work. But the money is, in essence, sponsorship:

> Zimin understands very well I need something to live on, and that politics is where I put most of my energy. We have a legal contract, I really do some work ... This is not entirely like sponsorship, but, of course, he does not completely need my services. He wants first to support us.[150]

Investigations not just for their own sake

Navalny's work is political. The investigations name and shame high-level officials—and this, in turn, helps Navalny's calls for mobilisation on the streets and in elections. For Navalny, exposing elite corruption helps create a division between 'us'—the 'normal, patriotic' citizenry—and 'them'—the authorities. An investigation into the mayor of Nizhny Novgorod, for example, is introduced in this manner:

> One of the questions I heard the most was how I intended to campaign for people to vote for me if I don't have access to TV, to the federal press, and if they won't let me buy ads [there] … OK. These are all weaknesses of our campaign. Let's have a look at the strengths. What kind of campaign can we make that the authorities or other candidates cannot? *Tell the truth.* Let's try a small experiment together without television, but with the truth. I'm going to try right now to convince the inhabitants of a big Russian city to support my candidacy.[151]

The self-professed 'patriotic' mayor from United Russia, Navalny says, owns two apartments in Miami—a stark contrast with the poverty and low quality of public services in the city.[152] Navalny concludes his post and video with a call to share the investigation and support him in an upcoming election, because the authorities 'won't change on their own'.[153]

Although the FBK uses the techniques of investigative journalism, it is not a journalistic outfit—it has a political mission. As FBK team member Maria Pevchikh has said, 'We are using investigative reporting as a tool to achieve our political ends.'[154]

Mistakes were made

At the start of 'Don't Call Him "Dimon"', Navalny points to the written investigation that the video summarises, saying that it 'contains irrefutable evidence of everything you'll see'. But the FBK does not always get things right.

In May 2017, the FBK deleted a video—'Putin's Friend Who Owns ALL of Television'.[155] Yarmysh—Navalny's press secretary and the lead on the video—posted a note on Facebook, saying that 'some of the information about the [investigated] ownership structure is outdated', leading her to delete the video.[156]

But it has not always been the FBK itself pointing out mistakes. In December 2019, the online independent media outlet The Bell published an article fact-checking one of the FBK's investigations. And this was their summary, generalising from what they found in this particular investigation to all of the FBK's work: 'Navalny is a politician. Anti-corruption investigations are a part of his political activities.'[157] Some details may not be watertight, some interpretations may be strained, argued The Bell. But they were based on open data and documents—they weren't just rumours; the details could be checked.

The FBK—an NGO with a political purpose

Navalny had started RosPil in 2011 with a handful of lawyers. Nearly ten years later, the Anti-Corruption Foundation employed dozens of people.[158] Many of them—lawyers and investigators—were in charge of the core business of the FBK. But the Foundation had evolved into something far bigger.

There was a whole team beyond this core group, dedicated to the production, direction, and diffusion of Navalny's content. A press secretary, an art director, a producer of the Navalny LIVE channel on YouTube, a video production manager, a video editor, a graphic designer. And, of course, a whole team responsible for the IT behind Navalny's activity, from web development to social media.

In short, this was a serious operation. Yes, Navalny was the front man as he had always been. But he was no longer leading a small activist collective. Instead, FBK had employees who received a proper salary of 70–80,000 roubles (then about £700–800) on average a month, even if this was fairly low for Moscow professionals.[159] The whole thing—complete with project managers and an executive director—had turned into a professional NGO.

And one that brought together all the things that an independent politician needed: money, cadres, and outreach.

First, it combined two sources of stable funding: permanent, larger contributions from Zimin, Ashurkov, and other businesspeople, some of whom remained anonymous for fear of persecution; and a crowd-funding platform that secured stable monthly payments from ordinary Russians. By the end of 2013, the FBK claimed it had raised twenty-three million roubles (then about £430,000).[160] In 2019, this had grown to over eighty-two million roubles (about £1 million at the time).[161]

Second, the FBK had evolved into a training unit for future opposition politicians. Sobol—hired as a lawyer—announced in October 2020 her plan to run in the State Duma elections of 2021.[162] And this path is not accidental. It shows how the FBK has been able to attract talented and undaunted individuals, able to take on tasks that ended up being far more than what they had initially applied for.

Finally, professionalising its investigations, the FBK team had also become experts at presenting their message—and timing their release to maximise impact. Considering that Navalny was banned from the state-controlled airwaves and could only use social media, his outreach was remarkable.

The FBK had, put simply, become a fully political beast. And it's no surprise, therefore, that the Kremlin treated it as exactly that: a real enemy.

The screws tighten

The FBK had a target on its back—and faced a mix of formal restrictions and informal pressures.

On the evening of 25 November 2016, Sergei Mokhov—Sobol's second husband—was coming home. A young man was waiting by the entrance to his building, holding flowers. When

Mokhov passed by, the young man stabbed him with a syringe. Mokhov immediately started convulsing and lost consciousness.

After hospitalisation, doctors declared he had been poisoned with an unknown substance—but he survived the attack.[163] Mokhov thought that it might have been related to his own investigative work into the funeral business in Russia—according to *The Economist*, '[t]o bury a loved one in Russia often means entering an underworld of corruption and red tape'.[164] But Sobol and Navalny thought it more likely to be related to one of their investigations. The poisoning of Sobol's husband has never, however, been fully explained.

The FBK also faced problems in court. Early in 2019, for instance, the Foundation released details of an investigation into catering companies and an outbreak of food poisoning at several Moscow schools. Following the FBK's probe, one of the companies pursued a defamation case against Navalny, Sobol, and the FBK for damaging its business reputation. And, in the autumn of 2019, a court ordered the Foundation, along with Navalny and Sobol personally, to pay a third each of eighty-eight million roubles (then about £1,100,000) to the company.[165]

'Foreign agent'

In 2012, the State Duma passed the so-called 'foreign agents' law. It obliged all civic organisations that receive foreign funding and engage in 'political activity' to register as a 'foreign agent'— and to print a statement to that effect on all their materials.[166] What constitutes political activity, meanwhile, was defined by the Ministry of Justice—which means it could be almost anything, from defending human rights to social protection and opinion polling.

In 2019, the authorities found a way to apply the law to the FBK. The Ministry of Justice claimed that the Foundation had received payments from two foreign donors. One private Russian citizen in Florida had donated US$50. The other donor was, as the independent online outlet Meduza found out, a professional boxer from Spain.[167] He told the journalists that he had transferred just over 138,000 roubles (about £1,700 at the time). When the Meduza journalists rang him up, he confirmed that he sent the money—but he did not recall the FBK's name or any other details of the case. These were not the foreign donors that one might think Russia seeks to bar, such as EU pro-democracy initiatives or American NGOs.

Navalny, of course, suspected a planned provocation by the Kremlin to get the FBK in trouble. Like many similarly bizarre stories, that cannot be proven. But the case clearly shows how easily the law can be instrumentalised.

Doors and debts

Sparks fly. The angry whir of a grinder fills the air as it cuts through a tough metal office door. People wait anxiously inside.[168]

It's 26 December 2019—and the FBK's office in Moscow is being raided by law enforcement. Officers cover security cameras before taking computers, with the Foundation's staff watching on. And this raid was not a one-off. But the team responds with characteristic, defiant humour. A Twitter account is set up for the office door, which comments in the first person: 'I haven't been broken today. It's been three days. I'm beginning to recover psychologically.'[169]

Navalny linked the December raid to the Foundation's investigation into Medvedev. But it wasn't just the Medvedev video that was giving the FBK trouble. The defamation suit in the Moscow food poisoning case had not ended well for the Foundation. It had to pay about £367,000—an enormous sum for the Foundation. As a result, in July 2020, Navalny announced that the FBK would close—it was, he said, the only way to deal with the enormous financial penalty, which was crippling their activities.[170]

In August 2020, an individual mentioned in the FBK's original investigation, Evgeny Prigozhin, bought the whole eighty-eight-million-rouble civil-suit debt. Often referred to by the moniker 'Putin's chef', Prigozhin denied allegations by the Foundation linking him to the food poisonings—and declared that he wanted to reduce 'this group of dishonest people to pennilessness and shoelessness'.[171]

But all was not lost. Navalny and his team simply set up a new NGO—the 'Foundation for the Protection of Citizens' Rights'—and continued to use the FBK brand publicly. The team kept working and the name could remain on the door—even if it was being smashed down all the time.

* * *

Duck ponds and politics

Ivanovo Region, near the town of Plyos on the bank of the Volga—a six-hour drive from Moscow.

A drone with a camera flies above the river, edging closer to the shore. In front, tree-covered land—and a grand estate the size of '30 Red Squares combined'.[172]

Two hovercraft. A ski slope. Three helipads. A renovated historical manor house, originally built in 1775. A cascading swimming pool. Is this another palace linked to Vladimir Putin?

No. This is the 'Milovka' estate, which FBK investigators allege is the 'secret dacha' of former president and then prime minister Dmitry Medvedev. Navalny publishes the video on YouTube in September 2016, a few days before elections to the State Duma. And he ends the video with a call to action:

> It's very strange that our country is poor but its officials live 300 times more luxuriously than other countries' leaders. All of this

corruption is only possible thanks to those who vote for United Russia. Please don't be like these people. And if you end up going to the elections this coming weekend, then make sure to vote against United Russia and ask as many people as you can to do the same.[173]

One detail of Navalny's video captured people's imagination: the presence of a duck house on a pond next to the manor building. Subsequently, yellow rubber ducks became a symbol of protests. And, at the start of 2018, one St Petersburg activist is even arrested after placing an enormous inflatable yellow duck in the window of his apartment along with a sign saying 'The police are waiting for us'.[174]

Navalny first achieved prominence as an anti-corruption blogger. We have shown how his journey began and evolved, moving from shareholder activism to crowd-sourcing scrutiny of state procurements, to in-depth investigations into the alleged hidden luxuries of Russia's officialdom. This earned him admirers and enemies alike.

He grew from a one-man-band to the head of a large group of professionals and volunteers. In assembling his team—the 'collective Navalny'—he has always stressed what he calls his 'meritocratic' approach, where skills, not connections, matter.

Navalny built a professional NGO with a political purpose. But he wasn't satisfied with simply calling for change as a civil society activist. He wanted to change things from within. He wanted to be president of the Russian Federation.

3

THE POLITICIAN

Navalny is wearing a dark suit and tie. He's sitting behind a desk in the grey office of a skyscraper overlooking Moscow. To his right, the Russian flag; to his left, pictures of his wife and children.

It's 13 December 2016. And it's official: Navalny is running for president of the Russian Federation. He releases a short video on YouTube and launches his campaign website, 'NAVALNY2018'—the year of the coming election. Looking straight to camera, composed and serious, candidate Navalny has 'long thought' about running. Can he and his supporters make their 'country better'?[1]

He's come to a conclusion: yes. He's thought about the issues. He has a whole 'programme of development' touching on inequality, wages, mortgage rates, taxes, and foreign policy. A 'difficult path' lies ahead, but he's convinced: 'We can succeed ... We'll fight together to give our beloved country a better future.'[2]

This is an ambitious forty-year-old with a long career in politics announcing he wants to become the leader of his country. He and his team have chosen a 'traditional format that fits what people are expecting from a presidential candidate'—a suit and tie.[3] Nothing out of the ordinary there.

Except Russian elections aren't normal or ordinary, by which Navalny means 'democratic'. Opposition candidates face a range of hurdles that unlevel the electoral playing field. Incumbents of the ruling elite—which in this presidential race means Putin himself—don't usually lose elections. True, opposition candidates are usually on the ballot—communists, liberals, populists, left wing, right wing. But, for them, success is not really a possibility.

Votes do matter—this is not the Soviet Union anymore. But so do what Russians call 'administrative resources': the levers the authorities have to deliver the votes they need—or to suppress those they do not. In a democracy, national television would probably have shown Navalny's three-minute video. Russian television does not.

Navalny says he wants to be a 'normal politician'. He wants to represent people, fight for power, for his supporters, for himself. And he believes he has all the necessary qualities to succeed. He stands for values—anti-corruption, yes, but also what he calls 'the European way of development' that Russia should follow: a democratic, rule-of-law state, with free markets and social policies.[4] His political programme reflects all of this.[5]

On the surface, Navalny's 2018 presidential campaign is about the politics people are familiar with in the West: personalities, issues, ideas, and policies. But it is actually about something harder: how to make this all happen in Russia. How to turn a plebiscite for Putin, with its handful of weak opponents, into democracy, into a real election, into a genuine fight for power—for the future of Russia.

And these difficulties become all too clear in late 2017, when, after a year of campaigning, Navalny is barred from running.

Navalny's political journey to this presidential campaign was long and far from straightforward. He has called himself a liberal, a democrat, a nationalist—until he abandoned political labels altogether. Why? Do these labels not fit Russia's complicated politics? Is it because he feels 'at home among strangers, and a stranger among his own', as he's keen to say when asked about his political identity?[6] Does he not want to alienate any potential supporters? Or, maybe, is his own brand now original and well known enough, making traditional labels irrelevant?

Navalny's political career spans some twenty years. But what are Navalny's politics? What does he stand for, besides his trademark fight against corruption? We track his journey from liberal party functionary in the early 2000s to a leading figure of the Russian opposition. We make sense of his many initiatives to transform his country, his twists and turns, his contradictions, and his friends and enemies. In these twenty years, only one man stood at the top of Russian politics—Putin. But underneath, people were organising and fighting—with Putin of course, but with each other as well.

A conflicted Russian liberal

Navalny was a teenager when the Soviet Union fell apart and a new Russia was born—in incredible pain. As the economy collapsed and plunged millions into misery, Russia was torn by a bloody political crisis that defined its future perhaps even more than the end of the Soviet Union itself.

In the early post-Soviet years, President Boris Yeltsin and his team of radical reformers were implementing brutal market reforms. In the Russian parliament—still called the Supreme Soviet—opposition to these reforms was growing. Two powers faced each other, irreconcilable: Yeltsin in the Kremlin, and parliament in the White House—the name of its building—around two-and-a-half kilometres away in the centre of Moscow.

The standoff ended when Yeltsin ordered tanks to fire on the White House in October 1993. The capital was shaken by violence. The clashes killed between 187 people (according to official sources) and 1,000 (according to supporters of the Supreme Soviet).[7] The country was on the brink of civil war.

But Yeltsin won. Muscovites came to look at the parliament building in flames by the Moskva River.

Among them was a first-year university student, cheering as special forces cracked down on the Supreme Soviet's insurgency. 'Crush the infamous', Navalny remembered shouting, quoting Voltaire. At the time, he called himself a 'market fundamentalist'; his friends joked he was a 'right-wing punk'.[8] He believed in Yeltsin and the reformers—in other words, in the promises of the West, in democracy, and in markets. 'Now we're going to wreck everything, privatise it, and a wonderful life will begin', he noted later, ironically.[9]

The 'wild 1990s'

In the 1990s, millions of Russians saw their savings destroyed by hyper-inflation. Many were made redundant and fell into poverty. Crime was rife. But, as he later admitted, Navalny thought the price was worth paying at the time.

For all but a minority of Russians, the years following the collapse of the Soviet Union were not times of promise, but a cursed decade. These were the 'wild 1990s'. Whatever they called themselves—communists or nationalists or patriots or nothing at all—they blamed the liberals or the democrats in power, even though not all liberals approved of the methods or specifics of Yeltsin's reforms.

Navalny was an aspiring businessman in the 1990s. He was part of the very constituency liberals targeted—or, rather, thought that their jolting reforms would create: a capitalist-minded middle class. He didn't get involved in politics until the end of the 1990s, after his business endeavours had proved less successful than he'd originally imagined: 'Market fundamentalists of my kind thought they'd all become millionaires. We all thought: since we're so smart, we'll get rich really quickly.' He did make money, but he didn't become a millionaire.

Navalny credits his experiences as a businessman in shaping his political views. He soon understood that, in Russia, 'money grows from power'. In rigged privatisation auctions—aimed, on the surface, at transferring wealth from the state to the people— Soviet factory directors, as well as young and ambitious communist officials, could get hold of businesses, as could those well connected to Yeltsin's team. In the process, a tiny minority became fabulously wealthy.

But Navalny's generation came too late to the party. And he realised that Yeltsin and the reformers had paved the way to Putin. With the complicity of their supporters—like Navalny himself—the 'democratic' reformers had laid the ground for an authoritarian and corrupt system. Many of them had believed that the Russian people were 'not ready for free elections'—and, in their eyes, this justified manipulating elections so that 'democratic' candidates won.[10]

Navalny became actively involved in Russian politics when Putin was rising to the heights of Russian power. Yeltsin made Putin his prime minister in August 1999 and soon his successor, with Putin becoming acting president on 31 December 1999.

Meanwhile, following the heady days of reform in the early to mid-1990s, liberals were in steady decline as a political force. Yeltsin had implemented liberal policies but had refused to support liberal parties, for fear of being constrained by them. In the 1999 legislative elections, liberal parties had managed to squeeze into parliament, but not by much. They were unpopular already—and their prospects didn't look good.

Navalny joins the party

In spite of this lack of popularity, Navalny decided to join a liberal party in 2000. Liberals were under threat and Navalny claimed he wanted to support them. The party he chose, Yabloko—meaning 'apple' in Russian—was small and slightly left-leaning.[11] The party's leader, Grigory Yavlinsky—an economist—had proposed an alternative plan to achieve the transition to a market economy. He was a constant critic of Yeltsin and his administration.

Yabloko had a principled reputation, contrary to its rival on the liberal flank, the Union of Right Forces (SPS)—a party closer to the Kremlin. In Navalny's words, Yabloko was 'the only consistently democratic party that talked about ideas and that didn't trade them for money or offices'.[12]

Despite its decent reputation, Navalny found the party to be a 'total mess', full of idlers.[13] Nevertheless—or, perhaps, precisely for that reason—he quickly rose through the ranks in the Moscow branch: from member of the regional council to campaign manager for the national parliamentary elections, deputy to the chairman, chief of staff, and up to a national position in the party's federal council.

The Moscow branch of Yabloko proved to be an excellent position to start a political career in a centralised country like Russia. Navalny showed clear abilities as a party functionary. He drew a salary from the party, complemented his income with legal work, and claimed he learned a lot there.[14]

But Navalny did not limit himself to party work. At the time, he already showed interest in blending civil-society activism and traditional politics. In 2003, the Moscow branch of Yabloko launched the Committee for the Defence of Muscovites, fighting against the boom in illegal, corrupt construction under the patronage of then boss of Moscow, Mayor Yuri Luzhkov. Navalny's trademark demonstrative courage—his bravado—was already on display: 'We're the only ones who don't fear Luzhkov'.[15] He would later claim that fighting developers could easily have had him killed.[16]

THE POLITICIAN

Climbing aboard a sinking ship

In 2006, alongside Maria Gaidar—opposition activist and daughter of the former 1990s liberal prime minister, Yegor Gaidar—Navalny started organising political debates.[17] They were soon a sensation, featuring prominent politicians from across the political spectrum. They were also an occasion for scandal: one of the debates was derailed by neo-Nazis.[18] At another, a brawl erupted, and Navalny shot one of his attackers with a rubber bullet pistol.[19]

As his reputation in Moscow grew—albeit not without controversy—it also started to become global. In 2010, he became a Yale World Fellow—a prestigious international programme for 'young leaders', with a four-month stay at the Ivy League university. For his application, he could count on support from the Russian capital's intelligentsia and liberal politics scene—leading journalist, Yevgenia Albats; economist and rector of the New Economic School, Sergei Guriev; chess master and opposition politician, Garry Kasparov; and Maxim Trudolyubov, a columnist for *Vedomosti*—the Russian equivalent of the *Financial Times*.[20]

Navalny was building a solid network in Moscow. He started to become a regular feature on the Ekho Moskvy radio station and to be mentioned for his party work in the capital's newspapers. The leading business daily *Kommersant* quoted him for the first time in June 2004. He was, in short, making a name for himself in that small world of liberal politicians, academics, and journalists called the *tusovka*—the clique.

But while his star was rising, his political camp all but disappeared. The fortunes of liberal politicians did not improve during Putin's first two terms as president, from 2000 to 2008. At the 2003 legislative elections, both Yabloko and SPS failed to pass the threshold of votes needed to enter the Duma. And at the next elections in 2007, they fared even worse: 1.59 per cent for Yabloko, and less than 1 per cent for SPS. Navalny was starting to think that liberalism looked like a 'political corpse'.[21]

After toeing the Yabloko party line for years as a loyal activist and party functionary, Navalny now had ideas as to how he might revive the party, liberalism, and the opposition in general. And these ideas came under a simple label: nationalism. In 2007, he opened what remains one of the most controversial chapters in his political career.

Political alchemy: trying to fuse nationalism and liberalism

At first sight, a liberal in Russia cannot be a nationalist—the two categories exclude one another. When perestroika reopened long-closed political debates in the Soviet Union, liberals found their models in the West—and, in their enthusiasm for democracy and the rule of law, they cursed Soviet and Russian imperialism. Liberals believed that nationalism could only end with Russia dominating its neighbours.

For most Russian liberals, nationalism might be acceptable if it meant freeing one's nation from Russian imperialism—as in, say, Poland or Latvia. In Russia, this wouldn't work—and, to this day, the word 'nationalism' carries connotations of bigotry, superiority, and chauvinism. A liberal might call themself a patriot, but not a 'nationalist'. This does not mean that liberals cannot have racial prejudices. What crossed a red line was to embrace an explicitly nationalist agenda.

But Navalny believed precisely in crossing that line: the future of liberalism lay in embracing nationalism.

In the mid-2000s, a new nationalism was on the rise in Russia. In the 1990s, most nationalists—or 'national-patriots', as they often called themselves—cultivated nostalgia for the Soviet Union. Some of them imagined that Russia would dominate Eurasia, the vast landmass between Western Europe and East Asia where, some argued, Slavic and Turkic people shared a common culture alien to European values.[22] They were usually accused of being 'red-brown'—that is, mixing far-left and far-right authoritarian ideas.

Now, a new generation of nationalists looked to the West—to the successful populist and far-right parties of Europe, the French National Front or the Austrian People's Party (ÖVP). And as Putin's hold on power seemed unassailable, some liberals were also opening up to the idea of collaborating with nationalists in common protest. In the mid-2000s, the 'Other Russia' coalition aimed to unite all manner of opponents to Putin's rule on a minimal, democratic platform: from liberals like Kasparov, to National Bolsheviks like Eduard Limonov—a dissident writer whose political platform mixed fascism and socialism with provocative direct action.[23]

NAROD—the people

Navalny did not limit himself, however, to mere tactical collaboration with nationalists. Since 2005, nationalists of all hues had been organising an annual rally in Moscow—the Russian March. Navalny started attending in 2006 as an 'observer' from Yabloko, then as a fully-fledged participant the following year.[24] He wanted to build an alliance that blended liberalism and nationalism. The result was NAROD, a movement that called itself national-democratic.

Navalny created NAROD with Sergei Gulyayev—a liberal politician from St Petersburg—and Zakhar Prilepin—a veteran of the Chechen wars, a National Bolshevik, and one of Russia's most famous writers. The initiative benefitted from a generous investor: political consultant Stanislav Belkovsky. On the lookout for fresh anti-Putin faces, he funded Navalny with 'tens of thousands of US dollars' to launch a movement.[25]

The name of the movement co-founded by Navalny set the bar very high. The acronym for the Russian National Movement of

Liberation forms the word *narod*—the 'people' in Russian. NAROD's goal was to unite people beyond their party affiliations, hoping that 'national-democratic' ideals might provide broad appeal and set the stage for a wide political coalition. Its manifesto was written in a dense style, blending nationalist clichés—'the population of Russia is degrading and dying'—and denunciations of corruption, lawlessness, and cynicism. NAROD aimed to create the 'conditions for the conservation and development of the Russian people, its culture, language, and historical territory'. The movement opposed the idea that Russia should be 'multinational'—a 'chimera', it claimed.[26]

While in Yabloko Navalny was mostly in charge of organisational matters, his role in NAROD allowed him to flesh out a concrete political programme. The NAROD manifesto articulated democratic reforms and remained vague, policy-wise, about what 'nationalism' would mean in practice. What it did call for was a 'sensible' immigration policy: 'Those who come to our home but do not want to respect our laws and traditions must be thrown out.'[27]

Jumping ship—or walking the plank

Putin is often branded a 'Russian nationalist' in the West. Where did Navalny's ideas stand in relation to the president's? Putin had promised to rebuild a strong and respected Russia and was never shy in praising the Motherland. But he steered clear of embracing ethnic Russians too closely. To him, those who chanted 'Russia for ethnic Russians' were either 'idiots' or 'provocateurs', as he sternly declared in 2003.[28] Putin never failed to praise Russia's multinational character—and never bent to the nationalists' calls for a stricter immigration regime.

This type of nationalism also proved intolerable to the leadership of Yabloko. Uniting nationalists with liberals, as Navalny proposed, crossed a red line. His immediate superior in the party, Sergei Mitrokhin—chair of the Moscow branch of the party—called on Navalny to resign from his position, which he did. But Navalny remained a member of the party for a while, even though he now considered the 'left-liberal tendency' of the party to be a 'mistake' and continued to advocate for a 'national-democratic ideology within its ranks'.[29]

But, in December 2007, the national bureau of Yabloko had had enough. It expelled Navalny 'for having caused political damage to the party, including for his nationalist activity'.[30] Nationalism certainly played its part in that decision—Yabloko is not known for accommodating this kind of ideological deviation. But many pointed out—including Navalny himself—that he had also called for the domineering founder and leader of the party, Yavlinsky, to step down, which may have precipitated his downfall.[31]

Nationalism on the rise

Nationalism was then a scene bustling with groups vying for an audience. And gaining respectability was especially crucial: the word itself carried toxic connotations, and many nationalists were not helping on that front.

Nationalists back then sought inspiration in the West, but some of them were looking to a darker European past: Nazi Germany. The 2000s saw a dramatic rise in skinhead groups committing racist attacks in Russia. Underground terrorist organisations were also established.[32] In 2011, members of one of the deadliest such groups, the National-Socialist Society– North, were found guilty of twenty-seven murders.[33]

Navalny wanted nothing whatsoever to do with that. In 2008, the New Political Nationalism conference brought together representatives from NAROD and several other groups.[34] They adopted a resolution crafted to offer voters nationalism with a human face. No to 'crazy Soviet patriots', no to 'skinheads', no to 'Orthodox banner-bearers with beards'. Yes to 'respectable' politicians of the 'modern Western European' kind—lounge suits for all.

Some liberals, like Ilya Yashin—a friend of Navalny and no sympathiser of nationalism—approved of this trend, hoping it would offer a peaceful space for nationalists to congregate. Better this than 'baseball bats', he thought.[35] Likewise, Yevgenia Albats claimed she encouraged him to attend the Russian March, and even went there with him.[36] This strategy has been called the 'normalisation' of nationalism.[37]

But, at the time, it meant more: it was an attempt to create a fusion of liberalism and nationalism—a creed that could unite the majority of the population against the Putin regime. The aim was to overcome what Navalny thought was an 'artificial division' and 'political nonsense from the early 1990s ... when "democrats" were fighting "communists-nationalists"'. In short, the goal was to make a renewed nationalism the ideology of the opposition.[38]

There were good reasons why Navalny and other nationalists thought their time had come. The 2000s saw a massive spike in anti-immigrant sentiment in Russia. This was directed first and foremost against migrant workers from Central Asia and the Caucasus, who often did menial jobs in retail or construction. This hostility also targeted Russian citizens—especially people from the North Caucasus, including the republics of Chechnya and Dagestan, who had moved to big cities in central Russia.[39] Across the country, xenophobia inspired large-scale riots.[40]

Those videos…

NAROD came to nothing in the end. It organised a few conferences, penned a manifesto, and that was about it. One lasting impact, however, was the production of infamous videos published in 2007 that are still debated as of 2021. In one of these, Navalny plays a dentist—a 'certified nationalist'—in his office, weaving a metaphor between 'teeth' and 'Russia': a tooth without a root is dead, and so will Russia be if it's deprived of its Russian roots. In order for Russia to keep its Russian roots, the clip advocates deporting illegal immigrants, although denouncing neo-Nazi violence. It concludes: 'We have the right to be Russians in Russia, and we'll defend that right.'[41]

The other infamous NAROD video presents another metaphor. Sitting at a desk, Navalny mentions how cockroaches or flies can be disgusting, and how you can chase them with a fly-swatter. But what should you do, asks Navalny, if the cockroach is too aggressive or too big? The video shows a picture of Chechen terrorists, with Shamil Basayev—one of the most well known—in the centre. A frightening character enters; Navalny shoots him and concludes: 'I recommend using a handgun.'[42] NAROD then stood for gun-rights. 'Artistic license' was Navalny's reply when asked if he regretted these videos.[43]

The failure of NAROD did not convince Navalny to abandon nationalism, however. His mission was to convince the population that the Kremlin was just 'pseudo-nationalist', while his own kind of nationalism could unite people in protest. For this, however, you needed issues and campaign slogans.

Navalny believed that nationalism was about the real, concrete problems of ordinary people. Take immigration: 'There is a great number of illegal immigrants. It's a fact that on this indicator, Russia is second only to the United States', he told a journalist.[44] In order to reduce immigration, Navalny advocated for the introduction of a visa regime with countries of Central Asia. Under Russian law, citizens of Kazakhstan, Kyrgyzstan, Uzbekistan, and Tajikistan can enter Russia without a visa and remain in the country for ninety days.[45]

These problems are all self-evident to the average person on the street—so thought Navalny. But 'politically correct' liberals fell into irrelevance by not acknowledging this: 'As a matter of principle, they considered certain topics as dangerous to discuss.'[46] And one of those pressing topics was the situation in the Caucasus.

'Stop feeding the Caucasus'

When the Soviet Union collapsed, Chechnya—a republic in the North Caucasus—had attempted to break free from Russian rule. Moscow's refusal to grant the region independence resulted in extraordinarily brutal wars, with active Islamist militancy, the devastation of the region, and terror attacks that hit big cities, including Moscow. By the end of the 2000s, most insurgents had been crushed and Moscow was rebuilding Chechnya—ruled semi-autonomously with an iron fist by President Ramzan Kadyrov.

Navalny resented the leadership that had turned Chechnya into a fiefdom.[47] Nationalists held that Kadyrov had built his own dictatorship in Chechnya, lavishly bankrolled by Moscow— and, yet, was allowed to live, in practice, outside the laws of the Russian Federation.

The question of the Caucasus had always proved contentious to Russian nationalists. But in 2011, several came up with a simply named campaign designed to bring them new supporters: 'Stop feeding the Caucasus'. The campaign, joined by Navalny for a while, mixed a xenophobic dog whistle against people in the Caucasus with a political critique of Kadyrov's rule—and, by implication, Vladimir Putin.

The associations of the campaign and its xenophobic, racist undertones were obvious to many in Russia.[48] Navalny did, however, attempt to distance himself from the stigmatisation of the peoples of the Caucasus, saying that the enormous resources transferred to Chechnya were simply embezzled by local elites— and that local populations who did not see 'anything of that rainfall of money' were certainly 'not happy about this'.[49]

THE POLITICIAN

A rising star of the opposition

By 2010, Navalny was one of the rising figures of the opposition scene. His anti-corruption activism had established him as an original player in that world. His blog on LiveJournal was one of the most popular on the Russian internet. He was getting his first profiles in the press, both in Russia and in the West—'tall and blond, Navalny, who is thirty-four years old, cuts a striking figure', wrote Julia Ioffe for *The New Yorker*.[50] *The New York Times* first mentioned his name in 2010 as a 'prominent blogger' and would feature its first profile of him in March 2011, noting his 'blue-eyed good looks and acidic sense of humour'.[51] He was a fixture on Ekho Moskvy, appearing five times as a guest in 2010, thirteen times in 2011.

By this point, he had already established a distinctive approach: straightforward, blunt, ironic, acerbic, brash. His blog was full of Russian and American memes and pop culture. It had facts, too. Here's how Leonid Volkov—one of Navalny's closest and oldest associates—described it in 2011: 'Appropriate and much needed. No endless musings about who was right in 1993, or about the merits of some person in 1989, no foaming-at-the-mouth indictments of the bloody regime. Applied politics: setting concrete problems, proposing concrete alternatives, meaningful criticism, with figures in hand.'[52] And many found it fun.

As a politician of the internet age, Navalny wasn't alone. The turn of the 2000s and the 2010s saw the coming of age of a number of young politicians eager to dislodge the old guard of opposition leaders. Many had come to the realisation that whatever their talents, these older leaders had been tainted by their involvement with politics in the 1990s. Their involvement in the reforms of the 1990s, as well as the devastating consequences of the resulting upheavals, made these figures dead wood in the eyes of the population—or they were just too stale.

A new generation had to come—and it created movements and coalitions challenging old-style parties. Among liberals, Yashin—born in 1983—became one of the leaders of the Solidarnost movement—a coalition of activists from small, liberal parties—after having tried to oust Yavlinsky from the leadership of Yabloko. Roman Dobrokhotov—also born in 1983—led the democratic youth movement 'We'. All these leaders and movements were challenging the regime in an atmosphere of stifling stability—and hoping they would be able to exploit any chance they might get.

Against Putin's 'party of crooks and thieves'

Politically, 2011 was a peculiar year in Russia. Everything seemed up in the air. Russia might become more modern, open, and liberal—as President Dmitry Medvedev gave some reasons to hope. Or it might slide deeper into authoritarianism.

Medvedev had ruled Russia as president since 2008 in an awkward tandem with Putin as his prime minister—and Medvedev's four-year term was coming to a close: the presidential election was set for spring the following year. But, before that, legislative elections were scheduled for December 2011.

The ratings of United Russia—the authorities' formidable 'party of power'—were on the wane. Both Putin's allies and his opponents were looking to the December elections as a general rehearsal for the presidential election. The fates of Medvedev and Putin hung in the balance—as did that of Russia.

Navalny also had his eyes on the 2011 elections, which were hardly promising for the liberal opposition. Many liberals had deluded themselves into thinking that their demise was due simply to authoritarianism—to believing, in other words, that Putin ruled by force alone.

Russian liberalism also had a distinctive elitist bent: the Russian people were ungrateful, dark masses, unable to see the light of progress. If only they could understand how democracy and markets were good for them. That's what some liberal elites appeared to think, at least. And if the people couldn't see the 'right' way forward, some even argued that they might need a strong hand—a Pinochet or a Lee Kuan Yew.[53]

Navalny was not among them. He admitted that there was an 'elite' with special responsibility. But this didn't reflect fundamental differences in values, he thought. Everyone—from the 'drunk' in a small town to the 'television worker in Moscow'—shared the same values. They understood that corruption is bad and that abiding by the law is good: 'Let's not fool ourselves into thinking that there's cattle and elites.'[54]

Navalny thought that the 'real' opposition had to be appealing to the people. And that helped explain his forays into nationalism. He also thought that Putin had real support in the country.[55] True, there is fraud at the polls, he noted, but the regime's power is based on its popularity—a popularity that translates into votes: 'The power of Putin is not based on some mythical "siloviki" [i.e., on coercive actors] ... it's based on the real ratings of Putin. He's the most popular politician in Russia, and he'll remain so in the future, even with fair elections and free media.'[56]

Putin was popular, but his party, United Russia, less so. And it was losing ground in local and regional elections. Could it be the weak link in the regime? That is precisely what Navalny thought. In order to win, the opposition would have to drive down the ratings of United Russia: 'The opposition must work systematically to bring the ratings of United Russia back to where they belong: around 20–25 per cent', said Navalny.[57] This would translate into bad electoral results for the authorities, thereby weakening the ruling group. That was the plan—simple, but ambitious.

Revealing corruption was the first part of Navalny's plan. And it got a serious boost when he started calling United Russia the 'party of crooks and thieves'. The slogan stuck. It was simple and in line with Navalny's core issue: corruption—the issue that was designed to unite everybody against Putin and his cronies. Navalny used the slogan relentlessly.

A slogan is not enough

Lowering Putin's popularity and discrediting his party with a catchy slogan was one thing, but what about elections? The regime looked strong, liberal parties had faded into irrelevance—and there was no unity among liberals on the horizon.

Worse, with elections being ever less free, the opposition faced a basic dilemma, leading to endless debate. Boycotting elections was an option—and had the advantage of being principled. Navalny had, in fact, advocated this approach in the past, along with NAROD.[58] But, by boycotting, wouldn't liberals run the risk of disappearing completely from public view? On the other hand, when they did participate in elections, they were humiliated.

A year before the 2011 elections, Navalny concluded that the boycott strategy had failed. United Russia had a supermajority in the State Duma—the lower chamber of the national legislature—and Medvedev had been elected in the first round of the 2008 elections. Something else was needed. If you can't boycott elections, then you have to participate in them—but how?

Tactical voting was the answer. People needed to go to the polls to 'destroy' United Russia by whatever means necessary.[59] 'To vote for any party but United Russia'—this was the slogan and the strategy. And Navalny put so much effort into popularising it that it became known as 'Navalny's option'.[60] But what did it mean in practice?

Authoritarian regimes leave opposition-minded citizens with bad options only—and the need to make compromises. For Navalny, this meant voting for parties of the 'systemic opposition'—those parties willing to work within the system. When he came to power, Putin did not ban opposition. He chose to manage it. And the result of this 'management' was the systemic opposition. These parties accept that there are red lines they shouldn't cross. They receive help—money, airtime, the right to participate in elections—in return for their loyal opposition, for making Russia look like a democracy. On the surface, at least.

But voting for the systemic opposition is not palatable to everyone opposed to the ruling elite. And Navalny was conscious of this. In a February 2011 blog post, he told his readers: 'You don't need to explain to me that "A Just Russia" is no different from "United Russia", and that Zhirinovsky is bad, and that the Communist Party is decrepit.'[61]

These were the only three nominally opposition parties with national parliamentary seats in 2011. The most powerful was the Communist Party of the Russian Federation (KPRF). It stood on a platform mixing socialism—with a heavy dose of Stalinist nostalgia—and Russian imperialism, suffused with Christian Orthodoxy.[62] It has been led by Gennady Zyuganov—a former Soviet apparatchik—since its founding in 1993.

The nominally left-wing A Just Russia was created by the Kremlin in order to siphon off votes from the Communist Party—a party that has sometimes ventured into real opposition. Vladimir Zhirinovsky, finally, was better known than his party, the Liberal Democratic Party of Russia (LDPR). Arguably the least aptly named party in the history of politics, LDPR was neither liberal nor democratic—but, if anything, of the far-right, populist kind. Its leader, Zhirinovsky, is widely considered to be a professional 'buffoon'.[63]

For many voters, these parties hardly made for an appealing option. But Navalny believed that, as unattractive as these parties may be, the benefits of voting for them were worth it. It would cause stress to the system. Any decrease in United Russia's results would be perceived as a loss for the Kremlin. Navalny believed that the more votes were cast, the harder it would be for the authorities to rig the elections. And it might embolden their more opposition-minded members, turning these nominal opposition parties into real allies.[64]

The return—of Putin and protests

On 24 September 2011, a question on the minds of many Russians was answered. Would Putin return to the presidency? He would. Medvedev declared that, according to what the two subsequently claimed was a long-planned decision, Putin would run in the 2012 presidential election. Medvedev would head the United Russia list in the upcoming Duma elections and become prime minister. The move caused outrage among the opposition-minded, and even those who had believed in Medvedev's promises of modernisation. For them, his whole presidency now looked even more like a sham, simply keeping Putin's seat warm and following the letter, but not the spirit, of the Constitution.

Not everything was under the Kremlin's control, however. The parliamentary elections held on 4 December 2011 were a blow to United Russia: its official share of the vote fell to less than 50 per cent for the first time since the 2003 elections, in spite of manipulation. Documented by an active movement of observers using smartphones, details of electoral fraud were spread around Russia—and the world—on social media.

The first protest was organised the next day by the liberal movement Solidarnost—and it caught Navalny by surprise. Solidarnost had advocated spoiling ballot papers in the elections, rather than adopting Navalny's tactical voting approach—and that angered him. As a result, Navalny did not want to attend the rally, he recalled. 'But when I saw the numbers for United Russia in Moscow, that they "invented" 46.5 per cent, when even in Vladivostok they got only 25–30 per cent, I went into a crazy rage. I went there thinking the rally would be a disaster'—that nobody would show up.[65]

But they did. Several thousand people gathered in Chistye Prudy—a grand boulevard in the very centre of Moscow. As is usual in Russia, the police had erected a perimeter with barriers and metal-detectors—but the space they had cordoned off was too small. Navalny remembered seeing many 'new faces', so many that Yashin recalled that it took him half an hour to make his way through the dense crowd to the stage.[66]

The rally on 5 December 2011 had been authorised by the authorities. What had not been authorised was to march to the Central Electoral Commission, a few hundred metres from the Kremlin. Three hundred demonstrators were detained for doing so—including Navalny, for fifteen days. He would follow subsequent events from a jail cell, seeing the scale of the protests, but not participating directly in their organisation.

Navalny was released on 21 December 2011 and his first LiveJournal post was full of optimism: 'We went to jail in one country and woke up in another.' He claimed the Kremlin had lost the support of the majority: 'Before: yes, there's cheating, theft and illegality, but the majority still supports them. After: there's cheating, theft and illegality, but without support, and with the anger of the majority.'[67]

Navalny was not alone in feeling optimistic. In terms of numbers, demonstrations had not been held on this scale in a long time. But the protests also showed that new leaders had appeared—and from a younger generation, even if older leaders, such as Boris Nemtsov, a former deputy prime minister, were still prominent. The movement grouped old and new, civil society organisations and political parties.

What was also striking was the ideological diversity beneath the common demand for free and fair elections. Liberals, socialists, communists, and nationalists stood side by side in the demonstrations. The protests took place in a joyful, optimistic atmosphere, with slogans and placards full of humour. Many journalists, writers, and artists—the intelligentsia—were prominent speakers.

Becoming an opposition leader

Navalny was a leader of the protest movement already—in Moscow, at least. On 24 December, he participated in a demonstration on Sakharov Avenue—named after the famous Soviet dissident, Andrei Sakharov, just up the road from Chistye Prudy. It gathered between 30,000 and more than 100,000 people.[68] (As always with opposition protest numbers in Russia, the lower figure comes from the authorities, the higher from the organisers.)

Navalny's words on 24 December were provocative and memorable—but non-committal: 'I see here enough people to take the Kremlin right now. But we're a peaceful force, we won't do that—yet! But if these crooks and thieves try again to trick and lie to us, we will take it! It's ours.'[69] Writing on his blog after the rally, Navalny seemed to believe the authorities were ready to reform for 'the sake of survival'.[70]

Navalny articulated a four-point strategy. First, the State Duma elections were illegitimate and he demanded immediate political reform, followed by new elections. Second, the protest movement should grow—and get prepared not to leave the streets. Third, the next presidential election, scheduled for March 2012, would not be legitimate until the registration of candidates was liberalised. Fourth, he called for negotiations between the protest movement and the authorities. They should be public, and the protest movement should elect delegates through an internet voting procedure. The goal was to answer the criticism that the opposition didn't represent the multiple viewpoints on the streets.[71]

More demonstrations followed. But so did counter-demonstrations. The Kremlin decided to mobilise massive crowds in support of Putin. Their fear was clear: a Russian version of the 'Orange Revolution'—mass protests in Ukraine in 2004–5 that resulted in regime change, and that the Kremlin thought were instigated by the West. With this heightened pressure, and their own rallies mobilising fewer and fewer people, the opposition found itself at a loss.

President Medvedev had announced political reforms in December, hoping to defuse the protest. He promised to ease the restrictive legislation on political party registration, allowing more parties to form. He also promised to return direct elections for governors—that is, the heads of the Russian regions. Since 2005, they had been appointed by the president without a popular vote. But the authorities clearly had no intention of negotiating directly with the protesters.

Navalny's strategy concentrated, therefore, on expanding and organising the protest movement—and calling to vote for any candidate but Putin.

Protest peters out

There was no momentum for the second point of Navalny's plan: to prepare people 'not to leave the streets'—as had been the case in Ukraine in 2004, when a tent city was quickly erected and stayed put in central Kyiv on Maidan Square. It seems that Navalny did not, in fact, 'get prepared' for such a scenario.

A few days before the presidential election, four journalists grilled him on the topic on the independent TV channel Dozhd (Rain). Would tents be distributed on election night? People, Navalny replied, were 'spontaneously' getting ready for that, and it 'would happen'.[72] But the tents did not appear.

The presidential election took place on 4 March 2012. According to official results, the election was a triumph for

Putin, who avoided a run-off, winning more than 63 per cent in the first round. On his blog, Navalny declared: 'We can only repeat the obvious. From today, Russia lives without legitimate, legal authorities. The crooks who usurped the Kremlin acknowledge it. This is why they launched a real military operation. The city hasn't seen such a number of soldiers since 1993.'[73]

The next day, a sanctioned rally took place on Pushkin Square—a traditional site of protest about a mile away from the Kremlin—gathering between 10,000 and 25,000 people.[74] When it came to its end, some 1,500 protesters remained on the square, along with Navalny, Sergei Udaltsov—the leader of the Left Front, a coalition of socialist movements—Yashin, and other leaders of the protests. Riot police dispersed the demonstration and detained 400 people.[75]

In an interview, Navalny claimed he had hoped for a repetition of what happened on the night of the Duma elections—a spontaneous march through the centre of Moscow—but that the massive presence of police forces on that day prevented the move.[76] But he also claimed he didn't believe a revolution was in sight. The authorities had 'regrouped' and reinforced support for Putin that Navalny believed to be real. The long-term goal would involve much work to chip away at this popularity.

The Kremlin, for its part, stepped up repression against the protest movement. On 6 May, a new demonstration was organised, this time on Bolotnaya Square—a large open space on an island in the Moskva River facing the Kremlin. Putin's inauguration ceremony was due the following day. The demonstration—organised by Navalny, Udaltsov, and Nemtsov—ended in confusion, violence, and repression. Some 450 demonstrators were detained. While in previous demonstrations short administrative arrests were the most common punishment, this time the authorities reacted with full-scale criminal prosecutions. Twenty-eight activists, representing the whole ideological spectrum, ended up being sentenced to prison terms ranging from two-and-a-half to four-and-a-half years.[77] There would be no Maidan in Moscow.

Back to the liberal mainstream?

These protests—known as the For Fair Elections movement—were remarkable in uniting forces across the political spectrum. Early on, numerous organising committees had been set up, none of them very efficient. This diversity proved difficult for the long-term prospects of the movement, something the fate of the Coordination Council of the Opposition only confirmed.

The Council was elected online in October 2012, coordinated by Leonid Volkov. This was a bottom-up experiment with online direct democracy. And the elections were a technical success, attracting more than 80,000 participants.[78]

But, from the start, the Council's job was frustrated by the vagueness of its objectives. Ideological diversity had certainly helped to swell the ranks of the protesters, but it stunted any wide-ranging organisation. As a result, the Coordination Council soon fell into irrelevance, with endless debates and conflicts.[79]

The For Fair Elections movement had provided Navalny with a unique platform, and he emerged from it as one of its leaders. It also transformed his strategy, ideas-wise. Nationalists were present in the movement—but as a minority. Elections were the focus, and nationalist themes had receded to the background.

Nationalism, it seems, did not live up to expectations. Navalny reflected to the journalist Ben Judah: 'I have some conservative views, but I joined Yabloko for a reason ... I'm more or less a liberal kind of guy.' He was not a fan, in general, of 'ideological mumbo-jumbo'.[80] Navalny has never been very specific about where he stands on the issues that matter most to the nationalist scene. As Russian nationalism expert Marlène

Laruelle has written, Navalny 'can only disappoint those who expect from him a modicum of theoretical construction: he is a doer, not a thinker'.[81]

Navalny is an ordinary politician in that he does not readily admit when he is wrong. Whether he really changed his mind or not on the question of nationalism remains unclear. He himself claimed his views had not changed, and he continued to use some nationalist talking points. But his next moves revealed that he was back firmly at the centre of the liberal opposition.

Navalny on the ballot—for the first and last time

During the protest movement, Medvedev had promised that regional heads would be elected again—and it started with Moscow. Sergei Sobyanin was appointed mayor of Moscow in 2010, replacing Luzhkov—a colourful character who had ruled over the Russian capital since 1992. In 2013, the Kremlin decided that the technocratic figure of Sobyanin needed fresh electoral legitimacy. On 4 June, Sobyanin resigned and announced a snap election, scheduled for September. Polls predicted a landslide victory.[82]

On the opposition side, Volkov was bullish. The same day as Sobyanin's resignation, he proclaimed on Twitter: 'No boycott. In itself a campaign is an important mobilising story, a way to rock the boat. Just let's not raise expectations too much.'[83] Navalny immediately announced he would run if he could.[84] The liberal party RPR–PARNAS endorsed Navalny's candidacy and even managed to have him registered with the support of United Russia.

The authorities had a not-so-secret hope that Navalny would be routed in the process.[85] The Kremlin was then in the habit of allowing weak candidates on to the ballot. That way, it could reap the reputational rewards of holding elections without running the risk of losing them. Wasn't Navalny just a liberal blogger unable to attract the votes of ordinary Russians?

Even in Moscow, Navalny's ratings were fairly low at the start of the race: in July, the independent pollster the Levada Center estimated them at merely 8 per cent, while Sobyanin polled at an impressive 78 per cent. But expectations for Navalny quickly picked up—and polls would soon confirm the trend.[86]

That he would be allowed to participate was far from guaranteed, however. At this very moment, Navalny was being tried for embezzlement in the Kirovles case. Few doubted what the verdict would be—especially since the prosecution had struck a plea bargain deal with Vyacheslav Opalev, the former head of Kirovles. He would 'actively provide the investigation with information' about Navalny's 'criminal plan'.[87]

On 18 July 2013—the day after being registered as a candidate for the mayoral election—Navalny was convicted and sentenced to five years in prison, which barred him from running. And he was immediately taken into custody. But then, in a move that surprised many, the prosecution decided to ask the court to release Navalny pending appeal. What was going on? Proekt—a leading Russian investigative website—claimed that officials in the Kremlin had apparently made a mistake: they had not 'thought to call the court' to prevent Navalny from being locked up—something that would prevent him from continuing to take part in the Moscow election.[88] The prosecution's request was, perhaps, simply correcting this mistake. And that meant that Navalny was a free man—for now. This all seemed like a classic case of 'telephone justice', when political authorities interfere in high-profile cases, although somewhat messier than usual this time.[89]

Navalny could campaign. He received the support of some nationalists. But he was also endorsed by an impressive array of representatives of the Russian liberal intelligentsia. Among them, writer Lyudmila Ulitskaya ('My ideal is not Navalny. It's Vaclav

Havel. We don't have Havel, but we have Navalny'); journalist Leonid Parfyonov ('We haven't had new politicians for so long!'); and gallerist Marat Guelman ('Absolutely everything is transparent, with passionate young people').[90]

Vying for the support of the same constituency, Navalny's former party, Yabloko, did not support him and ran its own candidate—Sergei Mitrokhin, for whom Navalny used to work. In an interview, Mitrokhin reiterated his hostility to Navalny's nationalism—an ideology he deemed 'extremely destructive' for Russia as a multi-ethnic state, besides being 'unbecoming to us, the party of the intelligentsia'.[91] Even though Navalny had been supported by some of the Moscow intelligentsia, many did not consider him one of them.

The campaign was a sensation. No local or regional election had attracted this much attention for a while. Leonid Volkov boasted that, contrary to opposition candidates in previous races, their team had chosen, 'as an experiment, to work, and not just to write in blogs'. Speaking to journalist Ilya Azar in his campaign office, Volkov claimed: 'Look around, everyone's working, there are 300 people already in our headquarters, on a 24/7 regime, a shitload.' And Azar remarked that, while waiting for Volkov for twenty minutes, six people had come into his office to sign up to help with the campaign.[92]

Navalny's electoral campaign recruited thousands of volunteers and set up stands across Moscow to distribute leaflets. The inspiration was decidedly Western. Volkov imagined 'campaign meetings like in the American movies'.[93] And Navalny claimed he was inspired by the third season of the US television series *The Wire*, which depicted the election of the mayor of Baltimore.[94]

But, inside the team, not everything was going well. Several years later, Ekaterina Patyulina—a staffer in 2013—accused Volkov of what she termed 'sexual harassment (in its Western understanding)' during the campaign.[95] In text messages that she later made public, it appeared that he had pressured her to date him. When she refused Volkov's advances, he fired her friend Maxim Katz from the campaign—out of 'jealousy', she claimed.[96] In his reaction to the allegations, Volkov cited several substantive reasons why Katz was fired. He also admitted that he had been in love with Patyulina and that his text messages now seemed 'stupid' to him—but he denied having harassed her. Navalny dismissed Patyulina's accusations and supported Volkov— although Navalny later claimed he would not tolerate sexual harassment in his team.[97]

A victory in defeat

Navalny's programme did not limit itself to narrow urban problems—as its slogan made plain: 'Change Russia, start with Moscow'. His programme was designed with the help of the economist and former rector of the New Economic School, Sergei Guriev—then exiled in France.[98] It promised a 'comfortable city' up to 'European standards', but also one 'where free citizens have a feeling of personal dignity and can directly influence municipal authorities'. In order to achieve these goals, Navalny and his team advocated direct democracy (referendums), a drive towards transparency, and more neoliberal solutions: 'Competition in housing and utilities, health and education'—in other words, privatisations.[99]

Navalny did not seem particularly keen on support from nationalists, but his campaign did include positions courting those receptive to nationalist themes, including strict positions on immigration.[100] He also suggested banning the 'Lezginka'—a traditional Caucasian dance—in the centre of Moscow, claiming that Muscovites considered it a 'challenge to society' that did not correspond to the 'cultural code' of the city.[101]

The results were a triumph for Navalny. On 8 September, he officially received 27.24 per cent of the vote, nearly forcing the incumbent Sobyanin—with 51.37 per cent—into a run-off. Though turnout was low—fewer than a third of the seven million registered voters turned out—the result was widely held as a success. Navalny now stood above any opposition leader of his generation.

Navalny, party-builder

Normal politicians usually belong to a political party. Navalny didn't.

As his national profile rose, Navalny was asked again and again whether he would join a party—or create his own. In June 2011, he declared: 'If you want to create a party, you need to get two million per year to support it and go to the Ministry of Justice to register it. This is not a struggle for power. It's a senseless waste of time.'[102] Until partial liberalisation in 2012, laws on political parties in Russia were restrictive—something reflected in a simple number: there were only seven official parties registered in 2011.

Navalny proclaimed: 'I'm taking another route. Weakening the legitimate support for United Russia—the fight against crooks and thieves: this is my political campaign, my struggle for power. It is many times more effective than any party.'[103]

Meanwhile, friends from the Urals—Volkov and Fyodor Krasheninnikov, a political consultant—were busy designing the party of the future. In April 2012, they announced that they would form a new political party on the basis of their online voting platform 'Demokratiya2'. Both were interested in radical, tech-driven ideas: they had published a book, *Cloud Democracy*, that extolled the virtues of IT for party structures. Volkov and Krasheninnikov believed that new technologies had dramatically lowered the cost of parties, allowing crowdfunding to help create these structures from the bottom up.[104]

The party's founders had even imagined that direct democracy could help design their programme:

> Are we, as a party, 'for' or 'against', same-sex marriage, a flat income tax, or immigrants? Every party must have a thought-out, ready answer. But not a party that builds its activities on electronic democracy. If we were asked, we could determine the opinion of the party in a couple of hours, and if it's necessary, even quicker! We vote, we get the opinion. Today we're for same-sex marriage (or against), and a week after...[105]

But these ideas were soon abandoned as the party adopted a conventional platform. That platform was recognisable: the party—soon named the People's Alliance—was a 'party of the opposition'. Though it eschewed traditional labels, where the party stood was quite obvious: it aimed 'to transform Putin's regime into a modern European democracy'.[106]

Notably, the party's platform did not include any nationalist rallying points, even though Volkov and Vladimir Ashurkov—executive director of the Anti-Corruption Foundation—both supported a visa regime with Central Asia. If needed, its focus on liberal and democratic institutions, and the 'effectiveness of the state', confirmed that orientation—a 'centrist' one: 'We should be at the centre and capture people's attention to the maximum', said Ashurkov in August.[107] Internet politics was giving way to traditional politics.

In September 2013, Navalny announced that he was ready to lead the People's Alliance—and they chose him as their leader. Navalny now had a party. But he still needed to register it—no small step for an opposition project in Russia.

One last attempt for unity

2013 was a good year for the Russian opposition—at least as far as elections were concerned. Even though the For Fair Elections

NAVALNY

movement was over, opposition candidates had managed to win in several big cities. Yekaterinburg, Novosibirsk, and Petrozavodsk elected opposition mayors—and Navalny made a strong showing in the Moscow mayoral race.

But this was all too much for the Kremlin. These wins were a reality check—and the country's political leadership decided to do something about it.

The following year looked tougher as a result. The Kremlin had increased its control over the opposition by barring candidates from participating in many local and regional elections—the surest way not to lose. In St Petersburg, for instance, even a popular candidate, Oksana Dmitrieva, from A Just Russia—a systemic opposition party—could not register in the September 2014 elections.

These new rules made the 'Vote for any party but United Russia' strategy more difficult. This approach was built on the assumption that it was possible to support and embolden the systemic opposition. But now that they were again deprived of strong candidates—candidates with at least a certain amount of popularity, competence, and stamina—it became close to impossible to advocate voting for them.[108]

All this called for new ideas. Alluding to his own earlier strategy of encouraging people to vote for political parties other than United Russia, Navalny now believed there could not be 'simple strategies that can be described with a slogan anymore'. The opposition needed to stand on 'moral positions', not simply on politicking. Now, Navalny argued that they should boycott elections when real opposition candidates were barred from running: 'We are not fighting for this or that candidate to be elected, we are fighting for the rule of law in Russia.'[109]

At the same time, developments abroad were putting the opposition in a difficult position. In Kyiv, the 2013–14 Maidan protests had resulted in the ousting of President Yanukovych, precipitating a deep crisis in relations between Russia, Ukraine, and the West. The annexation of Crimea, conflict in Donbas in eastern Ukraine, and sanctions were now dominating the agenda in Russia. And this did not bode well for the opposition in general—and liberals in particular. All parties of the systemic opposition had supported the annexation of Crimea—or its 'reunification' with Russia, as they called it—as had the vast majority of the population.

Liberals had organised marches calling for peace in Ukraine—but they looked more and more like an embattled minority. They were routinely presented as a fifth column representing the interests of Ukraine and the West. This was forcing hard choices for liberals—and leading them to consider unity, again.

Unifying liberal forces was their holy grail. It had been discussed frequently since the beginning of the 2000s—and failed each and every time.

All the most important liberal groups met in Moscow in November 2014 to discuss this perennial issue. The conference was organised by Nemtsov's RPR–PARNAS party, which came up with a classic theme for Russian liberals: the choice of Europe.

According to Nemtsov, Russia was facing a geopolitical and civilisational choice. On one side, 'the party of the Chinese choice'. Putin and his allies—the 'party of war, international isolation, repression, censorship, corruption'—was turning Russia into a 'natural resources colony of China'. On the other side, 'the party of the European choice'—the democratic opposition. Facing such an epochal decision, liberals should unite.[110]

Yabloko refused outright to participate in any alliance that would include 'nationalists, left-wing radicals, or parties that tolerate them'—an unmistakable allusion to Navalny.[111] He himself had been fairly sceptical about unification in the past but warmed to the idea in the following months, becoming an advocate of uniting those who stood for the 'European choice'.[112]

Besides, pessimism about the chances of getting candidates from his own party registered were mounting—a coalition might be a good alternative strategy.

The Democratic Coalition

Then, in February 2015, Boris Nemtsov—a leading figure of the opposition, who had been pushing for unity among liberals—was assassinated, right next to the Kremlin. Two months after this dramatic event, the leader of RPR-PARNAS, Mikhail Kasyanov, and Navalny announced that they would form a coalition to compete in the next Duma elections.[113]

According to Navalny, the Coalition's main goal was to represent people with democratic views: 'A huge number of people in the country think that Russia must develop according to the European way, that we need alternation in power, independent courts and free media.'[114] Despite that support, 'people with democratic views' were not in parliament—and the goal was to change this.

But that would be no small feat. Politicians from liberal parties had not held seats in the Duma since 2007. The Democratic Coalition hoped it could win seats in the September 2016 legislative elections. In the meantime, the 2015 regional elections were a first step in that direction. The Coalition planned to run in four regions, but was only allowed to field candidates in one—the Kostroma Region, a sparsely populated, rural region some 300 kilometres north-east of Moscow, worlds apart from the capital.[115]

Campaigning in a rural region with virtually no liberal support on the ground proved extremely difficult. Even though opposition numbers were small, the authorities used a wide array of dirty tricks and 'administrative resources' against the Democratic Coalition. For instance, at a meeting with voters, a black man arrived in a car with fake US diplomatic plates in an attempt to discredit the candidates as American stooges.[116] With only 2 per cent of the vote, the result of the elections was an unequivocal disappointment for the Coalition.

The September 2016 Duma elections should have been the next challenge—but the Democratic Coalition did not live to see them. The Coalition's strategy was heavily dependent on RPR–PARNAS being a registered party that could participate in elections—contrary to Navalny's party.

But RPR–PARNAS was in deep crisis. One of its founders, Vladimir Ryzhkov, had already left and the party was renamed 'PARNAS'. Nemtsov had been assassinated. Mikhail Kasyanov—a former prime minister to Putin—was now in full control of the party.

The Coalition now comprised mostly supporters of Navalny, the PARNAS party, and a few smaller groups.[117] Navalny and his allies hoped that primaries could determine who would lead the Democratic Coalition's list in the next Duma elections—and, no doubt, that he would come out on top. But the Russian law on parties and elections gave Kasyanov control of the party and, therefore, the list. His allies had to give him the top spot.

But Kasyanov was not the obvious vote-getting choice. He was widely considered an uninspiring, technocratic figure. In the end, however, Navalny and his team agreed to compromise with Kasyanov's demand to be on top—reluctantly.

Scandal in a hotel room

But, in April 2016, a devastating blow came from Kremlin-controlled television. The NTV channel released an investigation programme showing videos of the married Kasyanov half-naked with a female member of the party in a hotel bedroom. A former employee of that channel would later claim his bosses 'didn't hide' the Kremlin's role in ordering the film and that the FSB provided the videos.[118]

The sex scandal was the tipping point for the Democratic Coalition. The opposition criticised the unseemly attack on Kasyanov, but it damaged his reputation significantly. Navalny lashed out at Kasyanov, calling on him to organise primary elections to determine who would lead the democratic list—and remarked that even United Russia organised primaries.[119] He repeated that Kasyanov was not a charismatic politician. But Kasyanov did not bend; the Coalition collapsed as Navalny and his supporters abandoned it.[120]

Navalny had invested quite some time and resources into this coalition strategy—and it was over. He concluded that working with liberal parties in Russia was out of the question.

Yabloko had already decided that its 2018 presidential candidate would be its founder, Grigory Yavlinsky—despite the disaster of the 2016 Duma same elections, where his party received a mere 2 per cent of the vote. In these same elections, Kasyanov's PARNAS party ended up with even less: 0.73 per cent of the vote.

Navalny blamed the 'old guard' leadership of liberal parties:

> For the last thirteen years ... they have only lost ... There has never been in world politics an example of a party with the same name and leaders losing for thirteen years and then, boom! Winning. It's impossible. After such defeats, parties must change their names, their leaders must leave ... This is what voters want. This is how parties live. This is how politics is done in democratic countries.[121]

Navalny accused Russian liberal parties of being inept. In between elections, 'they're in a state of lethargic sleep, and then, a month before the election, they pop up to say: vote for us, we're the best that there is. Then they lose.'[122] And when they lose, Navalny claimed, they blame voters.

Navalny's strategic musings were also a way to take stock of the shortcomings of the For Fair Elections movement. The protest movement was mostly about voting procedures—'my vote counts'. Now, the fight should concentrate on allowing real candidates on the ballot—starting with him and his movement. Navalny was already looking to the next presidential election scheduled in 2018, and he would not be dragged down by coalitions he could not control.

Everywhere but on the ballot—the 2018 presidential campaign

The 2018 presidential election promised to be a plebiscite. Putin's re-election was never in doubt. The date itself—18 March—had symbolic significance: on that day in 2014, Putin had signed into law the 'reunification' of Crimea with Russia.

There was no alternative to Putin in sight. The systemic opposition represented in the State Duma had publicly supported the president's Ukraine policy. Zhirinovsky, the far-right populist who had his first presidential run in 1991, would be on the ballot. But he was mostly now seen as a 'clown' who always ended up siding with the Kremlin.[123] Navalny never took him and his party, LDPR, seriously. The Communist Party managed to come up with a surprise. Instead of their leader—a four-time presidential candidate already—the party went for an unknown businessman, Pavel Grudinin.

Though the Communists were the most significant party of the systemic opposition, this was certainly not enough to make the race competitive. Putin enjoyed sky-high popularity, still riding the wave of support following the annexation of Crimea. He was seen as above the fray—not an ordinary candidate. The Presidential Administration was aiming for 70 per cent for Putin in the first round, with 70 per cent turnout—and hoping it could achieve it without too much falsification.

The end of the Democratic Coalition had shattered any hopes that the liberal opposition might run a single candidate. Yavlinsky would be on the ballot—after runs in 1996 and 2000. Although he had stepped down from the chairmanship of Yabloko in 2008, he still held significant authority within the party. The Kremlin pushed its business ombudsman, Boris Titov, to run in the name of loyal liberalism—but he would barely campaign at all.

The only surprise came from Ksenia Sobchak. Born in 1981, the daughter of Anatoly Sobchak—the first elected mayor of St Petersburg and Putin's mentor—Ksenia Sobchak was a celebrity. She was known to virtually all Russians as a television presenter and producer, as a socialite and successful businesswoman. Sobchak had joined the 2011–12 protests—causing her to lose many television contracts—and turned to opposition politics and journalism.[124]

After this stint at opposition, Sobchak was now widely rumoured to be a candidate planted by the Kremlin to enliven the race—a claim she denied.[125] The other candidates—a total of eight names ended up on the ballot—were unpromising.

When Navalny announced his candidacy in December 2016, he stated that this would be no ordinary campaign. Wary that he would not be allowed to run—he was well aware of the nature of elections in Russia—he set his sights high:

> I call us all to organise a real election in 2018. This task is not an easy one, because real elections have not taken place in Russia since 1996. To transform a procedure that for twenty years has been meaningless into a real confrontation of ideas, programmes, approaches, and campaigns. And I want to be your voice, your representative in this election. A real politician, connected with people, representing their interests.[126]

Navalny was now running for the nation's highest office. And, as a politician, he had several liabilities. The first, paradoxically, was his reputation as a corruption-fighter: many saw him as a one-trick pony. In 2012, he had released a programme proclaiming that fighting corruption was his main aim: 'That's my economic programme'—and not much else, for which he was widely criticised.[127]

The second liability was that the economic policies of liberals did not appeal to the majority of the people—and that's an understatement. This was the criticism he directed at Sobchak, too—a 'caricature' of democrats from the 1990s with 'cannibalistic views on politics and the economy' ('cannibalism' meaning here radical, pro-market policies, contemptuous of the lives of ordinary Russians).[128] Navalny needed to look like a competent politician, while not alienating people who were wary of economic liberalism.

'Stop feeding the oligarchs'

The solution to this conundrum was inequality. When he announced his candidacy, Navalny devoted much attention to the 'monstrous inequality of wealth and opportunities' that plagued Russia—the main point of his programme. Power has been 'usurped' by a 'narrow group of people', he said—the '0.1 per cent' who own '88 per cent of national wealth'. These people are not 'wonderful entrepreneurs who have created businesses but the participants of large-scale privatisation and bureaucrats'.[129]

Navalny's programme amounted to a third way between economic liberalism and a fully left-wing approach. He contrasted his programme to the three groups of economic policymakers that dominated the Russian debate. These were neoliberals wishing to raise the pension age, supporters of state planning and isolation, and Putin's government that was just happy with 'doing nothing' and 'enriching officials'.[130]

Volkov confirmed that the plan was to shatter the association between 'liberals' and right-wing economic policy.[131] To tackle inequality, Navalny proposed increasing the minimum wage and benefits, and making housing affordable. His programme also proposed taxing privatised infrastructure. The slogan 'Stop feeding the oligarchs' offered the benefits of fighting against reviled groups (oligarchs and bureaucrats) and broadening his social appeal. This was a slogan that was 'both left-wing (for social justice), and right-wing (against monopolies) ... both conservative and liberal'.[132]

Was this populism? In the most widely used academic definition, populists pit a 'pure people' against a 'corrupt elite' and argue that politics should be an expression of the 'general will of the people'. That Navalny opposes the 'corrupt elite' goes without saying. He also wants politics to be about the will of the people against the usurpation of power by the ruling elite. But his solutions to these issues are liberal—rule of law, separation of powers, and pluralism of political forces. He has also proposed shifting powers away from the president to parliament.[133]

In other words, Navalny views the current standoff between a corrupt elite and a united people as temporary. He and Volkov have made clear many times that their political ideal is a system where different democratic forces compete—Navalny's party as one among many.[134]

If part of the economic programme leaned left, another part leaned right, towards neoliberalism—an ideology centred on markets, competition, and private initiative. It called for transparency, the fight against monopolies, competition, de-bureaucratisation, and lower taxes on labour and small business. But these neoliberal measures were supposed to foster a 'transition from oligarchic capitalism to social capitalism'.[135] One of his advisers told a journalist: 'If you ask him, business is good, competition is good, mainstream western advice is good ... But now he believes more in socially inclusive policies and fairness. So if you want to define him, in the US he would be a Democrat, in Europe he would be centre-right.'[136]

THE POLITICIAN

Nationalism, dropped?

Navalny's campaign confirmed that he had mostly abandoned nationalism as a path for the opposition. He claimed he was still a Russian nationalist, that his positions had 'not changed a millimetre' since 2011.[137] But nationalism was clearly no longer his public ideology.

On the most contentious issue of Crimea, Navalny had already struck a pragmatic tone. In 2014, he declared:

> Even though Crimea was seized in a gross violation of all international norms, it is now a part of the Russian Federation—these are the realities. Let's not fool ourselves. And I strongly advise Ukrainians not to fool themselves either. Crimea will remain a part of Russia and will never be Ukrainian in the foreseeable future.[138]

The declaration struck a middle ground between liberals and nationalists. Some liberals were advocating returning Crimea to Ukraine unilaterally. Not Navalny. Many nationalists were claiming everything was fine with what happened in Crimea—it was not an 'annexation' but a legal and legitimate reunification with Russia. Not Navalny.

Never was this pragmatic attitude better illustrated than during his July 2017 debate with Igor Strelkov, one of the leaders of the insurrection in Donbas. On the issue of the war in Ukraine, Navalny claimed that 'a bad peace is better than a good war'.[139] Russians are a 'divided people'—but he opposed any 'chimeric' foreign adventures to defend them in Russia's 'near abroad'. Navalny felt that Russians and Ukrainians were one and the same people.

But Navalny's position on Ukraine was determined by considerations about the interests of Russian citizens, not those of the 'Russian people' in an ethnic sense, he said. These interests, for Navalny, were mostly material: subsidising the war in Donbas would be too big a burden for the Russian taxpayer—not to mention the tragedy of the conflict more broadly. This position was miles away from the emotional appeal to national greatness that surrounded the events in official discourse and state media. In a choice between guns and butter, Navalny was going for butter.[140] The only point suggestive of his nationalist agenda was his proposal for a visa regime with the countries of Central Asia. Navalny was now campaigning on issues quite far from the traditional nationalist platform.

His political programme was lengthy, with lots of data and graphs in order to signal its seriousness. He claimed that the programme had been 'elaborated and written' by 'opinion leaders, professionals in the fields of economics, law and culture'. On his campaign website, they were presented as guaranteeing a 'balanced and realistic programme'. Among them were Vladimir Milov, economist and former deputy minister for energy; Pavel Chikov, director of the human rights group 'Agora'; Yelena Lukyanova, a professor of law; and Sergei Aleksashenko, an economist and former first deputy chairman of the board of the Central Bank.[141] These were decidedly liberal figures.

Navalny ran a campaign similar to the one he had run in Moscow in 2013. This time, however, it was on a different scale—that of Russia itself. Volkov served again as his campaign manager. It was professional and centralised, relying heavily on volunteers and paid staff.

After a year on the road, Navalny struck a satisfied chord: 'For the first time in recent Russian history, we have created a real, massive political structure, whose basis is made up of headquarters in eighty-three cities, and almost 200,000 volunteers across the whole country.'[142] Even allowing for the possible exaggeration that is sometimes involved in such accounts, this was an accomplishment. In the end, the campaign claimed to have raised—in a transparent manner—368 million roubles (more than £4 million at the time).[143]

The campaign's main thrust was to show mass support through multiple campaign rallies—attendance ranged between several hundred and a few thousand.[144] Mass, visible support helped to underline another one of Navalny's main points: that the Kremlin is afraid of him and his supporters. That his supporters were also harassed and arrested helped make this point: why the repression if he's not a threat?

In the end, the real election Navalny was hoping for did not take place. He could not participate in the presidential contest— the Kirovles case had struck again. After his conviction in 2013, Navalny had taken the case to the European Court of Human Rights—and won. In 2016, the Court ruled that the Russian 'domestic courts applied criminal law arbitrarily'.[145]

The Russian courts did not give up, however. They tried Navalny again, and sentenced him in early 2017 to a suspended term of five years.[146] The law now prevented him from running in elections for about a decade.[147] The chairwoman of the Central Electoral Commission downplayed the significance of this: Navalny 'is a young, promising politician … [W]hen this period of ten years is over, around 2028 … he'll be able to run in elections … Let him show, not with pressure from the street but with his ideas, that he's worthy of the office of president'.[148]

The meaning of success

Navalny reacted to the decision by announcing that 'elections are not taking place because Vladimir Putin is terribly scared, fears competition with me … and has given orders to his servants in the Central Electoral Commission to deny my registration'.[149] Navalny chose to boycott the election and organise it as a 'voters' strike'. The expression alluded to something more active than the image of the boycotter simply sitting on their couch on election day— and it involved mass efforts at organising observers and protests.

It's difficult to assess whether this 'strike' was a success. Navalny himself claimed it was—but 'normal' politicians are usually loath to admit defeat.[150] Turnout for the 2018 presidential election was high: above 67 per cent—by official measures, at least. Putin was re-elected in the first round, with more than 76 per cent of the vote.

What was obvious was the poor showing of liberal candidates. Sobchak and Yavlinsky managed to attract less than 2 per cent of the vote. Navalny was dismissive of what he considered remnants of the past. And he was ambitious about his plans: 'We should not discuss the unification of the opposition, but its creation. First in terms of ideas, and then, in terms of organisation ... We should discuss how we can win 60 per cent.'[151]

Navalny had been in politics for close to twenty years, and he was now known throughout the country—a politician of national importance. He wasn't on the ballot in 2018, but the campaign itself was a success. Navalny did not have a party, but he could mobilise thousands of supporters across Russia. His campaign website concluded: 'We created and maintained a network of headquarters across the whole country. They will continue their political activity further, they will fight for our rights and not let the authorities rest. Join us.'

The impossible politician

The story of Navalny's journey as a politician can be bewildering. At some points, he has called for the liberal opposition to unite. Then he opted to go alone. Regarding elections, he has sometimes called for boycotts, but then for the fielding of opposition candidates—and then for protest voting. Sometimes, slogans are central. At other times, they're rejected as simplistic. Then they're back in favour once again.

How should we make sense of these zig-zags—of this inconsistency?

One answer is that the back and forth is not inconsistent at all—that it reflects adaptation to a political system that may seem static from a distance, but that is, in fact, constantly changing. When the Kremlin—itself responding to the For Fair Elections protests—relaxed party registration laws, this prompted Navalny to try participating in elections, even though, up to this point, he had considered them meaningless. But when the Kremlin returned to banning hopeful candidates, Navalny was prepared to shift course again.

Such adaptations also concern ideology. When Navalny realised that nationalism was not a platform to win over the masses, he started to emphasise the issue of economic inequality.

One may call him inconsistent and an opportunist for these turns, like his less pragmatic colleagues in the liberal opposition have constantly done. But, in reality, they appear to reflect Navalny's readiness to subordinate both tactics and substantive demands to the one thing that he has been remarkably consistent about: the need to fight an authoritarian system that uses corruption and repression to secure its power.

Navalny's story also sheds light on the perennial difficulties facing Russia's political opposition. Why have they experienced such problems in working together? One answer relates to a basic feature of politics and politicians of all stripes: egos. Yavlinsky's insistence on being a presidential candidate for Yabloko, despite his unpopularity, is one such example of political vanity—and it led to intense friction with Navalny.

But that is far from the whole story. Another factor is the sheer variety of political positions in the opposition camp—as, for example, was on display during the December 2011 protests in Moscow. Opposition to Putin and in support of free and fair elections might bring people together in the short term, but longer-term cooperation has often proved impossible.

Given the nature of Russia's authoritarian political system, even people sharing the same goals can disagree quite significantly over the best ways to achieve them. A boycott might be backed for its moral purity—that is, for not endorsing sham elections by taking part in them—but other opposition forces have tried to engage with elections, attempting to make them freer and fairer through tactical voting. In contrast to completely closed dictatorships, therefore, systems like Russia's offer different—if limited—entry points. And all of these are bad options, leading to disagreements within the opposition as to which path to take.

Also, mistrust can run deep in the opposition camp—and this is far from unfounded. The Kremlin has courted and co-opted people and organisations of various stripes. And that means that people can be paranoid as a result—even in cases where the Kremlin is not involved at all.

Beneath the seemingly monotonous surface of Putin's dominance, politics in Russia is far from dull and boring. Both the Kremlin and opposition adapt constantly. But, when Navalny was barred from the 2018 presidential race, it was clear to all that the Kremlin had blocked off his chances of becoming a 'normal' politician.

One thing was now clear to him: protest was crucial. And he wasn't starting from scratch. Navalny had been a protester for most of his political career, and, when running for president, he had started building a movement across the country. To tell this story—of Navalny as protest leader—we now need to leave Moscow and head to the regions—and to the activists on the ground.

4

THE PROTESTER

'We are not afraid!'

Vladivostok, 23 January 2021. Thousands of protesters block Svetlanskaya Street—a major thoroughfare lined with shops and historic buildings in the heart of Russia's main port city in the Far East. Close to the borders with China and North Korea, Vladivostok is Russia's main gateway to the Pacific.[1]

As the sun moves westward, lighting up the vast space that is Russia, city after city joins the protests. Tens of thousands of demonstrators are on the streets.

But one man is missing. Navalny is in custody, awaiting his 2 February court appearance that will decide whether he will go to prison.

Across Russia, people are calling for Putin to leave office. They're also demanding that the Russian president 'give the palace back to the people', responding to the 'Putin's Palace' video posted by the Anti-Corruption Foundation on 19 January. After documenting the complex web of finances and the unbelievable splendour of the palace on the Black Sea, allegedly built and maintained for Putin himself, Navalny turns to the camera:

Putin and everyone who guards him, steals for him, and falsifies elections for him—these are a few hundred thousand people at the very maximum. But we are tens of millions. We don't just believe in our strength ... When 10 per cent of the unsatisfied take to the streets, they won't dare to falsify elections ... All we have to do is stop being patient.[2]

The film is part of a dramatic series of events. Navalny returns to Russia and is arrested, as expected. While the world is watching, his team releases the video, adding fuel to the flames. And then, a few days later, the protests.

Their spread is unprecedented. Some cities have not seen a sizable crowd on the streets in decades.

And all of this does not just happen by chance. People's anger is real and genuine. But that they turn out onto the streets at this very moment reflects years of work by Navalny's team to channel and consolidate protest potential.

We now trace Navalny's evolution from a Moscow politician without a party to the leader of Russia's largest political movement fully independent of the Kremlin. We show how protest became such a vital part of Navalny's toolkit—in part because street mobilisation was one of the few things still possible in the restricted political environment of Vladimir Putin's third presidential term. We trace how Navalny, learning from the For Fair Elections protests of 2011–12, consciously used protest to mobilise support and inspire activists for his country-wide organisation.[3]

But mobilisation has not been a one-way street—of Navalny using people for his own goals. Discontented Russian citizens from all sections of society faced the ever-increasing costs the authorities have placed on political activism—threats, arrests, surveillance, and violence—not because Navalny manipulated them into blindly following his call, but because they see in him somebody they themselves can use in their own push for political change.

In other words, we show how Navalny the man became Navalny the movement.

A politician derailed

Protest is central to Navalny's activities. Beyond his YouTube videos, he has been most prominent when appearing in demonstrations calling for 'Russia without Putin', decrying election fraud, and calling out corruption.

But he has paid the price. Not counting his 2021 sentence, he has spent over 250 days in jail.[4] This includes many short periods of arrest, when he was punished for violating some of the many complex rules the authorities have built to contain protest. Examples of these violations include calling for a rally that has not been approved by authorities, or an alleged 'failure to comply with a lawful request of a police officer'. But Navalny has often put a good spin on his time in jail, saying he has time to read and get to know people from all walks of life.[5]

This is what we see when the media covers Navalny and his movement. But, if you dig a bit deeper, it's clear that protest is fundamental to Navalny's life as an opposition politician. Without protest, his opposition activities would look very different—and might not even exist.

Opposition in Russia is not forbidden as such. But Russia is also not a democracy. We can tell democracies from non-democracies by asking one basic question: do ruling parties sometimes lose elections? In Russia—and other non-democracies—only opposition parties tend to lose important elections. And politicians who refuse to accept the Kremlin's dominance face a very hard time. The Kremlin uses an array of tools to ensure it gets the election results it wants, drawing from a 'menu of manipulation'—a series of ways to unlevel the electoral playing field.[6] Ballot stuffing might be one element—and social media is often saturated with images of such falsifications around elections in Russia. But other forms of manipulation are likely to be even more important: from blocking opposition candidates getting onto ballots in the first place to skewed media coverage favouring the authorities' picks.

The possibilities for an aspiring opposition politician like Navalny were limited from the beginning. And this was bad news for someone who sees themselves as a 'normal' politician working inside political institutions—a campaigner, a party leader, even a president. All of that was out of the question.

Protest as the solution

But politics is not just about elections. Even in the world's liberal democracies, voting is only one form of political activity. Protest is another—and it is the one that Navalny was drawn to, given the informal but strict constraints the authorities placed on institutional politics.

In a system intolerant of opposition, protest becomes a key way to engage in politics. When opposition politicians are barred from ballots, kept off the air, and pursued by law enforcement, mobilising on the streets is one of the few channels left to make yourself heard, gain new supporters, and build pressure on the authorities.

This is not to say that protesting has been easy. Protesters in Russia have faced increasing restrictions over time, especially after the shockwaves that the For Fair Elections movement sent through the Kremlin in 2011 and early 2012. But, even if constrained, protest itself was—and still is, to some degree—possible. Navalny, then, increasingly focused on protest simply because it was one of the few channels left open to him.

And Navalny made the best out of a bad situation. Being forced into street politics made him take it seriously. And that meant transforming protest from an occasional outburst of dissatisfaction—lively but uncoordinated—into a political strategy.

Two stories from the provinces

Rostov-on-Don, 10 December 2011. Six days have passed since the national parliamentary elections—and protests are spreading rapidly through the country. In Rostov, several hundred young people march through the city, holding up blank sheets of paper. The message is simple: why write anything when everyone knows what's going on?

Rostov is a large city—a metropolis of more than one million inhabitants in the south of Russia. Its central streets, lined with imposing white houses, speak of its past as an imperial trading hub. And it is still a rich city. But, unlike other places where growing wealth coincided with the emergence of politically independent business and media in the post-Soviet period, Rostov's political sphere has always been tightly controlled.

During the first two decades after the fall of the Soviet Union, the governor, Vladimir Chub, a political heavyweight, did not shy away from direct pressure on anyone questioning his power, including journalists and politically engaged businesses.

Because of these challenges, political opposition in Rostov has largely been confined to a small circle of battle-hardened activists of different political stripes. When they gathered for their small demonstrations, *pikety* (pickets), liberals stood next to National Bolsheviks, the radical group led by Eduard Limonov that blends fascism with state socialism and punk aesthetics. These kinds of coalitions—built on personal connections and common opposition to the authorities much more than ideology—are not untypical in Russia.

But in Rostov, solidarity among dissidents is even more essential—because there are so few of them.

As young people carry their white paper sheets along the grand city boulevards, the veteran activists are stunned: where did these people come from? For weeks, they struggle to build a connection to these young protesters, partly because authorities are quick to shut down the social media groups where protest marches are coordinated, arrest their administrators, and pre-emptively threaten students of Rostov's state university not to take part. Nonetheless, established activists and newcomers manage to co-organise rallies in the winter of 2011–12—and, for a time, it looks as though there is real potential for Rostov's opposition to grow.

But the group of veteran activists does not know how to engage the newcomers in anything beyond their small, regular pickets. As a result, the rallies that were so inspiring, unexpected and shocking, even—in the beginning at least—peter out amid repression and frustration. When Leonid Volkov organises the Coordination Council of the Opposition in October 2012 to give the national movement an organisational base, Daria, one of the few remaining newcomers, is hopeful: 'We need something like this for Rostov, too!' But Boris, a long-term liberal activist, replies: 'Why bother? It would be the same five people anyway.'

Perm, 11 December 2011. The For Fair Elections wave of protest engulfing the country arrives in the city on a Sunday, one day after most other cities, including Rostov. But the nature of protest is remarkably similar. Based on a social media group, people in their twenties and thirties coordinate a vibrant demonstration that stuns observers and long-term civic activists.

In Perm, existing activism is much more professional than in Rostov. The city—an industrial centre of one million inhabitants in the Urals—has a history of liberal voting; repression is on a much lower level. More importantly still, it is home to a unique coalition of NGOs and civic groups that regularly cooperate with authorities on local matters, sometimes even co-drafting legislation.

But they know how to protest, too.

When the newly mobilised protesters cheerfully fill the city's spaces with their banners—not empty, like Rostov, but with home-drawn slogans—the old guard of activists are sceptical at first. 'We were afraid they would turn protest into a game, a fake', recalls Sergei, an established liberal organiser. But they also see the potential. They, therefore, engage the leaders of the social media group and, in time, build an ad hoc organisation together—the 'Council of 24 December', named after the day of the largest rally in 2011.

The Council organises many new initiatives, like a local electoral monitoring group that still exists as of 2021. It is a hub of activity, fusing the experience and resources of Perm's established civil society with the motivation of a new generation of protesters.

But it is also a place of conflict. The newcomers demand new national parliamentary elections and more honesty in politics. They press for broad, sweeping changes but have no clear political programme. Sergei and his colleagues, while sympathetic to the newcomers, have their own, much more specific local goals. Most of all, they are fighting the region's governor, Oleg Chirkunov—a smart and approachable manager who nonetheless carries out Moscow's undermining of local self-government, reducing the city's political clout.[7]

Some of the inexperienced members get the impression that their initiatives are 'exploited by people who have their own interests', as one of the young organisers recalls. Although the Council established democratic procedures, the new protesters feel personally excluded from the real decision-making—and, after the protests have quietened down, withdraw in frustration about 'politics'.

We are not alone

These stories from late 2011 and early 2012 contain important lessons about protest in Russia—and for Navalny.

The first is that protest has an enormous capacity to inspire and unite previously disparate social groups. The protests of 2011–12 were not coordinated by anyone in particular. Opposition groups had organised the monitoring of the elections, but the mobilisation itself—of people coming out onto the streets—was largely spontaneous.

Many protesters did not attend the rallies with a concrete goal in mind. When protests began, people vented their anger over electoral falsification and the September 2011 announcement that Putin would run to become president yet again. But, at the same time, many protesters did not have a precise political identity—they were not 'liberals', 'democrats', or 'socialists' as much as curious and concerned citizens not used to engaging with politics directly, never mind protesting on the streets. Political outlooks developed during the protests much more than they drove them at the outset.

In 2011, many protested for the first time in their lives. And when they stood on the squares and walked the streets of their hometowns, many could not believe their own eyes: 'This was so amazing,' recalls Tanya from Perm, 'you saw that there are so many like-minded people.' From Tahrir Square in Cairo to Maidan in Ukraine, these moments of realisation are often the first steps to a large and sustained wave of mobilisation.

The experience of protest can transform people's understanding of themselves and their place in society, creating a collective identity. In the end, the For Fair Elections protests brought little positive change in terms of politics. On the contrary, once Putin was president again in 2012, he initiated a crackdown on the timid liberalisations introduced during Dmitry Medvedev's presidency—and protest participants were sentenced to lengthy jail terms. But, for many, it was their first step into politics—and it was the moment when they realised that they were not alone.

Protest—and then what?

This realisation can be incredibly motivating. But the story from Rostov shows that protest can, nevertheless, recede quickly. The second lesson for Navalny was, therefore, that, to have real political impact, the inspiration and enthusiasm that protest generates needs to be captured, channelled, and consolidated—that protest needs organisation.

The Council in Perm did just that. It offered those who were motivated by the protests a structure for sustained activism. And it connected newly mobilised protesters with those who, through decades of civil society work, had built up the knowledge and the network needed for effective activism.

Material resources were also key. The Council included some independent local businessmen who provided a small salary for the Council's secretary, and the new monitoring organisation was allowed to set up its headquarters in a building owned by one of the Council's members.

This, like so many other examples from different regions, showed how much knowledge and experience there was in the provinces. Contrary to what the stereotypical liberal in Moscow might have believed, not only was there life beyond the capital but there existed the necessary conditions for political work. There was, in other words, a glimpse that protest politics in Russia was not necessarily restricted to Moscow and St Petersburg.

However, these episodes also showed the problems of relying on protest for long-term political projects. How they played out depended to a large degree on local specifics. When, as in Rostov, there was no initiative to structure the protests early on, they did not last for long. And even in Perm, the Council could not realise its full potential, as the conflict over its agenda and the dominating role of older activists frustrated some of the newcomers.[8]

If Navalny was to make protest work for his fight against autocracy and corruption, what he needed was something that blended the best of both worlds. Protests that inspired and motivated long-term engagement, and a structure that drew upon the experience and knowledge in the regions while not being dependent on any particular circle of local activists. In his year-long campaign for the 2018 presidential election, Navalny set out to build exactly that.

But he was not alone.

The movement's architect

'First entry—so that this space isn't completely empty.'[9] With these deeply uninspiring words on his new blog, Leonid Volkov set foot on a path that changed his life entirely.

Born in 1980, Volkov witnessed the economic turmoil and social catastrophes of the 1990s as a teenager, but his own professional life began when things started to get better. Still under thirty years old, he had risen through the ranks of SKB Kontur—a large IT company in his hometown of Yekaterinburg. Born into a family of mathematicians, he started out as a programmer, but quickly took on managerial roles. And, in the heyday of Russian blogging, he began to experiment with LiveJournal, the same platform that Navalny and countless others used at the time for public writing.

Undecided at first what his blog was going to be about, Volkov's topics quickly developed from personal stories to politics. In December 2007—less than three months after the first entry—Volkov tells the story of how he attended an introductory course for volunteer election observers: 'Yesterday I went to a training session for observers and heard a lot about possible types of violations. I tried to remember everything. I was very impressed. There's a lot I hadn't imagined before—and how easy it is to end up with the kind of result you need!'[10]

Witnessing the 2007 parliamentary elections made a great impression on Volkov. In an entry posted only hours after polling stations closed, he provided a detailed analysis of the falsifications he observed. Volkov concluded that Putin's allies wanted both a good result for their candidates and a high turnout, but that they couldn't achieve both at the same time without manipulations. Volkov's blog provides a record of his politicisation in real time.

Over the next two years, Volkov's blog turned from a personal, experimental space into an important local source of commentary and information in Yekaterinburg. Volkov was able to speak to a section of Russian society that had not previously been interested in politics: the very group that would, four years later, fill the streets of Moscow to protest the parliamentary election results. In Yekaterinburg, these highly educated and relatively well-off urbanites slowly began to politicise in 2007—in part inspired by Volkov's blog.

Before long, he decides to run for the city council as an independent candidate. This is the first time Volkov organises an electoral campaign, something that will soon enough become his job. A blog entry lists what this campaign did and did not include: 'Number of volunteers—36. Total circulation of campaign materials—61,548 copies ... Number of gifts distributed—0.'[11]

Volkov here ridicules the established practice of buying votes with 'gifts' and contrasts it with his own democratic, 'normal' campaign.

He wins the seat and gets to work. Membership in the city council's finance committee gives him access to the city's budget plans that he discusses on the blog. He organises livestreams of parliamentary sessions. He popularises local politics. And, at the same time, he leads the local branch of the liberal Solidarnost coalition and heads the local branch of Golos, the electoral monitoring organisation. Volkov now embodies liberal activism in Yekaterinburg.

When listening to friends and aides, the air is thick with praise. 'Active, competent, intelligent', says one. 'A smart guy who quickly teaches himself everything', says another. In the eyes of the local business community, a third recalls, Volkov appeared to be a 'decent young man'. They liked interacting with Volkov and he convinced them to contribute to his campaigns.

But there are those with other views. Volkov was always a liberal extremist, says Dmitry, a former ally turned editor-in-chief of the regional administration's official newspaper. Volkov can be harsh, 'intolerant of those who do not immediately agree with his views'. But even Dmitry admits that, in 2009, Volkov became the 'epicentre of the movement'.

An essential component of that movement is protest. In 2010, Volkov organises large, colourful rallies against the construction of a new cathedral on a central square in Yekaterinburg and for keeping direct elections for the city's mayor. As a local Communist deputy puts it, these were the first protests that were not primarily driven by economic or social concerns like prices, pensions, and welfare benefits. Instead, Volkov's middle-class audience turned out for urban issues and for political freedom, changing the demands of protest. And Volkov was, if not the cause of that change, then certainly its catalyst.

A leader meets his strategist

These events did not go unnoticed in Moscow. Later, Navalny recalled that Yekaterinburg had been crucial in his effort to reach an audience beyond Moscow.[12] And it was in Yekaterinburg where he forged a personal connection that would prove decisive.

In the autumn of 2011, Volkov decides to take things a step further. He wants to become a deputy in the region's parliament—one rung up the ladder in Russia's federal political system compared to his seat on Yekaterinburg's city council. Again, he campaigns, now with two years' experience on the council and with the help of several aides. He is also financially well supported: when asked to leave his firm in 2010—possibly because his political profile was proving increasingly tricky—his generous severance package allows him to invest in political projects.

But the authorities know him by now. In their eyes, he is no longer the harmless, 'smart Jewish programmer boy'—an impression relayed by his political scientist friend, Fyodor Krasheninnikov. He has become a threat. And when someone is a threat, the safety measures in the system kick in: Volkov's candidacy is declined, allegedly because of faulty signatures.

With the support of Yekaterinburg's liberal activists, Volkov organises a demonstration to protest the decision—and Navalny travels to Yekaterinburg. They have met before at least once, in Moscow, at Garry Kasparov's apartment. But this is Navalny's first political appearance on stage anywhere outside the capital.[13]

From now on, Volkov and Navalny work as a team. And soon, Volkov—until 2012 an aspiring local politician hoping one day to become mayor of Yekaterinburg—decides that constantly being in the spotlight is not his thing. He has campaigned and given speeches, but he has always thrived most when organising. In the current political environment, moreover, building competing liberal opposition platforms—one led by Navalny, one led by Volkov—does not make sense. And so Volkov decides to do what he does best. Navalny the politician has met Volkov the strategist.

How to build a movement?

Fast forward to December 2016. The protests of 2011–12 are long gone, Navalny's party has not been allowed to register, and the Democratic Coalition with Yashin and Kasyanov has collapsed. But, by now, Navalny and Volkov have years of teamwork experience—and the Anti-Corruption Foundation has developed into a professional political machine. It was time for the next step.

When Navalny announces his plan in December 2016 to run for president in the 2018 election, he knows the authorities are likely to block him. When they let him run in the 2013 Moscow mayoral election, it was clearly a strategic mistake that they are unlikely to repeat. What is entirely possible, however, even when Navalny's candidacy ultimately fails, is to use this campaign to finally reach beyond Moscow and build a truly Russia-wide political structure. This is at the heart of the plan from the outset in late 2016.

Volkov gets to work. The goal is simple enough: mobilise those who might support Navalny—or, at least, back his anti-Putin course—and open campaign offices in the country's larger cities that can coordinate Navalny's future actions. As Navalny repeatedly says, this is simply what presidential candidates do in 'normal' democracies: travel the country, open campaign branches, talk to potential voters. Be a politician.

But building the largest political structure independent of the Kremlin is not a normal thing to do in modern Russia. In a country where political resources—even of nominally opposition parties—are tightly controlled, and the non-systemic opposition has little to no chance of appearing on nationwide traditional media, nobody has dared to put a plan of these proportions into action. But there is a way—and that way is through protest.

THE PROTESTER

Four circles of resistance

To understand how Navalny approached this huge task, it is helpful to view his campaign as four concentric circles. Navalny and his core FBK team are in the centre. This is where the decisions are taken. The first circle consists of the regional offices, their staff, and the volunteer activists who do the everyday work of the campaign. The second circle contains the sympathisers—those who may not be activists themselves, but who are ready to vocally support Navalny and spread his cause to their families, schools, and workplaces. The two outermost circles are made up of the general population, the potential electorate—those on whose support the success of any politician ultimately depends. Circle three consists of those who might vote for Navalny, while circle four, finally, contains those who either distrust or oppose him—or are not even aware of his existence.

Protest is the primary vehicle to pull people closer to the centre.

One way it does that is by raising attention. When hundreds or thousands walk through a neighbourhood chanting and holding signs, when dozens of police vans pull up in the city centre and the everyday course of life is interrupted, when journalists interview participants and pictures of crowds fill online spaces, then people pay attention, even if they do not directly engage.

Navalny's visibility has, indeed, been boosted by a few high-profile episodes.[14] Before 2011, only 6 per cent of respondents in nationally representative surveys knew his name. After the For Fair Elections protests of 2011–12, that figure had risen to 34 per cent. It increased again to over 50 per cent during his 2013 mayoral campaign in Moscow, rising again during his presidential campaign in 2017–18 and in 2020–21 following his poisoning. In 2021, those who knew nothing of Navalny were in the minority—25 per cent.[15] In all these periods, protest was an important factor raising Navalny's profile: it drove media attention—some positive, some negative—which in turn drove name recognition.

Name recognition is, of course, not the same as support. But it is a necessary condition. And, in contrast to earlier periods, in 2017 Navalny's visibility and his support grew in parallel.[16] His campaign—to a large extent driven by protest—not only made him better known but also made him more popular.

Another way in which protest can draw people into the movement is the experience itself. Protest socialises and inspires. As seen already during the For Fair Elections movement, protest can profoundly change people's perceptions of their surroundings— and the views of their fellow citizens. Those who previously thought they were alone with their views, isolated dissidents in a city of indifferent bores—or, worse, hostile Putin fans—now suddenly see that there are, to quote Tanya from Perm again, 'so many like-minded people'.

In 2017, protests formed part of a three-stage mobilisation strategy to get Navalny's presidential campaign rolling: social media PR, nation-wide protest mobilisation, and the opening of local campaign offices. Stage one involved the 'Don't Call Him "Dimon"' video exposing allegations of corruption against former prime minister Dmitry Medvedev, posted on YouTube on 2 March.

Stage two followed a few weeks later, when Navalny demanded answers from Medvedev.

On 26 March, Navalny's team held rallies in ninety-seven cities, the largest protest wave since 2012. On 12 June, when a second round of protests was called, the number of cities with people on the streets grew to an unprecedented 154.[17] As in 2011, the rallies brought together many people who had never protested before. In most regions, they were the largest rallies since at least 2012; in some, they were the first large protests in decades. And Navalny's team was shrewd enough to frame them broadly and inclusively.

Navalny was conscious that people opposing corruption, a politicised justice system, and the absence of political competition would not automatically translate into support for him. And so, instead of placing the protests in the context of his own run for president, he and his team framed them as protests against political corruption in general. They were fuelled, no doubt, by the video on Medvedev, but spoke to a broader anger at the lavish lifestyle of the elites and the seeming impossibility of getting rid of United Russia—and Putin. They attracted a much broader crowd than Navalny's core fans: concerned, sometimes angry citizens and activists from across the political spectrum. Many openly distanced themselves from Navalny personally but nonetheless used the occasion to voice their discontent—something that would occur again in early 2021.

The 2017 protests came at exactly the right moment. Just like those of five years earlier, they infused many with renewed optimism, a sense of agency, and the drive to get involved. But unlike 2011–12, there was now a movement to join. No longer did the growth of opposition in the regions depend on the complex, and often conflictual, interactions between established activists and enthused newcomers.

Stage three, then, was the creation of regional campaign offices. In a few places like Moscow, St Petersburg, Yekaterinburg, and Samara, these offices had already formally opened in February or March—often with a visit from either Volkov or Navalny. In most cities, however, the opening was planned for April, May, or June 2017. And even for those already launched, recruitment of permanent staff and campaign volunteers was only just beginning. Now, those who wanted to join the movement could simply knock on the door of Navalny's new office or check their local social media to see when it was going to open. The protests had the desired effect: of pulling people inwards, from the outer circle of those who had never heard Navalny's name to the circle of potential supporters, and further inwards into the circle of activists.

The making of an activist

Sometimes, that inward transition proceeded very quickly. Sitting at one of the white IKEA tables that filled Navalny's offices across the country, twenty-one-year-old Oleg describes how he moved from a passive consumer of YouTube videos to paid staffer of Navalny's campaign in less than four months. 'I first learned about the campaign in the beginning of March through the video "Don't Call Him 'Dimon'"', he says. 'Back then I had no idea about the opening of the office here.' Oleg chuckles in disbelief at his own activist career.

The film captivated him. And when he heard a few days later that there was going to be a protest in his hometown, he decided to go. 'My friends weren't really up for it, but I went anyway. There, I met a few people who told me of this office here.' Oleg checked it out, liked what he saw, and became a volunteer with all that entailed: organising events, distributing flyers, and hiding campaign material when the police came to seize it. He socialised, met new friends, and, when a paid position opened, he took it.

There are numerous stories like this. An online survey conducted among Navalny's social media groups in early 2018 showed that a full 35 per cent had first heard of the campaign through the YouTube video on Medvedev.[18] Of those respondents who took part in the protests of 26 March or 12 June 2017, half had never protested before, just like Oleg. And of those who then went on to become volunteers or staffers, 60 per cent had no prior activist experience.[19] It is no exaggeration to say, then, that the protests marked the birth of a new generation of activists in Russia.

THE PROTESTER

Enlisting the regions

Enthused activists and IKEA tables were not the only recurring features, however. In any of the offices that popped up around the country—in Volgograd, Moscow, or Krasnodar—you got the impression of stepping into a branch of a hip national retail chain. But, instead of trainers, these places traded in politics.

The colour scheme ran throughout all campaign materials, including the office walls, evoking a refreshed, modernised Russian flag: white, red with a hint of salmon pink, and a light blue that was almost, but not quite, green. The colours subtly underscored how Navalny wanted his campaign to be seen: as a patriotic attempt to refresh rather than revolutionise Russia, to help it develop its full potential.

Navalny himself was everywhere. The campaign slogan 'NAVALNY2018' covered the walls, the light grey sweatshirts of staff and volunteers, and merchandise items. Passers-by were greeted from the windows with his programme statements, like 'Affluence for all, not wealth for the 0.1%'. And Navalny's face was on countless brochures that activists handed out to visitors.

The highly standardised branding ensured not only that people got the same impression of Navalny's campaign across the country. It also made sure that the campaign did not depend too much on local resources—a problem that plagued the activist projects coming out of the 2011–12 protests. Here, the campaign's headquarters made sure that the basic setup was in place everywhere—a functional and visually appealing space, enough campaign materials to distribute, and two to three paid staff, including a 'coordinator' and someone with legal knowledge to help wrestle with authorities when they seized equipment, cancelled rallies, or pressured landlords. All of this made sure that first-time activists always had a fully set-up place to go and immediately start working, without much prior knowledge or experience. This was the definition of professional political organising.

But for all the standardisation, Volkov and Navalny's team also made sure that the offices integrated into the local activist spheres. This made sense not just to avoid the impression of colonisation and remote control from Moscow, but also because there was a lot of activist potential and local experience to draw upon.

Soon, the offices turned into hubs of activity. Local activists frequently gave guest lectures on electoral monitoring, interaction with police, or even deeply theoretical topics. An activist from the liberal PARNAS party in Kazan, for instance, held a two-series lecture on social theory, and, in Yekaterinburg, a veteran activist discussed 'varieties of liberalism'.

But even more important were the practical resources. When Navalny toured the country in the autumn of 2017, the authorities declined most requests to hold public gatherings, often in violation of the Russian Constitution. Going ahead and holding unsanctioned events would give the police a pretext to arrest and repress, which the campaign sought to avoid. They, therefore, looked for large private spaces. In Perm, they found a slightly unusual one: Navalny, a controversial liberal, set up a stage in the courtyard of a socialist-led housing commune. This would not have been possible without the local connections that routinely cross political alignments.

Tapping into the potential of the regions also included the recruitment of personnel. Although there were cases, like Volgograd, in which the local office's head came from Volkov's orbit and without connections to the city, most were locals—and most were deeply rooted in various activist projects.

The selection process for personnel, meanwhile, resembled the practices of a large commercial firm more than those of a social movement. Usually, the campaign announced the opening of a local office and invited interested candidates to submit a CV. Volkov made clear that the selection was competitive and followed clear criteria. This was not just due to Volkov's background in business. It also had a signalling function: in everything Navalny's team did, they sought to set an example of how the 'wonderful Russia of the future'—one of Navalny's preferred slogans—would be working. The goals are precise and the institutions are fair—and that is the image they wanted to project to the outside, too.

As Volkov made clear, leading a regional office was not so much political as it was organisational. Although experienced activists had valuable resources to contribute and were, therefore, privileged, the main selection criterion was managerial competence. When in the southern city of Krasnodar the campaign selected a coordinator who had been organising the local 'Russian Marches' and was involved in the nationalist 'Movement Against Illegal Immigration', Volkov simply said that there had been an open competition in which the candidate had convinced the campaign leaders that he was best qualified for the task.[20]

Not a grass-roots movement

Realising objectives is perhaps not exactly what comes to mind when thinking about activism. But this was the goal of the campaign: grow fast, mobilise as many supporters as possible, and gather signatures for Navalny's presidential candidacy. Although it relied on local knowledge and experience, the regional offices had little leeway in choosing their activities or their strategy. One staffer in a region on the Volga complained that the campaign style was too fixed on a young, urban audience. They had wanted to adapt their activities to reach out to pensioners. For instance, the imagery of yellow ducks—alluding to the duck pond featuring in the FBK's investigation into Medvedev's alleged 'secret dacha'—just didn't work for people outside the metropolises, he squirmed. And yet, directions from Moscow were clear: no changes to the campaign material.

A young activist from a southern city had a similar complaint. One of Navalny's six major demands during the 2017–18 campaign was 'Trust the people, don't decide everything in Moscow'. But that is not what he observed in the running of the campaign itself. 'It's all very professional', he said—but also somewhat 'authoritarian'. Every post, every video he made as a social media manager he had to send to the central headquarters for approval. When he worked for the liberal party Yabloko, he recalled, things were different. This lack of trust from the Navalny campaign in their own local staff made him think: 'I don't know whether they will be more democratic, more liberal on other questions, I'm just not sure.'

But he and most others with similar objections understood the reasons for the tight top-down organisation. The campaign was operating in a hostile environment, with just a tiny fraction of the resources that its adversary—the authorities—commanded. If they wanted to stand a chance, quick reactions—rather than drawn-out, democratic discussions—were key. Why are the offices called *shtaby*—the Russian word for military headquarters—asks one coordinator, and immediately gives the answer: 'Because we are fully mobilised here for the fight.'

Nonetheless, there was certainly tension between the local embeddedness of activists—the grass-roots spirit emanating from the rallies—on the one hand, and the tight working of a well-oiled political machine on the other. It was that combination that made the campaign strong, attractive, and adaptable—but it also provoked a clash of philosophies that not everybody was happy with.

'Manipulating the country's youth'

For years, the Kremlin has accused Navalny of using the country's youth for his own self-interested goals. When Putin talks about him—albeit never actually using his name—an image of Navalny pulling strings is often lurking in the background.

The Kremlin sees no problem in making teenage school children attend marches for United Russia or in enlisting the nation's teachers—who often operate polling stations during elections—in the orchestration of electoral fraud.[21] But Putin makes clear that he views himself and the Russian state as the protector of the country's 'naïve and misled' youth, manipulated by Navalny for his own power games.

With this accusation, the Kremlin taps into the idea that politics as such is a bad thing. In Russia and other post-communist countries, where political competition is often associated with the chaos and hardship of the 1990s, this conviction is widespread. In that reading, politics is not the art of the possible, but the art of deception: an immoral game of cynics, in which all players focus on nothing but their own individual gain. Politics is, therefore, something to stay away from or something best left to the grown-ups—those in power.

Many people in Russia are genuinely convinced of that idea—in part, for good reason. But the Kremlin has also done everything to cultivate it. It is one of the favourite exercises of government-friendly outlets to expose opposition infighting—the sordid airing of Kasyanov's pillow talk is just one example. And even the justice system is enlisted to provide proof: in January 2021, shortly after the first wave of large protests against Navalny's imprisonment, authorities opened a criminal case against Volkov for 'encouraging minors to participate in unauthorised rallies in Moscow and other Russian cities'.[22]

The charge of instrumentalisation—that Navalny is using people for his own ends, including by putting them in harm's way—assumes that people at Navalny's protests are blind followers of his, ignorant of possible consequences, and without any agency. We now ask whether that is indeed the case.

Not a rich kids' movement

The polls show that Navalny has amassed a sizable group of potential voters—were he ever again to appear on a ballot. To return to the image of concentric circles, these make up circle three. But any political force needs the rank-and-file—those who are more than simply potential voters. Who are these people? Are they different from the rest of Russia? If so, in what ways?

Since this group of vocal followers is, naturally, much smaller than the group of potential voters, it is impossible to rely on general population surveys for information about them. However, the results of a survey conducted by one of the authors in early 2018—when Navalny's presidential campaign was at its peak—offers an insight. The survey engaged with subscribers to Navalny's social media groups in Moscow, St Petersburg, and other cities like Vladivostok, Barnaul, and Ivanovo. Since these people had joined explicitly pro-Navalny groups with their publicly visible profile, we can assume that they are more strongly committed than respondents in general polls. They, therefore, do not represent the 'average Navalny supporter', which is helpful if we want to zoom in on his movement.[23]

To better understand how this group differs from other Russians, they can be compared to the participants of surveys conducted at a similar point in time.[24] Because the 2018 survey was conducted online and only in large cities, the results should be compared to survey responses from those who live in cities with over 500,000 inhabitants and who regularly use the internet.

In general, Navalny's core online supporters are younger and better educated than other urban internet users.[25] But the data clearly debunk one of the Kremlin's stereotypes—of Navalny's followership being fanatic minors. The 'fanatic' part will be addressed below, but the numbers on age clearly show that people under eighteen make up less than one fifth of all respondents.

Men are clearly overrepresented, making up two thirds of the group. This mirrors the impression of the interviews taken at the campaign offices. It does not necessarily mean that Navalny's ideas are more attractive to men, but men expressed their support for Navalny more openly.

Another stereotype that has haunted the liberal opposition since the protests of 2011–12 is that this is simply a movement of the affluent—of the urban middle classes who are out of touch with the hopes and fears of real Russia. From what we know about the composition of protests back then, there is a grain of truth in this: protesters in Moscow were indeed better off than other Moscow residents.

But, for Navalny's movement, this does not hold. The data show that Navalny's group is better off than people in the countryside, but a little poorer on average than those who live in big cities.[26] This really is striking. Combined with the findings on age, it shows that the narrative of a rich kids' movement is simply wrong: these are neither kids, nor are they rich.[27]

It takes guts to be an activist

In January 2021, shortly after Navalny had been detained upon arrival by plane to Moscow, TikTok—a social network not exactly known for politics up to that point—burst with pro-Navalny content. Many videos appeared in which secondary school students—fifteen or sixteen years old—replaced official portraits of President Putin in classrooms and hallways with portraits of Navalny. The videos were often set to music, like the all-time protest classic 'Changes' written by the late Soviet rock singer Viktor Tsoi, or a recent tune by the rapper FACE with the distinctive line 'To be against the authorities doesn't mean to be against the Motherland'.

The Kremlin was worried. Based on a hasty decision by the Procuracy, Roskomnadzor—the Russian state agency responsible for regulating telecommunications—demanded that TikTok stop distributing information 'that aims to involve minors in illegal activities'—similar to the charge that Volkov faced.[28]

The videos became so popular that they eventually spilled over into other social networks. The Kremlin, meanwhile, tried to frame the movement as one of misguided school children. What is it, then, that drives people—young and older—to support Navalny publicly? And what risks do they face by supporting him?

The 2018 survey shows that more than half of respondents had argued with others about their support for Navalny—in their families, at school, or at work. That number grows to more than two thirds for those who, like Oleg from Yekaterinburg, were actively involved in Navalny's campaign, distributing leaflets and coordinating protest—that is, conducting a 'normal' campaign in abnormal circumstances.

Of course, private conflict is unpleasant and may keep many potential activists from ever engaging in activism, but the impact on Navalny supporters extends beyond arguing with a pro-Putin parent or a work colleague. The organisation OVD-Info—which legally supports people who get into trouble for their political activism—documents the repression against Navalny supporters in painful detail.[29]

The list is long and disheartening. During the 2017–18 campaign alone, there were hundreds of arrests and police searches at Navalny's regional offices. Police threatened volunteers, staffers, and their relatives. Universities held 'preventive conversations' with students. Unknown assailants and openly pro-Putin groups like the 'National Liberation Movement' (NOD) attacked volunteers while police looked the other way. And, after protest rallies, regional coordinators regularly spent five to seven days in detention for violating one or more of the complex protest regulations. In all, the survey shows that one in two activists had experienced at least one of these forms of repression.

When asked about potential consequences for their own lives, most activists replied that they hoped repercussions would be minimal, but that they were ready to put up with what's coming their way. 'Of course, I expect problems', said one activist from Rostov. 'I was already convicted once of an administrative offence'—for attending a non-sanctioned rally—'and I know that if I'm convicted two more times, I can be criminally charged.' And, besides concrete legal threats, there is constant surveillance by the 'Anti-Extremism Centre'—a unit within the Ministry of Interior, established by Putin in 2008, that is frequently used for intimidation. But the activist shrugs it off: 'When we talk to these agents, they say things like, "I know you didn't spend the night at home." But that doesn't scare me at all: "If you're interested in such things, feel free to observe me"', he quips.

Polina, twenty-six—an energetic staffer and experienced Yekaterinburg activist since the 2012 protests—shows a similarly cool attitude when interviewed in 2017. Perhaps, she concedes, a future employer could be wary that, due to her political engagement, authorities would harass the business with excessive tax inspections or health requirements. 'But no boss in his right mind will be afraid of that—and working for someone who's not in their right mind isn't a good idea anyway', she laughs.

When talking to an interviewer, some of these people may understate their level of fear in an effort to impress. But it obviously takes guts to be an opposition activist in today's Russia. These are exceptionally brave people, but they're not superheroes. They are ordinary Russians from all walks of life. But, at some point, they decided to accept the conflict, the threats, the potential problems for their professional future. Why? What is it that drives them? What do Navalny's supporters see in him?

The personal in the political

There is not one reason that unites all of Navalny's supporters. The movement is diverse, as the personal backgrounds of supporters above suggest. But a general rule is that those who are closest to the action, those who invest themselves most into the campaign work, are usually not simply driven by personal admiration for Navalny the man.

Of course, Navalny has real fans—those who admire him mainly as a charismatic figure and who engage positively with every Instagram post from him and his family. A former coordinator of a regional office talks about his own teenage daughters: 'They strongly feel everything that happens to him as a human tragedy. My eldest daughter—she's seventeen—cried when she heard that Navalny was sent to prison. They feel a lot of sympathy for Navalny's wife Yulia, too.'

Support for Navalny the man is also something that drives his campaign activists. For instance, when he held his 2013 campaign in Moscow, Polina from Yekaterinburg thought that Navalny was different from any other opposition politician she had seen so far. 'When I looked at the candidates for governor or for parliament, they were all fake to me, insincere. But in Navalny's campaign I saw sincerity, I saw that the man really wants to do something good.' A survey respondent agreed: 'I like that he suggests things which many in this country, for some reason, think are unattainable and utopian.'

Navalny can be very inspiring. In a system that has long sought to depoliticise and sow doubts about politics as a legitimate endeavour, somebody who calls on people to trust their own ability to change things stands out. That optimism, combined with his dry humour and readiness to face challenges, are the things that come up most when talking to his supporters. Asked about Navalny's most important personal qualities, Yuri—a former campaign coordinator in Yekaterinburg—simply says: 'I might not agree with all of his views, but I've never met a braver person.'

It's no surprise, then, that many survey respondents list personal features as a reason to support Navalny's cause. 'He is brave and charismatic', writes one; 'I believe in him!', writes another; and a third is certain that 'he is the only person I would trust with the leadership of the country. I've lost faith in all others.'

An alternative without alternatives

These and many other statements underline that there is much about Navalny himself that attracts people. But for most individuals—regardless of whether they are online subscribers, campaign volunteers, or paid staff—their personal support for him is an expression of a larger goal. For many people, Navalny is an exceptional person and an inspiring politician. However, they do not support him simply for these qualities, but because he is the best-placed person to challenge the current political order. A survey respondent combines the personal and the political in the most concise way: 'Honest, smart, strong, energetic, brave. And there's no alternative.'

This statement may seem paradoxical. When someone likes Navalny because he is strong and brave, why would they care whether there are other able politicians or not? But the apparent paradox underlines that, for most people, their political goals come first, and Navalny, the person to enact them, comes second.

In the survey, the word 'alternative' is one of the most frequent terms people use in connection to Navalny—and they use it in two ways. The first presents him as a challenger to the existing political system. 'Navalny is an alternative to the current authorities', 'I can no longer stand the unchangeable regime. We need an alternative; we need political competition.' In this reading, Navalny simply provides something different. It is not so much about him as it is about a challenge to Putin, United Russia, and the authoritarian political system that conflates Putin with Russia itself. This is the meaning that FACE echoes, rapping that 'To be against the authorities doesn't mean to be against the Motherland'.

The second perspective views Navalny—for now, at least—as the only person capable of bringing about such change. Just as Polina expressed it when sharing her frustration about 'fake' opposition candidates, many activists and supporters are convinced that there is nobody but Navalny who can mount an effective challenge to the Putin-led political system.

Combined, these two meanings of 'alternative' describe Navalny's position in Russian politics. He provides an alternative to Putin's authoritarianism—and he is the only one doing so with a country-wide profile and the appropriate resources. He is an alternative without alternatives.

Who's using whom?

The staffers in the regional offices share this perspective. Some express admiration for Navalny, like the employee who admits that his approach to politics is always personal. 'I follow personalities', he says, 'and Navalny is someone who does not abandon or betray—a person who has ideals and pursues them.'[30] But most, at the same time, are keen to emphasise their devotion to the cause rather than the figure.

A theme that runs through many interviews is that staffers view their alliance with Navalny as temporary. Right now, they say, Navalny deserves Russians' support because he has built the only movement that can strengthen political competition, fight for an independent judiciary, and root out corruption and political favouritism. Any differences we might have, many claim, don't count as long as there is a whole authoritarian system that we're up against.

For example, an activist from Perm—who was already fighting for better local housing policies when Navalny was still a blogger—smiles when asked whether he disagrees with Navalny politically. Navalny is all wrong about housing, he says, 'but I forgive him, because that's secondary right now'.

Statements like these abound. Some left-wingers are not content with Navalny's call for a visa regime with former Soviet republics in Central Asia, some centre-right liberals do not agree with his demands for greater social protection and higher state investments—and some criticise Navalny for conceding that Crimea will remain Russian. But all are ready to sacrifice these kinds of disagreements for the greater, more urgent good as they see it.

Viktor, the first-appointed coordinator in Yekaterinburg, puts a name to this idea: Navalny 'is an instrument', he says, a weapon in the fight against authoritarianism and corruption. For many, Navalny is the best-placed figure right now, and that clearly has to do with his personal abilities, but that does not mean unlimited, cult-like devotion to him personally.

This turns the Kremlin's idea of 'Navalny the manipulator' on its head. It's not Navalny who uses 'naïve' Russians for his sinister power games, nor is it the West, oligarchs, or Kremlin clans who use Navalny. It's ordinary Russians who use him. They invest their time, their money, and sometimes risk their health, because they view him as a driver of change, as somebody able to catalyse and channel their own push for a better future.

It's the economy—or is it?

What unites Navalny's movement is clear. It is the demand for a say in who governs the country, for a fairer justice system that cannot be used for political aims, a Russia that no longer beats and imprisons its own citizens for political motives. This makes sense in an authoritarian country: it seeks to create the conditions for political contestation, for a 'normal' representative democracy, where parties and candidates compete for the support of voters.

But is there more that Navalny's supporters share—on economic issues, on foreign policy, on immigration?

In classical Kremlin-speak, one criticism levelled against Navalny is that his battle against autocracy is just a 'negative agenda'. He does not provide anything positive. All he can do is criticise. That is clearly untrue, as the evolution of his political platform shows. But where do his supporters stand on issues?

To understand how ordinary people feel about complex political questions, survey researchers sometimes ask respondents to place themselves on a scale between two extreme positions: do they prefer a fully state-controlled or a completely market-based economy, or something in between? Navalny's supporters overwhelmingly choose the market: they are, in that sense, classical economic liberals, much more so than the Russian population as a whole.[31]

On the other hand, when asked whether the state should provide for people in need or whether people should take more responsibility for themselves, Navalny's supporters favour government intervention. Similarly, a large majority thinks that income inequality is too large. Only a small fraction agrees with the idea that 'we need larger income differences as incentives for individual effort'. Here, it seems, they locate themselves clearly on the left—this time in agreement with a majority in Russia.

Is this a contradiction? Does it simply reflect Navalny's liberal and more recent centre-left demands without revealing what his supporters actually want? Yes and no. It is true that Navalny is remarkably effective at attracting people with different political attitudes and uniting them under his anti-Putin and anti-corruption umbrella.

But there is more to it.

Both survey results and staffers' positions reflect what, in a Western European context, would be called a social democratic profile. His supporters believe the individual is the master of their fate, holding that the state should not interfere with people's economic choices. This is also why many activists hate corruption: using power positions for economic gain is bad for competition, depriving ambitious and talented people of what they deserve.

But, as Viktor from Yekaterinburg puts it, the state also has a responsibility: 'The state should let everybody make money who wants and is able to, but at the same time it should support those who really cannot earn money on their own.'

What most Navalny supporters could probably agree on, then, is an economy that is firmly in private hands, that rewards individual initiative, but that is controlled and tamed by a redistributing state. This fits well with Navalny's own positions as summarised by two Russian leftist thinkers: 'He advocates "normal" capitalism with functioning democracy, a large middle class, and a welfare state capable of smoothing out income inequality.'[32]

Whether or not this is a realistic goal in Russia in the near future is a different question. Another is whether Navalny would be able to uphold this position if he ever were to come to power—or whether he would succumb to pressure from his currently much more market-friendly advisors. But if the mood in his movement does not change, then his supporters would clearly be a force for an economy that is liberal but more redistributive than Putin's oligarchic state capitalism.

Nationalism and xenophobia

Navalny has demonstrated that a focus on corruption can bring together ideologically diverse groups. Finding a similarly inclusive position on nationalism—the topic that Navalny clearly has the most complicated relationship with—is more difficult.

Navalny's position on establishing a visa regime with countries of Central Asia hasn't changed. According to proponents, introducing such a regime would reduce illegal immigration. This measure is a crucial part of the nationalist platform in Russia. More broadly, Navalny has expressed some regrets about his nationalist past—but has never wholeheartedly distanced himself from it.[33] So, does his platform attract xeno-phobes and nationalists?

It does—but his supporters are no more nationalist or xeno-phobic than the rest of the Russian population. It is difficult to measure xenophobia directly because respondents will often con-ceal their real attitudes from researchers and pollsters.[34] But it is possible to ask slightly more subtle questions. To measure atti-tudes towards various socially marginalised groups, the World Values Survey—a global polling project—asks people whom they would not like to have as neighbours, including migrant work-ers—the direct target of Navalny's visa regime demand.

In a 2017 survey that is representative of the Russian popula-tion, a third of respondents claimed they would not like to have migrant workers as neighbours. This share is exactly the same among Navalny's supporters. So, if that question tells us any-thing, then, put simply, Navalny's supporters are neither more nor less xenophobic than the broader Russian population.

It is no wonder, then, that racist stereotypes regarding the alleged crimes of working migrants—the same stereotypes that Navalny sometimes used in the past—do pop up when talking to activists.

Interviewed in 2017, one activist ran through a variety of reasons why she fully supported the visa regime. One of the arguments she gave is that, as Navalny claimed, legal registra-tion would protect migrants from the severe exploitation at work sites that many currently face—because companies cannot be held accountable when they illegally employ unregistered workers. Viktor agrees: 'The current situation is mostly abused by unscrupulous employers. This is bad first and foremost for migrants themselves.'

But a second reason for the young female activist is what she calls 'the criminal component'. When you walk through some parts of our city alone at night, she says, 'most likely someone will take your phone, your purse, or even your life ... And when you press charges, no one finds that person ever again.' She thinks that an official registration system, such as taking finger-prints upon entry into the country, might act as a deterrent.

Interviewed again on her positions in 2021, she still supports the visa regime—but says that neither her former colleagues from Navalny's office nor her Central Asian friends would par-ticularly like that. However, she makes clear now that, in her view, crime is not a question of ethnicity but simply results from migrants' status as legal incognitos.

These things, of course, are difficult to disentangle. Without insinuating a racist motivation on her part, the case shows that the demand for a visa regime is compatible with various posi-tions, including blatant racism: 'For sure', says another activist, 'if Uzbekistan and Tajikistan become civilised and rich countries that are no longer a threat, then welcome!'

That said, such ideas do not appear to drive many of Navalny's supporters. For one thing, asked about the special status of ethnic Russians in society, the vast majority distance themselves from such claims and stress the multinational character of Russian soci-ety. Emphasising ethnicity—'that's just nonsense', grunts Viktor, the coordinator in Yekaterinburg. 'I really don't like it when eth-nicity is excessively stressed. It makes absolutely no difference—you live and pay taxes in Russia? Then you're Russian.'[35]

In fact, some of Navalny's core activists are critical of the visa regime. 'It's a right-wing topic, and I consider myself on the left', says one. Another immediately names the visa policy when asked what elements of Navalny's programme he does not support: 'As a social liberal, I don't think this is that necessary.'

In contrast to socially responsible capitalism, where Navalny and most activists seem in agreement, the visa regime is—with notable exceptions—something that Navalny's base tolerates more than they champion. But it is also not an issue that drives many away.

All of this demonstrates Navalny's success in formulating positions that can be supported by a diverse group of people. On topics other than fighting corruption and autocracy, this sometimes means being consciously vague, providing a platform for people to project their own demands. This is clearly a strategic move—and one for which he can be, and is, criticised. But it only shows once more that Navalny cannot dictate viewpoints and agendas, that he depends on the support of Russia's people if he is to affect anything at all.

The man and the movement

Marching down St Petersburg's Nevsky Prospekt alongside 20,000 others protesting Navalny's arrest in early 2021, Stepan, a nineteen-year-old student, makes one thing very clear: 'I am no fan of Navalny's. I'm a fan of the rule of law.'[36]

Navalny has built his movement through protest. Over the years, he has very consciously employed it as a mobilising device, crafting—first and foremost with the help of Leonid Volkov—a formidable political force. But, as we have shown, this does not mean Navalny can count on unwavering, uncritical personal devotion from supporters and protest participants.

Navalny's supporters may be inspired by his courage and optimism, but they make their own choices. And so do people like Stepan, who do not count themselves among Navalny's partisans but nonetheless protest at his rallies. All of them pursue a goal that is greater than Navalny the individual: a Russia that is free of political repression, of elite corruption, and whose enormous wealth is more equally distributed.

But even though, ultimately, it's not always about Navalny, he has time and again consolidated and channelled people's push for change.

And his actions, it turns out, have also had a profound effect on the Kremlin.

5

THE KREMLIN V. NAVALNY

'Complete nonsense'.

So replied Putin's press secretary, Dmitry Peskov, to a question on everybody's mind: is Putin 'afraid of Alexei Navalny'?[1]

It's 19 January 2021—two days after Navalny's return to Russia. His plane was rerouted, his supporters were confronted by riot police, his associates were detained, and he was taken into custody as soon as he stepped foot on Russian soil. Given all of this, it seems that the journalist's question was a reasonable one to ask—but Peskov was having none of it. And the protests that were announced in support of Navalny for the coming days, he said, did not worry the Kremlin either.

But anyone on the streets of Moscow that Saturday—and a week later—could be forgiven for having a different impression. Police were everywhere. Van after van pulled into the city, metal crowd control fences went up across the centre, thousands of officers lined the streets. Central metro stations were closed, police in plain clothes patrolled cafés and 'urged' their owners to shut down Wi-Fi networks.[2] It looked as though the city was trying to prevent a revolution.

About 160,000 people turned out to non-sanctioned rallies across the country on 23 and around 66,000 on 31 January.[3] The revolution did not take place—but police did their best to prevent it anyway. Up to mid-February, OVD-Info documented over 11,000 detentions, 140 cases of police beating unarmed participants, and ninety criminal cases that were opened against protesters.[4]

These numbers were unprecedented for Russia under Putin. So was the president afraid of Navalny after all?

One thing is certain: the Kremlin takes Navalny very seriously. As journalists found out from sources in the Russian security services, the FSB looks into why people support Navalny and monitors protest turnout.[5] Also, Peskov has admitted that Putin is regularly informed about Navalny—and the Russian president himself even revealed that he gave his personal permission for Navalny to be taken abroad for treatment in August 2020.[6]

We might never know whether Putin is actually afraid of Navalny. But, perhaps, the more relevant question to ask is whether, and how, the Kremlin has reacted to the actions of a man it claims to be irrelevant.

Five dimensions of change

So far, we have shown how Navalny has reacted to the Kremlin and the evolution of politics under Putin. Both Navalny's anti-corruption activism and protest mobilisation were clear responses to the limited opportunities to be a 'normal' politician—to compete for power in free and fair elections. Navalny has tried to make the best of an increasingly dismal situation.

But Navalny has not been pushing back against a static political force—a Kremlin that is monolithic and immovable. Influence also runs the other way: from Navalny and his movement to the Kremlin.

In that process, the Kremlin has become more blatantly authoritarian. Since the end of Medvedev's presidency and the mass protests of 2011–12, Putin's system has made repression more severe and more visible to scare people away from protesting. It has limited access to information about officials, complicating the FBK's investigations. Without banning opposition outright, it has further restricted access to elections, even to those at the lowest level that matter least. And it has discredited opponents as traitors.

But as the Kremlin has become more repressive, it has also established emotional connections with parts of the population and built alliances with select parts of civil society. In other words, the Kremlin has tried to mobilise real support—and not without success.

All of these changes from the Kremlin are reactions to the challenges that Putin has faced during his rule. We have looked at many of them from the perspective of Navalny: how to build support in the population, how to fight corruption, how to organise protest, how to compete in elections. It's now time to look at how the authorities have adapted to these challenges, focusing on five dimensions: Putin's support, freedom of information, civil society, protest, and elections.

Navalny has become the main political counterforce in the country—its second most important politician, even though Peskov would never admit it. The Kremlin's reactions, therefore, have a lot to do with Navalny.

But Navalny did not appear in a vacuum—and the Kremlin does not react to him alone. As we show for each of the five dimensions, there is much more to Russian politics than Navalny. He is part of a broader movement of citizens and organisations—in Moscow as well as in the regions. The five cases illustrate this: sometimes Navalny is present, sometimes less so. But all of them convey the surprising dynamism underlying Putin's seemingly stable rule.

We now follow the Kremlin's search for social support and its quest for control—both of Navalny and those beyond.

Hearts and minds

Vladimir Putin enters the Kremlin's Georgievsky Hall. The largest hall in the Kremlin's Great Palace—built in the nineteenth century to host the family of the tsars—its walls are covered with tributes to Imperial Russia's military victories. Having arrived at the podium, Putin faces the audience with a calm, confident, determined expression—and a barely noticeable smile. What he is about to say will make history.

'Good afternoon, esteemed members of the Federation Council, State Duma deputies, representatives of the Republic of Crimea and Sevastopol who are here among us, citizens of Russia!'[7] Putin does not even get beyond this opening before the first standing ovation. On mentioning Crimea, everybody rises from their seat, applauding. Putin's expression is just as calm now, but the smile is wider.

It is 18 March 2014—and Russia is about to officially annex Crimea. Or, as Putin says, 'reunite it with Russia'.

The annexation is in clear violation of Ukrainian and international law. It will isolate Russia internationally, leading to economic sanctions from Western countries that will trigger highly damaging counter-sanctions. But the speech is about something else. It is, for Putin and those assembled, about historical justice and national greatness, a glorious past that is now connected to a glorious future.

Putin speaks about the roots of Christian Orthodoxy that unite the people of Russia, Ukraine, and Belarus, about the multinational character of Crimea that makes it similar to Russia, about the port city of Sevastopol and its heroic fight against the Nazis. 'Everything in Crimea speaks of our shared history and pride', he says. 'In people's hearts and minds, Crimea has always been an inseparable part of Russia.'

It is easy to dismiss the whole scene as a well-staged spectacle by Russian officialdom—parliamentarians, military figures, law enforcement, clerics from Russia's Orthodox, Muslim, and Jewish communities—who are eager to show their support for the national leader. And it is that—but it is also much more. These are not the dull, expressionless faces of subordinates receiving yet another lecture from Putin, as is often seen during broadcasts of other meetings. Here, people's eyes are filled with joy.

A turn to emotions

Putin's speech marks an emotional turn in the Kremlin's strategy to bolster its rule. The first decade of Putin's presidency was marked by strong economic recovery and the strengthening of the central state. Stability and growth were what convinced people of the Kremlin's leadership.

But the For Fair Elections protests in 2011–12 showed that not everybody was going to accept the implicit social contract, where the authorities promised rising living standards in return for political acquiescence. Even though the messages voiced at the protests were diverse, it was clear that many now demanded a say.

At some point in early 2012, the Kremlin decided that it could not please everybody. It turned to those people who did not support or understand the protests, who were still content with the existing social contract, or who were simply afraid of change. Trying to unite these very different sections of the population behind their leader, the Kremlin started to restructure 'Putin's majority'.

Emotions played a big part in that endeavour. And the events of 2013–14 in Ukraine provided unexpected help.

In November 2013, people in Ukraine rose to demand closer ties to Europe and an end to President Viktor Yanukovych's corrupt rule. Despite Putin's proclamations to the contrary, the Ukrainian Maidan—its violent climax and the fall of Yanukovych—were useful for the Kremlin, because they strengthened the emotional appeal of the Russian leadership's agenda.

Chaos in Kyiv—and, later, war in eastern Ukraine—re-ignited fears of revolutionary violence at home, in Russia. A pro-Western Ukrainian government aroused concerns over renewed NATO expansion. Russia, in the eyes of many, needed to be defended. But Russia's response—swiftly annexing Crimea according to a scenario that had been planned several weeks in advance[8]—also allowed the Kremlin to add pride and joy to the emotional mix. Putin, the message went, did not just protect Russia. He also restored its greatness.

Not just propaganda

All of this sounds as though the Kremlin carefully planned its response to the challenges it faced at home. It sounds as though Russia used special forces to annex Crimea, a loyal parliament to enact the needed laws, and state-controlled media to deliver the propaganda, forcing a strategy to legitimise its rule upon a passive and brainwashed population. But, just as Navalny does not simply use Russians for his own political goals, the Kremlin could not just manipulate them at will, either.

Power in Russia, as social scientists Samuel Greene and Graeme Robertson show, is 'co-constructed'.[9] This phrase captures a very important feature of Russian politics: even though formal democratic institutions are highly flawed, favouring the current authorities, Putin's power is rooted in the population itself. Far from simply flowing from propaganda and repression, the president's power depends on daily support from millions of Russian citizens. For some, that support takes the form of harassing Kremlin enemies or attending pro-Putin rallies. But, for most, that construction of power happens in the more mundane spaces of schools, workplaces, and families. That's the reason, after all, why Navalny's supporters have so often experienced conflict not just with the official organs of the state but with colleagues, friends, and family members. These seemingly non-political sites are, in fact, charged with politics.

Acknowledging that the president's power is dependent on popular support, the Kremlin regularly experiments with offers that it can make to the population to try to win them over. The turn to emotions was one such offer—and one that was particularly effective. Positive emotions like pride in Russia's renewed greatness—and negative ones like fear of chaos and foreign domination—were collectively experienced by millions of citizens, building emotional connections to each other as much as to their leadership.

'Putin is Russia, Russia is Putin'

What does all of this have to do with Navalny? The new emotional strategy was designed to construct a majority—and a minority. It was consciously excluding those who want Russia to take the 'European way'—to build closer alliances with Western countries, to tame presidential power, to make Russia a democratic country. It also excluded those with socially liberal attitudes, emphasising Russian Orthodox Christianity and associating homosexuality with the 'morally degraded' West.

This way, the Kremlin reinforced the polarisation of Russian society, trying to reduce society to two opposing camps—the 'patriotic majority' and everybody else.[10] This strategy was not targeted at Navalny alone, but it was a clear answer to the challenge that dissatisfied citizens had mounted against the Kremlin, both during the For Fair Elections protests and during Navalny's

Moscow campaign. The response was clear: You are a small, estranged minority.

This new Kremlin strategy was built on nationalism. Putin brought Crimea 'home'. And he finally 'raised Russia from its knees', after the humiliation of the 1990s when, many were convinced, Russia was subordinated to the West. Putin, therefore, established himself as the country's prime defender of national interests. Even more than that, he became equated with Russia itself. As parliamentary speaker Vyacheslav Volodin put it, 'if there's Putin, there's Russia, if there's no Putin, there's no Russia'.[11]

It was nationalism with a specific twist, as Putin continued to emphasise the multi-ethnic character of Russian society. But, still, he won over a large share of Russian nationalists, driving a deep wedge into that camp, much of which had previously harboured oppositional views. Boris, a far-right radical in Perm—who had been convicted of inciting racial hatred and categorically opposed Putin's 'awful migration policy'—said that, 'for Crimea, I forgive Putin a lot'.

Navalny, as we have shown, had mostly abandoned nationalism as a public ideology a few years before, but the annexation of Crimea ensured that the topic was not going to offer promise for the opposition any time soon.

Powerful but fragile

Emotional experiences create a sense of community and can, therefore, be a much more powerful way of winning people's hearts and minds than rational calculations of costs and benefits.[12] This is captured in the famous Russian phrase of the 'battle between the TV and the fridge', where propaganda can win despite deteriorating material conditions.

But the phrase is inaccurate, because it portrays the population as passive and easily misled, just as pro-Kremlin media sometimes portray Navalny's supporters. Controlling the most important media is an enormous advantage, but it does not allow the authorities to manipulate people at will. Putin's rule depends on the population accepting his offers. That makes it both powerful and fragile.[13]

The joy on people's faces in the Kremlin's Georgievsky Hall was real, as was the joy and pride of millions of Russians in 2014. But it is difficult to sustain such emotional highs. The euphoria that surrounded the annexation of Crimea was an enormously effective tool to bolster Putin's rule—but, since 2018, Putin's ratings have come down again from the astronomic heights they reached at that time. This decline in support was triggered by the government's decision to raise the retirement age, but the trend has been sustained by both stagnating economic prospects and a lack of positive emotional anchors.

This does not mean that the Kremlin's emotional strategy is over. In early 2021, Navalny was not just taken to court for having violated his parole conditions, but also for allegedly insulting a veteran of the Great Patriotic War—the Russian term for the Second World War.[14] Along with a cosmonaut, an actor, and other famous Russians, the ninety-four-year-old former soldier had appeared in a promotional video by the state-owned outlet RT that was designed to elicit support for Russia's 2020 constitutional changes.

In a characteristically sharp attack, Navalny had called the participants in the video 'corrupt lackeys'.[15] He had not mentioned the veteran personally, but his presence in the clip was enough. Navalny, so the accusation went, had committed a grave moral offence against a war hero—one that could, and should, be punished. It was again the emotional strategy in action. This time, however, it mobilised what is fundamental to the very identity of many Russians: the memory of the Great Patriotic War.

Classified information

'LSDU3' and 'YFYaU9'. These cryptic codes swept across the Russian internet in 2016. But why?

They are codenames for Artyom and Igor Chaika, respectively—the sons of Yuri Chaika, Russia's prosecutor general between 2006 and 2020.

The Chaika family was the focus of an Anti-Corruption Foundation investigation, released on 1 December 2015—two days before Putin's annual 'state of the nation' address.[16] Navalny's FBK presented evidence that, it claimed, showed the sons' extensive commercial empire. Peskov brushed the allegations aside, saying they did not relate directly to the prosecutor general himself—and Yuri Chaika said that the investigation was 'a hatchet job, not paid for by those who made it'.[17]

The investigation was crucially dependent on official records linking Artyom and Igor—along with their relatives—to property and businesses. One such source of information was 'Rosreestr'—Russia's Federal Service for State Registration, Cadastre, and Cartography—which manages information on property ownership.

On 9 June 2016, Navalny announced that Rosreestr had replaced the Chaika sons' actual names in official records.[18] Navalny provided a series of 'before and after' pictures on his website, showing the replacement of real names with the codes on official documents. And he was clear about what he saw as the purpose of these changes—to hide information that could be used to expose high-level corruption:

> We believe that Rosreestr officials are criminals, that what they are doing is completely illegal, and that they should be held responsible for this. They are clearly doing this on the orders of the Kremlin, but all the same. We're suing Rosreestr for each case of classifying/blackening out [the names of] officials and their children.[19]

Navalny included pictures of C-3PO and R2-D2—droid characters from *Star Wars*—next to photos of the Chaika sons and their father to hammer home the weirdness of the codenames. And Russian internet users followed suit, turning 'LSDU3' and 'YFYaU9' into memes. This once again showed Navalny's approach: packaging serious content in a light-hearted format—with a view to reaching as broad an audience as possible.

But the Kremlin wanted a less risky way to keep officials shielded from the glare of the FBK's investigators—one that reduced the likelihood of state bodies looking like fools.

From obscuring to classifying

'On the Introduction of Changes to the Federal Law "On State Protection" and Certain Legislative Acts of the Russian Federation'.[20] This was the boring, bureaucratic name of a draft law Putin introduced into the State Duma in February 2017 that threatened to strike a blow to the heart of the FBK's investigative approach.

The final version of the law that Putin signed in July 2017 gave grounds to classify the personal data of people with 'state protection', as well as their family members. According to Transparency International Russia, this legal change would allow information on top-level officials—including, for instance, Prosecutor General Yuri Chaika and his family—to be excluded from state registries.[21]

But this legal change was absent from the version of the draft law submitted by Putin in February. Instead, it was introduced as a last-minute amendment to the draft law during review in the State Duma. This is a classic technique often used in Russian law-making to sneak controversial legal changes past the scrutinising eyes of legislators and journalists—a practice that also reduces the opportunities for people to kick up a fuss.[22]

The FBK's Georgy Alburov wasn't too concerned, however. He said the Foundation would employ other means to discover the elite's property holdings. One technique involved matching the size of prestige property recently on the market to the data contained in officials' yearly asset declarations.[23] While this wasn't a perfect solution, it was another way to get the job done.

This was, then, a game of cat and mouse. The FBK would exploit one channel of information; the authorities would take steps to block access; and Navalny's team would find ways to overcome these difficulties. Navalny and the Kremlin responded to each other in a constant back-and-forth. Indeed, the grounds for classifying information were widened with another law, passed in December 2020,[24] which made it easier for the authorities to withhold information about a range of officials. Although the bill was approved by more than 70 per cent of deputies in its final vote in the State Duma, a Communist Party deputy asked the bill's authors whether they were 'closing the mouths of the remaining brave journalists who identify high-ranking corrupt officials'.[25]

The information in question up to this point has been open-source, accessed legally. But the response to Navalny's August 2020 poisoning raised the profile of a shadier type of information.

'Probiv'

Personal information, it seems, has a price.

The investigation by Bellingcat, The Insider, CNN, and *Der Spiegel* into Navalny's poisoning drew, in part, on leaked information sold in online black markets—a practice known in Russian, and now more broadly, as 'probiv'.[26] Such records include flight manifests, mobile phone records, and bank account details.

The use of probiv by Bellingcat and its partners did not go unnoticed by Russian law enforcement. In the first few months of 2021, several Russian police officers were arrested on suspicion of leaking information that might have been used in the Bellingcat investigation.[27] As noted by Russia analyst Mark Galeotti, '[t]hose very same security officers meant to be protecting the nation's data, are actually the most enthusiastic in monetising the capacity for probiv their positions offer'.[28]

But that didn't stop the authorities from trying to reduce the attractiveness of this market for personal data. In February 2021, a draft law was introduced into the State Duma, proposing criminal liability for law enforcement officials who disseminate information about their colleagues obtained through their positions.[29] The goal, it seemed, was to create a chilling effect.

This was yet another step by the authorities to restrict access to information that could be deployed against them. The FBK itself has claimed that 'only open sources of information' are used in its investigations.[30] But Navalny's poisoning and the steps taken to uncover the details of the attack underscored, more broadly, the possibilities—and perils for the Kremlin—of online information.

The 'Runet's' shrinking space

Upon assuming power as prime minister in 1999, Putin promised 'not to touch' the Russian internet for the foreseeable future.[31] And, although many would say that he has not kept his promise, the Russian internet—also known as the Runet—was for a long time an almost anarchic zone within an otherwise gradually tightening public sphere.

Nonetheless, as Navalny and many others perfected the use of social media for organising resistance and distributing information that the authorities would have preferred to stay under wraps, the Kremlin sensed the danger.

On 9 December 2011, the FSB urged Pavel Durov—a young tech entrepreneur and founder of the Russian Facebook equivalent, VKontakte (VK)—to block several pages on which protest events were coordinated. Durov did not comply. Instead, he used Twitter to publicise the FSB's letter and accompanied it with a photo of a dog in a hoodie, sticking out its tongue.[32]

But, in less than two years, Durov had sold his stake in VK—shortly after to be acquired by oligarch Alisher Usmanov's Mail.ru Group. Durov also stepped down as CEO of VK, complaining about the authorities' requests to shut down pages of Navalny's supporters and to provide information on opposition accounts.[33] Durov emigrated and founded the messenger app Telegram.

As an encrypted messaging app, the Russian authorities didn't like Telegram either. So much so that, in April 2018, Russia's communications regulator, Roskomnadzor, tried to block the platform. Chaos ensued. Instead of successfully disabling use of Telegram, the regulator's actions led to service disruptions for unassociated online services.[34] (Roskomnadzor lifted its ban in June 2020.)[35]

Navalny's website also faced difficulties in 2018. Access to it was temporarily blocked after he published an investigation into connections between oligarch Oleg Deripaska and then Deputy Prime Minister Sergei Prikhodko. Pictures of the two on Deripaska's yacht had appeared on the public Instagram account of the model Nastya Rybka, who was also on the boat.[36]

Navalny used the pictures, Deripaska sued Rybka for 'infringements of his private life', she deleted the pictures, and Roskomnadzor blocked Navalny's website—until, a week later, he deleted the post as well and his site was reinstated. Navalny, therefore, showed the capacity to compromise in order to keep his website accessible. And yet, he also showed the capacity for cheekiness: he reminded people that they could still access the video on YouTube.[37]

* * *

Navalny is who he is because of the internet. From his LiveJournal blog to his first forays into online crowd-sourcing, his website, and the FBK's YouTube hits, he has used online platforms to investigate—and make public—allegations of corruption and official wrongdoing. The relative freedom of the Runet allowed Navalny to spread his message without access to traditional media, especially television. His public persona is, to a large degree, his internet persona.

But this source of strength has also made Navalny—and the investigations conducted by his team—vulnerable to counter-measures taken by the Russian state. And yet, the episodes above show that the FBK has been able to respond to this evolving challenge.

Civilising society

Perm is a special city. A place of exile for dissidents in tsarist and Soviet times, it is home to one of the few Russian museums on Soviet forced labour colonies. But there is more to the city than that.

Andrei Nikitin, an enthusiastic commentator, once called Perm the home of Russian liberalism.[38] And while liberal parties used to fare slightly better here than they did elsewhere in the 1990s and 2000s, what made Perm liberal is first and foremost its civil society.

'Liberal' in this context relates to the idea that social organisation is independent of the state. Groups of citizens work together to keep the state in check, but also to assist it in providing services to its citizens. Such vibrant civic self-organising is what Tocqueville admired so much about the United States in the mid-nineteenth century and what he thought to be the basis of a healthy democracy. It is also what Nikitin admired about Perm.

During perestroika in the 1980s, the history department of Perm State University was a place where critical minds gathered.

Here, many of those who would later become the city's leading civil society activists met for the first time.

The 1990s witnessed a flourishing of self-organisation. In the beginning, this boom was supported by foreign aid designed specifically to move Russia's nascent civil society towards the Western ideal of a state-independent sphere. The Ford Foundation,[39] in particular, lent significant assistance, but later the regional government provided grants as well.

And, in contrast to some other places, where such money ended up being stolen, it fell on fertile ground in Perm. There was a group of people who made it their vocation to animate the ideal of civil society.

How to deal with the authorities

Various human rights organisations, like the Perm Civic Chamber and the Perm Regional Human Rights Centre, were founded in the 1990s. The local branch of the historical and civil rights society Memorial organised an unprecedented educational programme on Soviet repression, building up the Perm-36 Gulag museum around 100 kilometres outside the city.

But, in the 1990s, when the central state in Russia was weak and poor, the activities of these groups did not just mean defence against state overreach and education about state repression. They also meant helping people to get what was rightfully theirs—whether that was education, a pension, or welfare. Aleksandr Zotin, for example, led one of the most effective housing organisations in the country, helping thousands defend their rights against the authorities and utility companies. Human rights in Perm were—and still are—explicitly social rights, too.

All of this had an intellectual basis. Igor Averkiev, one of the central figures in Perm's NGO scene since the 1990s, maintained a blog where he reflected on much of what they did, some of it based on philosophical thought, some based on practical experience. Among these writings were 'Perm's rules of conduct'.[40]

The text, written in 2004, describes in self-confident terms how Perm's civil society challenged—but also how it collaborated with—local and regional authorities. In times when political opposition was gradually declining—even in liberal Perm—the idea was that civil society would take its place. Without ever seeking political office themselves, activists sought to influence policy in the interest of citizens and vulnerable groups. And they did: their decidedly pragmatic approach led to the adoption of several local and regional bills.[41]

'Foreign agents' everywhere

This model was largely unheard of in most other regions. And it eventually came to an end in Perm, too. Vsevolod Bederson, a young scholar and civic organiser from Perm, sees two reasons for this. Both of them have nothing to do with the city itself and everything to do with the changing political climate in the country, spurred by persistent challenges from Navalny and others. The first of these reasons was the notorious 'foreign agent' law that authorities also used to attack the FBK.

Introduced in 2012, the number of groups that could be subjected to the law grew steadily. From 2019, it applied not only to NGOs with foreign funding and allegedly political goals but also to media organisations. And, since 2020, it has applied to individuals, too. What's more, 'foreign support' is no longer limited to money. It can consist of any 'organisational and methodological assistance', as the law vaguely states. Moreover, everyone who mentions these organisations in the press and social media without pointing to their status as a 'foreign agent' can now be fined.[42] To the outside observer, this might seem petty but not draconian. But even the original version of the law had severe negative effects on organised civil society.

The second reason why Perm's civil society was in crisis related to the international context—a context that made the 'foreign agent' label particularly damaging. With the Ukraine crisis and the annexation of Crimea, the Kremlin ramped up its rhetoric against foreign interference. In this environment, being labelled a 'foreign agent' could cost you all the hard-earned trust of your constituency—as well as your connections to local authorities, if only because they themselves did not want to be accused of working with 'foreign agents'.

But it was not just reputation that was at stake. Organisations that did not comply with the rules faced high fines. Valentina Cherevatenko, head of Women of the Don—a long-established women's rights NGO that received funding from the German Heinrich Böll Foundation—was even criminally charged. She had, the accusation went, knowingly refrained from registering her NGO as a 'foreign agent'. For that, she faced two years in prison. The charges were later dropped, partly because she had already paid an administrative fine of 300,000 roubles (around £4,000 at the time).[43] But this case shows that the law is a constant Sword of Damocles for activists.

When the FBK fell victim to the law in 2019, authorities officially based the case on roughly £1,750 from two private donors, including the Spanish boxer apparently without any connection to Russia whatsoever. Whether authorities engineered these payments, as Navalny suspected, remains unclear—but they used the case to bolster their long-term claim that Navalny is a Western agent.

The FBK, meanwhile, got inventive. Being obliged to label themselves a 'foreign agent' on their website, they listed high-ranking officials and state media executives with residence permits in Europe, noting wryly: 'And yet it is us who have been labelled as a "non-profit organisation performing the functions of a foreign agent" by the Ministry of Justice.'[44]

Taking with one hand, giving with the other

But NGOs in Russia are not just shamed and repressed: they're also courted and funded. The state placed restrictions on many of the potentially critical portions of civil society. But, in parallel, it boosted domestic funding for NGOs. And Putin did not shy away from making it personal. Since their inception in 2006, the various programmes are known as 'presidential grants'.

In principle, any Russian organisation can apply. Sometimes, critical organisations have received funding, like the NGO For Human Rights of Lev Ponomaryov, who has tirelessly defended the rights of political and other prisoners. Even Cherevatenko's Women of the Don was awarded a grant in 2014 when it was already a 'foreign agent'.[45] But the bigger share usually goes to cultural and social organisations. These are not necessarily loyal or uncritical when interacting with the authorities, but most clearly view themselves as partners of the state rather than watchdogs, providing expertise rather than oversight.[46]

In Perm, too, organisations needed to decide whether they accepted the 'foreign agent' label—which was hardly an option—or whether they should try to attract domestic money. But Bederson points to an important catch: 'This is civil society in an authoritarian system: if you take money from the state, you can't criticise it the way you want.' Or that is at least what many felt, perhaps not without reason: Memorial has not received a grant since 2016 and Ponomaryov's For Human Rights lost its funding in 2018—and was dissolved by the Ministry of Justice shortly after on the grounds of alleged violations of the 'foreign agent' law.[47]

This double movement of restriction and stigmatisation on the one hand and increased investment in civil society on the other reveals a clear pattern. The state does not reject civic activity altogether. On the contrary, it often welcomes it—also because social NGOs help compensate for an insufficient welfare system. But the state tries to integrate civil society into its distinctive conservative worldview, in which society and the state act in concert in pursuit of common objectives. This, in principle, need not be authoritarian. The authoritarianism comes with the repression of those who disagree with this model.

Three strikes and you're out

Ildar Dadin was once an ordinary Russian citizen. Born in the outskirts of Moscow in 1982, he enrolled at a technical university, served in the army, and worked in private security. But, in 2011, he got involved in protests. And now, a repressive law is named after him.

His story shows how the Russian state changed its approach to protest—something closely connected to Navalny's role as a protest organiser.

In the 2000s, protest did not bother the Kremlin much. Most people were happy that Russia was getting out of the economic troubles of the 1990s, that the central state was no longer being pushed around by oligarchs and governors—that order was restored and life was improving. On the whole, few felt the need to complain.

The first challenge Putin faced from the streets came in early 2005, when the Kremlin sought to restructure the welfare system. Part of the logic of the existing Russian welfare state had been carried over from Soviet times, granting people benefits and privileges based on their belonging to certain social categories—students, pensioners, war veterans, Chernobyl liquidators, and so on. These benefits were often in-kind, like free public transport. Now, the government pushed neoliberal reforms, exchanging these benefits for cash payments, which often left people worse off.

When regional governments started to implement the law, protest erupted. Without political organisations leading the movement, people organised across the country, marching and some-times blocking roads. The Kremlin was taken by surprise. And some regions reversed course, halting or downsizing their reforms.

The movement gave a first taste that Russians—widely stereo-typed in post-Soviet times for being passive and apolitical—could force the authorities to compromise.[48] However, although the movement brought some local groups together, it did not grow into a political threat to the country's leadership.

The following years saw an increase in protest, however. In these times of recovery from the economic troubles of the 1990s, citizens usually turned out when the state was directly infringing on their lives. New import taxes on Japanese cars, for instance, inspired a movement of car owners in the Russian Far East. And, across the country, small protest initiatives fought environmental pollution or high-density urban development.[49]

These initiatives usually saw themselves as far away from 'politics'. They protested decisions of local administrations, they sometimes targeted specific mayors or governors—but they did not question Putin's rule. For many, politics was a dirty word, which is also why these initiatives rarely sought cooperation with politicians.

Openly political protest, however, was on the rise, too. In 2007 and 2008, for example, the 'Dissenters' Marches' brought together Putin's opponents across the political spectrum. More generally, there was a move away from the economic protest of the late 1990s towards more civic and political protest in the late 2000s—and a move away from the provinces and into the metropolises.[50] Towards the kind of protest, that is, that Navalny was then getting into.

Managed protest

None of this was to the liking of the Kremlin. And even though protest was generally small in scale and localised, the Kremlin took it seriously. Officials knew full well that, once protest reaches a stage that requires broad, visible repression to quell, it might be too late. Large, open dissent could help bring down Putin's ratings—and elites could turn their back on him. After all, the 'colour revolutions' in Ukraine and Georgia—which saw the toppling of political leaders—were fresh in people's minds.

So, just like it 'managed' political opposition, the Kremlin sought to 'manage' political protest in the 2000s.[51] That meant, first and foremost, preventing protest by pre-emptive arrests of leading activists. Where political protest did happen, repression was usually not sweeping but selective. This approach aimed to make dissent largely invisible—and broad repression unnecessary.

In addition, the Kremlin invested heavily in pro-Putin organisations and youth movements like Nashi (Ours) that could be quickly mobilised against street challenges. This strategy was a conscious reaction, again, to the 'colour revolutions' in other post-communist states, where oppositional youth movements had played major roles.

All these measures resembled the tools used to keep electoral opposition at bay. Managing both protest and opposition was done in such a way as to make the barriers in the system clear to those who challenged them directly, and, for everyone else, to create the impression that Putin rules largely unopposed.

From the Bolotnaya trials to Dadin's law

This nuanced approach came to an end after the For Fair Elections movement in 2011–12 when political protest exploded. There was no chance for the authorities to pre-empt it, partly because the movement was not just driven by the well-known protest leaders, but mobilised ad hoc on social media.

The Kremlin's first reaction was to embrace the new reality, albeit reluctantly. In most big cities, protesters were allowed to march, while police—unexpectedly for many opposition-minded citizens—stood by. The Kremlin might have been driven by the hope that letting off steam would calm people down, and that keeping police at bay might help to regain trust among protesters. And this appeared to work as protests gradually dissipated.[52]

But then came the rally on Bolotnaya Square in Moscow on 6 May 2012. The movement was already in decline, and the Kremlin made extra sure that protests like this would not emerge again. When the police cordoned off a section of the square—in violation of agreements with organisers[53]—Navalny and others called for a sit-in. Tensions built up, scuffles erupted, and police started beating unarmed protesters. Hundreds were detained.

In the wake of the event, the Procuracy opened criminal cases against dozens of demonstrators—mostly young and from different political camps, sometimes newcomers. Judges constantly violated procedural rules when dealing with these court cases.[54] Sometimes, even the police witnesses themselves could not remember any harm allegedly done to them.[55] In the end, many protesters were sent to prison, sometimes for several years.[56]

The 'Bolotnaya trials', as they came to be known, marked a decisive change in the Kremlin's approach to protest. In their wake, the State Duma passed several laws that restricted the conditions for legal protest. The ever-increasing complexity of rules regulating protest made it ever more difficult for activists not to violate them. And rule violation served as a pretext for repression. One move in this regard—a change in the Criminal Code—is today unofficially called 'Dadin's law'.

The law stipulates that individuals who are found to have violated administrative protest rules three or more times within 180 days can receive up to five years in jail. The trick with the law is that it works in conjunction with the many small restrictions on protest, which makes it relatively easy for a committed protester to receive two or more administrative fines for violating protest rules within half a year. Participated in a peaceful but officially non-sanctioned rally? Allegedly disobeyed the orders of a policeman? That's two offences.

Dadin—like so many others—attended his first rally in December 2011 and, after that, became an active protester. In early 2015, he was the first person to be convicted based on this new law that came, informally, to bear his name. Among the previous administrative fines were one received at a single-person protest in support of the accused at the Bolotnaya trials, and another from a rally in January 2015 in support of Navalny after his conviction in the Yves Rocher case.

Dadin received three years in prison, later reduced to two-and-a-half. After allegations of torture, and a domestic and international outcry, Russia's Supreme Court overturned the sentence in early 2017.[57] The Court did not, however, find a problem with the law itself, even though it punishes people twice for one and the same act, and has, thus, drawn heavy criticism from human rights lawyers.

Fearing protest

Dadin's law is used mainly to scare activists rather than imprison them.[58] But it has also been applied, for instance, against the Moscow-based Yabloko deputy Yulia Galyamina who, after protests in Moscow in 2019, received a suspended sentence and accordingly was barred from running for a seat on Moscow City Council.[59]

Protesters are still facing increasing repression, even without recourse to Dadin's law. Data collected by OVD-Info on administrative cases against protesters show a peak in 2011–12, and then a consistently high level since 2017 when Navalny started mobilising large rallies.[60] But even arrests at individual protests—the only form of protest that does not need prior agreement with the authorities—in Moscow and St Petersburg increased more than three-fold between 2013 and 2019. In 2020, arrests rose again sharply.[61]

Such is the reality of protest in today's Russia. Like political opposition, it is not banned outright. Authorities still sometimes give permission to hold rallies, and they do not always arrest everybody—but sometimes they do.

The Bolotnaya trials started a repressive trend that intensified with Navalny's rallies of 2017. Protest is no longer managed as it used to be in the 2000s. Instead, the Kremlin has become ever more creative at making protest difficult—and dangerous. Repression is more visible now and applied to random participants, rather than just protest leaders. Riot police arbitrarily snatching people from crowds is becoming a common sight.

The idea, then, is no longer to pre-empt protest by obstructing its organisation, but to scare everyone off from attending. To the extent that Navalny has developed protest as a political tool, the Kremlin has made sure that people hear their response loud and clear: if you take to the street, you might get into very serious trouble.

Khabarovsk: the exception?

In July 2020, Sergei Furgal, governor of the Khabarovsk Region in the country's Far East, was arrested, flown to Moscow, and charged with ordering the murder of two businessmen in 2004, well before he became governor. People spontaneously took to the streets, forming what became one of the largest and most sustained protest campaigns in a decade. Tens of thousands walked the streets of Khabarovsk every Saturday for months. What angered people was that federal authorities were interfering with their region, which had unequivocally voted against United Russia and the Khabarovsk governor Vyacheslav Shport in the 2018 gubernatorial election.

In that race, Furgal had run for the systemic opposition party LDPR. Nobody expected him to win—but then the protest vote against Shport, the recently announced pension reform, and years of being ignored by Moscow catapulted Furgal to victory. Although he ended up being surprisingly popular once in office, most people protested in 2020 less for Furgal himself and more to demand respect for their democratic choice.[62]

What was perhaps even more surprising than the sheer number of people who turned out week after week was the fact that, at first, police stood by—even though rallies were not sanctioned by the authorities. But when the protests waned in the autumn, police started arresting journalists and activists between rallies. Some were severely beaten.[63]

Was Khabarovsk an exception? If we look simply at law enforcement's initial response, yes. But with the subsequent crackdown, they returned to their established script. More generally, this shift shows how the authorities tailor their response to conditions on the ground. Where they deem it more appropriate, they can hold back. But most of the time, they don't.

Escalation game

Moscow, 11 September 2017. The team around Maxim Katz and Dmitry Gudkov is in celebration mode.

Katz is a Yabloko politician and former Navalny staffer. Gudkov used to be a State Duma deputy for the systemic opposition party A Just Russia—before he was expelled from the party for engaging in too much actual opposition. Together, the two have led the United Democrats—a coalition of various liberal groups and activists—into the 2017 Moscow municipal elections.

The outcome is a small sensation. Overall, United Russia receives most votes, but the coalition manages to win a majority in several municipal councils. In the Gagarinsky District, where Putin voted, all twelve seats are captured by Yabloko.

Why did the Kremlin not prevent this? Perhaps authorities were too distracted by Navalny's presidential campaign; perhaps they did not take this lowest of all levels of government seriously. Whatever the reason, many at the time see in this a sign that not all is lost for liberal politics in Russia.

Moscow, 13 March 2021. Police storm the Federal Forum of Municipal Deputies, detaining about 200 participants, many of them journalists and elected deputies, twisting their arms, pulling them into vans.[64] It is the first time that so many people have been detained outside of a street protest in post-Soviet Russia.

The conference was again organised by the United Democrats. Its objective was to share experiences and best practices before the municipal elections in September 2021, bringing together independent and oppositional municipal deputies from around the country.

Police justify their actions in terms of COVID-19 measures. They also say that some participants have links to an NGO founded by Mikhail Khodorkovsky—an organisation that was banned in Russia 2017 as an 'undesirable organisation'.[65] But, whatever the formal grounds, the goal of the raid is evidently to intimidate those who want to challenge United Russia—now even at the municipal level.

A change of heart

These two episodes feature the same people, the same city, the same level of elections. But, while the authorities looked the other way in 2017, they now made sure that everyone understood that times had changed. Why? What happened in between?

One reason might be the United Democrats' surprise 2017 victory itself. The Moscow authorities had failed to mobilise their own supporters. Turnout was low, benefitting the United

Democrats who had campaigned extensively. Perhaps Mayor Sergei Sobyanin and his colleagues in the Kremlin wanted to make sure that this could not happen again.

But there is another reason—a broader, more general one.

As authorities have made it more difficult for opposition forces to take part in elections on national and regional levels, many have moved to lower levels in search of remaining freedoms for independent politics.

In 2019—and in a rare moment of unity—different opposition forces, including Navalny's team, attempted to coordinate candidates for the elections to Moscow City Council, one level above the municipal councils. In contrast to 2021, they were allowed to campaign.

But at the very last moment, the authorities pulled the plug. Most candidates were denied registration, a decision that triggered protests—50,000 at a sanctioned rally in central Moscow on 10 August 2019.[66] As was becoming the norm, these protests were met with police beatings and resulted in criminal trials. The raid in March 2021 showed that authorities were now ready, if needed, to stamp out any challenge at the moment of its inception.

And this greater preparedness clearly has to do with Alexei Navalny.

A smart idea?

Navalny was frustrated at every turn when trying to take part in conventional electoral politics. Although he led a political party, the Ministry of Justice repeatedly rejected his requests to register it. He needed to get creative. But Navalny also faced problems of a less formal nature. For example, 'political technologists' more than once frustrated Navalny by registering parties using the names that he had planned to use himself.[67] Navalny needed, then, to find a way to outsmart the system.

THE KREMLIN V. NAVALNY

It's November 2018. Still in his presidential suit and tie, Navalny releases another YouTube video. This time, however, he does not report about yachts and vineyards. Instead, he presents an idea:

> The parties themselves cannot agree to put up a single candidate against United Russia. But we can. We are all different, but we have the same politics—we are against the monopoly of United Russia. The rest is mathematics. If we all do the smart thing and vote for the strongest candidate, then this candidate will win, and the United Russia candidate will lose.[68]

What Navalny advocates as 'Smart Voting' is his team's latest strategy to deal with the constantly shrinking space for the opposition in Russian elections. In a way, it harks back to Navalny's tactic of 2011 when he called for people to 'vote for any party except United Russia'. But there is an important twist: rather than just voting for anyone, Navalny's team would, for every race, identify the one candidate it thought would have the best chance of defeating the candidate from United Russia.

Opposition-minded voters could then enter their address into a website and get information on the recommended candidate in their area. This way, Smart Voting concentrates the protest vote to beat the Kremlin's choice. It is tactical voting in an authoritarian political system.

How does Navalny's team identify which candidates to back? According to Volkov, it's determined by many factors—surveys, the preceding electoral campaign, scandals. The exact mix is known only to Navalny's team. But one factor does not play a role by design: the candidate's ideology. This precipitates constant fights within the liberal camp. Katz, for instance, has been a vocal critic of the approach—but so are many others. Should we really vote for a communist or nationalist just to make United Russia lose? Should we not, rather, concentrate on getting our own candidates on the ballot—and, if we can't, denounce the elections for what they are: a farce?

Defending Smart Voting, Navalny borrows terms from political science—and interprets them with classic Navalny humour:

> Yes, of course, Smart Voting is not the ideal strategy. Clear as daylight. I want to remind everyone that our political system is called 'electoral authoritarianism'. The word 'electoral' kind of means that elections are manipulated so that only Putin wins. And the word authoritarianism means, guys, that there's no ideal strategy.[69]

Navalny and Volkov continually stressed that opponents of the Kremlin do not have the luxury of supporting their favourite political force. That is for the future. Today is about exerting pressure on the authorities.

Elections in Russia, Volkov said in 2019, were often cleansed of real contenders—to the extent that they have effectively turned into referendums on Putin. But that means that the Kremlin really cannot afford to lose these elections, given the reputational damage that would be inflicted on the president if they did. And, if it does start losing elections—in the provinces, in the municipalities, wherever—that may also make elites rethink whether they want to continue backing the Kremlin. And this, in turn, can spice things up considerably. In Volkov's thinking, Smart Voting is supposed to bring politics back to Russia—even without Navalny being on the ballot himself.

Action and reaction

Does Smart Voting work? When first trialled in September 2019, it was not a resounding success—United Russia still received a majority of seats in many regional and city parliaments. But the numbers suggest that, without Smart Voting, that victory would have been much larger.

In the municipal elections of St Petersburg of 2019, a study found that being recommended by Smart Voting gave candidates an average boost of 7 per cent—perhaps not a lot, but sometimes enough to win.[70] In Moscow in the same year, Smart Voting helped oust several prominent United Russia figures and helped candidates from Yabloko, the Communist Party, and A Just Russia win seats. And in 2020, oppositional candidates—with whom Navalny had been campaigning just before his poisoning—won a majority in the city council of the Siberian city of Tomsk thanks to Smart Voting.

These are small victories. But they are significant enough to worry the Kremlin, laying bare that its strategy to manage elections—in which systemic opposition is permitted and most other opposition forces filtered out—can backfire when anger and frustration is concentrated against the ruling party's candidate.

One of the reactions to Navalny's initiative did not even come from the Kremlin itself. All leaders of the systemic opposition parties distanced themselves from Navalny and Smart Voting at every possible occasion—even though their candidates only stood to benefit from it. Sergei Mironov of A Just Russia, for instance, was convinced that his party's performance in the 2019 elections in Moscow had nothing to do with Smart Voting—instead it was the party's own strong campaign that made their politicians attractive for Smart Voting in the first place.[71]

When the State Duma opened after the New Year break in 2021, all parties were in agreement that Navalny was a stooge, a demagogue—and utterly irrelevant. In a classic performance, Zhirinovsky called Navalny's supporters 'drug addicts and prostitutes'.[72]

But, in preparing for the 2021 Duma elections—in which Navalny's team planned to use Smart Voting, even with him in jail—the Kremlin needed more than discrediting statements from the old guard of systemic opposition politicians. And rather urgently, since, in spring, United Russia's ratings stood at their lowest level for many years.[73]

In March 2021, the online outlet Meduza published extracts from a document apparently intercepted from Moscow's United Russia branch on how to approach the September Duma elections.[74] The document identified Smart Voting as one of the main risks for the party's electoral success—together with possible investigations of the FBK into individual deputies. As a remedy, the document proposed setting up a website called 'Smart Vote' to confuse voters and increase the use of so-called 'technical candidates'. These candidates run under the label of a systemic opposition party but, in case they win, join United Russia's faction or drop out.

A downward spiral

In light of all this, the police raid on the conference of municipal deputies in March 2021 may seem more understandable. Since 2017, opposition forces have developed strategies to use the few remaining opportunities afforded by formal institutions. And authorities at all levels—mayors, governors, election officials—feel the need to act. After all, the Kremlin requires them to deliver majorities at the polls.

In this situation, Smart Voting takes the idea of tactical voting to its logical extreme. For it to work, no 'real' opposition even needs to be on the ballot. As long as there are elections with more than one candidate, Navalny's team can coordinate the protest vote. To undermine it, authorities would have to make elections completely controlled rather than just massively unfair.

That has not happened so far. But the Kremlin is edging towards it.

* * *

The shifting shapes of Russia's regime

In the past fifteen years, Navalny—as anti-corruption activist, politician, and protester—has evolved to adapt to the Kremlin.

The cases above have shown that the Kremlin has also evolved to adapt to Navalny.

But none of the above was a reaction to Navalny alone. Many other individuals, opposition activists, and movements pushed the Kremlin to react in various ways. The most important of these were the For Fair Elections protests—where Navalny was but one leader among many—that made authorities rethink the way they were holding on to power and searching for ways to gain citizens' genuine support. And this, more broadly, shows that Navalny has often escalated existing tensions rather than creating them in the first place.

A lot has changed, therefore, beneath the seeming stability of Putin's rule. Is it possible to assess—even if crudely—the general direction of that change?

The idea that democracy and autocracy are two radically different things is very much tied to the Cold War. Today, there is a consensus that there can be many types of regime—with 'regime' neutrally understood as a set of rules and practices by which countries are governed.

Some regimes are more democratic—they have functioning elections, protect the rule of law, and tolerate independent media—while others are less so. But undemocratic practices can and do happen in all kinds of regimes. To say that a country is a democracy is only a very crude way of saying that democratic practices prevail most of the time.

This also means that there is a large grey zone between liberal democracy and totalitarianism. Rulers in this zone try to get the best of both worlds: they attempt to look like democracies but manipulate rules so as to avoid real political competition.

Russia is one such case. It is far from being a totalitarian dictatorship. But it is also far from being a liberal democracy. There are elections—but authorities make them very unfair. The state does not censor all media—but it controls television and spreads disinformation. Protest and opposition are allowed—but are constrained and repressed.

Within this grey zone, however, Russia under Putin has edged towards dictatorship. We have shown that, partly in response to Navalny, the Kremlin has placed more restrictions on access to information, further encroached on the small freedoms that elections had provided, and ramped up repression against protesters. In its reactions to challenges, then, the Kremlin has decided to become less concerned with keeping up the appearance—and substance—of democracy.

This does not mean, however, that Putin rules by force alone. Just as Navalny diagnosed when he started his political career, Putin's power still rests on the support—both active and tacit—of a majority of citizens. The Russian political regime has become more brutal and authoritarian. But, at the same time, it has worked hard to gain the support of Russians, building emotional connections and presenting Putin as the guardian of Russian sovereignty.

In addition to these emotional strategies, the state continues to care for the welfare of Russians. It balances the corruption needed to keep elites happy with some sensible policies, including those that keep the state out of debt, provide basic healthcare, and deliver a minimum of social security.

In other words, Russia's authorities are much more adaptable and realistic than many observers and challengers make them out to be. This does not morally absolve them of their repression. But it helps explain why, despite the formidable challenges that Navalny and others have confronted the Kremlin with, it has retained the upper hand.

And yet, it seems that the Kremlin, despite all its adaptations, really does not want to take any risks when it comes to Navalny. His poisoning and later imprisonment clearly show that the authorities have made a decision: Navalny should be gone for good.

6

NAVALNY AND THE FUTURE OF RUSSIA

Moscow, 2 February 2021.

Alexei Navalny smiles as he traces a heart with his finger on the glass in front of him. Surrounded by officials, he gazes at his wife while standing in the defendant's box. With the world's media trained on him, he waits for the judge to announce his fate.[1]

Navalny is in court, again—and for a criminal case opened many years earlier. In late 2014, he and his brother Oleg had been sentenced to three-and-a-half years in the Yves Rocher case—a decision the European Court of Human Rights ruled in 2017 was 'arbitrary and manifestly unreasonable'.[2] Alexei was handed a suspended sentence, but Oleg Navalny was sent to jail. Although spared incarceration, Alexei still had to report twice a month to prison officials—something he did not do while undergoing treatment in Germany after his poisoning in August 2020. This was the formal reason for the court proceedings: the Russian prison authorities were asking for his suspended sentence to be revoked and for him to serve real time.[3]

But, for Navalny, this was not the real reason he was in court—he was now being punished for his failure to die of Novichok poisoning on the orders of Vladimir Putin:

I mortally offended him by surviving ... And then I committed an even more serious offense: I didn't run and hide. Then something truly terrifying happened: I participated in the investigation of my own poisoning, and we proved, in fact, that Putin, using Russia's Federal Security Service, was responsible for this attempted murder. And that's driving this thieving little man in his bunker out of his mind. He's simply going insane as a result.[4]

As is standard practice in Russian courts, the judge read off the sentence quickly and monotonously. It was as if the dull, grinding machinery of Russian justice had taken vocal form. Navalny looked on, resigned to the inevitable with a flicker of humour running across his face.

The verdict was widely anticipated—two years and eight months in a penal colony.[5]

At the end of court proceedings, Navalny said to his wife Yulia, 'Bye, don't be sad, everything's going to be OK.'

But his supporters on the streets outside the court were less calm. Coordinated by Navalny's team, they set off for Manezh Square in central Moscow—just in front of the Kremlin and Red Square. But the riot police—a sea of intimidating figures, dressed in black—were waiting for them.

This would be the third time since Navalny's return to Russia that his team had called for protests. The vast majority were unauthorised—the official reason being COVID-19-related health measures. The authorities had made it clear repeatedly that demonstrations were illegal and would be met with the full force of the law.

And they were. When Navalny's team announced the first nationwide demonstrations in January, a number of leading FBK figures—including Kira Yarmysh, Lyubov Sobol, and Georgy Alburov—were pre-emptively detained.[6] And so was every single head of Navalny's regional headquarters—either before, during, or after the protests. Many of them were eventually sentenced to short-term arrests or fines.[7]

Dozens of criminal cases were launched against participants and organisers, including Sobol.[8] Even family members were pressured by the authorities. The father of Ivan Zhdanov—the Anti-Corruption Foundation's director—was detained by law enforcement officers who accused him of abuse of office when he had served as a municipal official.[9]

The January protests also spurred a widespread crackdown on critical voices in Russia. The editor-in-chief of the online outlet Mediazona was sent to jail for twenty-five days. By retweeting a joke, authorities claimed he had 'organised' the non-sanctioned rally on 23 January.[10] And, on 14 April, three editors of the student outlet DOXA were charged with 'encouraging minors to engage in illegal activities'. In a video, they had demanded that authorities stop threatening students before the protests.[11]

And repression seemed to be working. Tens of thousands of protesters had shown up on 23 and 31 January across the country. On 2 February, the number was down to a few thousand at best, concentrated in Moscow and St Petersburg, with over 1,500 people detained by police.[12] Facing this sharp reduction in numbers, Navalny's team decided to declare a pause in protest.

We now pick up Navalny's story since his return to Russia—not as an activist, politician, or protester, however, but as a prisoner.

Navalny the prisoner

Even though Navalny had been sentenced on 2 February 2021 to serve time in a prison colony, he did not leave Moscow immediately. He was facing another trial. This time, he was accused of defaming a Second World War veteran. He was found guilty and sentenced to an 850,000-rouble fine (then about £8,200).

On 25 February, with court proceedings concluded, Navalny was finally moved from Moscow—destination unknown. For a few days, not even his family or lawyers knew where he was.

On 15 March, Navalny wrote for the first time from the place where he would serve his sentence—a 'corrective labour colony' in Pokrov, Vladimir Region, about 100 kilometres from Moscow. 'Three things do not cease to surprise me. The starry sky above us, the categorical imperative inside us, and that amazing sensation when you run your hand over your freshly shaved head.'[13]

Navalny wasn't beaten or threatened in prison. But he was constantly reprimanded for petty reasons: getting up ten minutes earlier than ordered or meeting his lawyer wearing a t-shirt.[14] Then, somehow, CCTV footage ended up in a Russian television report framing Navalny as a liar: he wasn't ill at all (he could walk 'with a cup of tea in his hand') and was condescending to a prison guard (he addressed him 'with his hand in his pocket').[15]

On top of this oppressive scrutiny, Navalny had been declared an 'escape risk'—a status used to add further pressure to inmates.[16] He was, for instance, woken up at night—every hour. And yet, Navalny noted that, armed with 'humour', it was 'possible to live' behind bars.[17]

But his health started to deteriorate. Navalny pointed to back pain and difficulties walking due to numbness in one leg.[18] He had, after all, still not fully recovered from his poisoning in August 2020. Through his lawyers, Navalny asked the prison authorities to grant him access to a specialist doctor—as was his legal right—and to stop what he called torture by sleep deprivation.[19]

When prison authorities blocked these requests, Navalny announced on 31 March 2021 that he would go on hunger strike. This was, for him, both the only option left and a symbol. Less than two years before, Lyubov Sobol had also been on hunger strike. In Navalny's own words at the time, this was a 'very powerful act of self-sacrifice'—and he noted how many great people, 'from suffragettes to Gandhi and Sakharov', had obtained their objectives by taking this route.[20]

A few days into the hunger strike, though, Navalny had an unwelcome visit: a whole crew from the state broadcaster RT.

Their report painted a rosy picture of life in jail: inmates could, they said, play table tennis (the table had not been brought in for the report, the journalist assured). The presenter, Maria Butina—also a member of the expert council for the Russian High Commissioner for Human Rights—had herself done jail time in the United States; conditions were, in her view, much better in Russia. But, what's more, they were even better than hotels in her hometown—something she said with venom to Navalny's face.[21]

When his wife visited him on 13 April, Navalny had lost 17 kilogrammes. Yulia Navalnaya wrote: 'he's still buoyant and cheerful'. But he had little energy, finding it difficult to speak.[22]

The pressure didn't let up. The newspaper he had subscribed to was censored—the old-fashioned way, with scissors.[23] He also said that sweets had been sneaked into his pockets and inmates were given poultry to cook in the common kitchen to tempt him out of his hunger strike.

And Navalny wouldn't be Navalny if he didn't see a political lesson here on the ideology of those in power. They can't understand, he said on Instagram through his representatives, that someone would choose ideas and principles over material comfort—they believe that everybody can simply be bribed into submission. But Navalny was determined to fight, and concluded with a winking emoji: 'don't you give up on important struggles either'.[24]

That fight included a call by Navalny's team for protests on 21 April. The goal was to pressure authorities into granting Navalny access to his own medical team. Fewer people turned out in April than in January, but numbers were still in the tens of thousands. In the end, Navalny did receive medical treatment, although he was still not granted a visit by his own doctor. He claimed that the protests had worked and announced he would terminate his hunger strike.[25]

As Navalny the man was struggling behind bars, Navalny's movement was being attacked with unprecedented severity across the country. On 16 April 2021, the Moscow Procuracy took legal steps against the FBK and Navalny's offices in the regions. It demanded that they be entered into the registry of 'extremist organisations' for planning to overthrow the constitutional order in Russia and carry out a 'colour revolution'.[26] By law, leaders of 'extremist organisations' can be imprisoned for up to ten years. Members—such as the FBK's employees—face up to six years. Donations are impossible, and all media have to use the 'extremist' label when mentioning the organisation.[27]

This destroyed Navalny's political structures—organisations he had been building for more than a decade. They were now being dismantled with dramatic speed. Was this the end for Navalny and his movement? To answer this question, we now reflect on what he achieved before this confrontation that appeared so final.

Three stories, one life

We have told the story of Alexei Navalny in three strands—as anti-corruption activist, politician, and protest leader. But these are simply dimensions of the same man—three threads running through more than twenty years of political struggle to transform his country.

In all three roles, Navalny started small, often not conscious of quite where these different paths would take him. His anti-corruption activism began with simple, non-activist steps as a minority shareholder. He just wanted to make money by investing shares, he said. But his frustrations grew when he couldn't access the information—and receive the dividends—he thought he was entitled to. And that created a cause. He started blogging, he gained an audience, and he turned his following into organisations that grew in ambition—from the Centre for the Protection of Shareholders, to RosPil, to the Anti-Corruption Foundation. Navalny the activist and blogger looked more and more like a politician.

Navalny had, in fact, been involved in politics before he was an activist. And his first forays into politics showed promise, but were ultimately hampered by clashes with the leadership of Yabloko—and his involvement with nationalism. His political career took off, however, after establishing himself as a leading anti-corruption blogger, finding a message that could unite disparate ideological positions around a common cause to attack the political elite. And it was his reputation as an online activist that helped him in the 2013 Moscow mayoral election. With this political success, he tried—for years—to register a political party, and, ultimately, to launch a campaign for the 2018 presidential election.

But Navalny faced hurdle after hurdle as his status rose—and as he became more troubling for the Kremlin. Facing these difficulties, he increasingly took on a leading role in protest. His first steps in the 2011–12 For Fair Elections movement showed charisma and enthusiasm—but not too much organisational nous. He took stock with his chief strategist, Volkov—and they set about creating a nationwide network to get Navalny's message beyond Moscow, to tap into the regions' potential.

Navalny's story since returning to Russia in January 2021 shows the same mix of activities—of the fight against corruption, of politics, and of protest. Except that Navalny was now behind bars—and his movement had come even more to the fore.

A matter of perspective

Has Navalny achieved what he wanted in politics?

Navalny's list of political victories is, perhaps, not impressive. What would be a footnote in someone else's biography—second place in the mayoral election of Moscow in 2013—stands as his best performance at the polls. His next best result is from 2020, when he—although not on the ballot himself—managed to get several activists from his regional offices elected to local and regional parliaments. Nothing to write home about, you might say.

But the deck was stacked against Navalny from day one. Everything he has achieved was done in the face of resistance from a political system in which principled opposition is actively marginalised or repressed.

When you cannot appear on state television—still by far the most important source of information for Russians[28]—a name recognition of 75 per cent is the result of many years of hard work and seizing every opportunity to get your message across. And, given the Kremlin's efforts to increase polarisation between the urban middle classes and the rest of the country, it is striking that Navalny's support is similar across the metropolises, smaller towns, and rural areas.

Navalny's aim has not just been to succeed in an unfair system, but to highlight the system's very unfairness. He has done that in part by presenting himself as a 'normal' politician—somebody who should be able to be on the ballot, register a party, and travel the country to meet supporters without being arrested or poisoned. By showing that his attempts to enter politics are obstructed or blocked entirely, Navalny forces people to focus on the reality of the Russian political regime.

Prodder-in-chief

Making the system's authoritarian features—and its corruption— apparent to as many as possible will increase the number of people willing to turn out to resist the status quo on the streets. That, at least, has been Navalny's hope.

But Navalny and his strategists have been well aware that pro- tests alone won't overturn the system. Disaffection with living standards, public services, and political stagnation is rife, but so is fear of change and chaos, as well as distrust in leaders—including Navalny.

Instead of concentrating all their energy on protesting, therefore, Navalny and Volkov have sought to challenge those in power by other means as well. Their goal is to divide the elites—and, by that, to increase political competition wherever possible. Smart Voting is a tool for that, trying to undermine Putin's power base, one election at a time. Rather than thwarting Putin right away—which he does not believe is possible—Navalny's strategy has always been to be a thorn in his side—to frustrate the exercise of power at every possible turn. For this reason, Navalny has aptly been referred to as the 'prodder-in-chief'.[29]

A revolutionary?

It's late March 2020. A young activist, Yegor Zhukov, faces Navalny in the studio of the radio station Ekho Moskvy.[30] He thanks Navalny for having inspired him to become an activist—just like he inspired so many others. But, today, Zhukov is in attack mode.

It is no wonder, he says, that rallies often don't achieve their goals when they aren't part of a larger plan of action. Protesting for two hours and then going home won't worry the authorities. What needs to happen instead, Zhukov is convinced, is something more disruptive—peaceful, but forceful: blocking roads, for instance, or occupying official buildings.

Navalny's answer is clear. According to the Constitution, people have the right to 'assemble peacefully and unarmed'—and Navalny is ready to defend that right even when the authorities have not given their formal authorisation. 'I call for protest, and I don't give a damn about what the Moscow mayor's office has to say.' But this is about as radical as he gets.

This is not because Navalny is allergic to revolution in principle. In 2011, for instance, he thought 'a confrontation between the corrupt elites and broad popular masses' that had just toppled regimes in the Middle East and North Africa as part of the 'Arab Spring' might also happen in Russia—a hope he repeated in 2016.[31] This makes him different from the old guard of Russian liberals, many of whom are principally opposed to any form of disorder.

But he is also different from the younger generation—people like Zhukov who sometimes endorse more radical measures. Pro-Kremlin media constantly accuse Navalny of wanting to bring a Ukrainian Maidan to Russia. In 2021, Putin himself likened pro-Navalny protests to the Bolshevik Revolution and its organisers to 'terrorists'.[32]

These accusations are what Navalny refers to when answering Zhukov. 'I'm realistic', he says. 'I just know that, as soon as I start calling to block roads, everyone in all my offices across the country will be arrested immediately.' The goal is to maximise protest turnout—and to create stress for the regime. But within the limits of the Constitution.

We might not know whether Navalny secretly dreams of leading people to the barricades. But his words and actions suggest he doesn't. Instead of a revolutionary, then, Navalny is better thought of as an uncompromising realist. But that has its downsides, too.

A dictatorial democrat?

We have shown how Navalny and his team built up the FBK and a network of offices around the country as political organisations. They gathered resources, they recruited talent, they orchestrated campaigns. But they lacked one thing that most other parties have: a mechanism for the rank and file to influence decisions at the top. And that has led to accusations of authoritarianism—both from other liberal politicians and journalists, and from activists in Navalny's own movement.

Navalny's structures work from the top down. This does not mean, however, that ideas and complaints from activists fall on deaf ears. It is in the leadership's best interest to listen to what people experience on the ground. But there has been no formal way for them to affect choices, let alone select and replace people at the top.

As activists have said themselves, the ability to implement decisions quickly across the whole network can be an important advantage in the current repressive environment. But sticking to a non-democratic structure has clearly been at odds with what the team otherwise has consciously attempted to do: design their own structures in a way that they want a modern, democratic Russia to look like.

A populist?

With this combination of authoritarianism and democracy, Navalny might be considered a populist—and he is by some.

Populists are often hostile to the intellectual elite and sceptical of expert opinion. But Navalny's platform is entirely devoid of this trait. He does not self-style as an intellectual himself, but, in contrast to many Western populists, he appears to value expert opinion. This speaks to an important difference between Navalny and populist movements in the West.

But still, Navalny is almost a textbook case of an anti-establishment politician. Relentlessly criticising the corruption and greed of political elites, his attacks sometimes include simplifications that might remind Western audiences of their own populists. So, is he one?

If we base the answer on his own statements, then he isn't. Navalny has stressed many times that he sees himself as being engaged in a two-stage battle. The anti-establishment part of his rhetoric concerns stage one, as it attacks the way power is organised in today's Russia. For now, he claims that politics is simple—that it is, in the words of Yevgenia Albats, 'black and white'. As Navalny told journalists at *Der Spiegel* in 2020,

> I don't see a problem in working together with all those who fundamentally represent anti-authoritarian positions. That's why I don't mind it if we now support communists in elections. I'm not scandalized just because one of the candidates we support wears a Lenin pin. You have a different system in Germany: You already have democracy, and the right and the left are fighting within its framework. We first have to create a coalition of all forces that stand for the alternation of power and for the independence of the courts.[33]

Then, Navalny is convinced there will be a second stage—a point at which this crude opposition between elites and people would dissolve and 'normal' politics would be possible.

When he thinks of himself as a politician in a parliamentary democracy, then, Navalny rejects populists' authoritarian claims to have direct access to the 'general will' of the people. In the version of Russia that he and his team imagine, Navalny's party would just be one of several.

A racist?

Navalny has made racist comments in the past. He has, for instance, used crude ethnic stereotypes, directed mainly at people from Central Asia and the Caucasus.[34] This has drawn much commentary from observers in the West, cautioning that Navalny is not the unequivocal democratic hero that some make him out to be.[35] But Navalny is not a Western politician. In this discussion, it is important to consider Russian perspectives.

Navalny's comments have, indeed, been controversial in Russia: many human rights defenders have been uneasy with Navalny precisely for that reason.[36] Alexander Verkhovsky, an expert on Russian nationalism, has said that Navalny harbours 'ethnic prejudice'.[37] And we have shown that some activists from Navalny's own movement distance themselves from his positions on immigration.

But, in contrast to racist comments made in today's Europe or the United States, in Russia, these remarks do not exclude Navalny from progressive politics.

Some might want him excluded if politics were 'normal'. But they view the issue as secondary—for the moment, at least. It may very well be that, in an open and free debate, 'Navalny the politician' would be called out more forcefully for his reluctance to renounce his earlier comments. But, as many point out, the more important problem now is to join forces against a brutal authoritarian regime.[38] His politics are for stage two.

* * *

A revolutionary, a dictator, a populist—and a racist. Navalny has been called many things. Although all of these labels capture something, none of them describes him well or completely. Navalny is a complex political figure. Consistent in his goal to replace Russia's corruption-fuelled autocracy with functioning democratic institutions, much else has been shifting—both around him and in his approach.

While sticking to his demands for regulating migration, his nationalism has moved to the background. In the past few years, centre-left elements have come to the fore in his programme—but these too might fade at some point. Navalny modifies his platform to connect with as broad a cross-section of society as possible. This could be called opportunist. But it is this flexibility that has made him dangerous to those in power.

NAVALNY

Is Putin afraid of Navalny?

Many of the questions asked about Navalny and his relationship with the Kremlin are, essentially, unanswerable. 'Is Putin afraid of Navalny?' is one such question. Answering it definitively would require access to Putin's inner thoughts—or, at least, to his closest confidants.

Facing these barriers, we have taken a different tack. Because what the Russian authorities say and what they do can often be at odds, we've looked at how the system has responded to particular incidents.

We might not know what Putin thinks of Navalny. But we can draw conclusions from the president's dogged refusal to use Navalny's name in public, his admission that Navalny was indeed being followed by security service personnel before falling ill in August 2020, and his insistence that Navalny is an agent of Western powers.

We might not know how troubled the authorities are by the Anti-Corruption Foundation's investigations. But we can draw conclusions from the official orders to take down YouTube videos, the frequent law enforcement raids on the Foundation, and, finally, the destruction of the FBK itself.

We might not know how seriously the Kremlin takes Smart Voting. But we can draw conclusions from the reported set-up of a spoiler initiative called 'Smart Vote' to confuse voters, the mass detention of municipal politicians in March 2021, and the full-frontal attack on Navalny's campaign offices across the country.

All of this suggests that, even if we don't know Putin's personal view, it is unquestionable that the Kremlin takes Navalny extremely seriously—that they see in him and his team's activities a clear threat to the current political order.

But the Kremlin also knows that Navalny is not its only problem.

Navalny has shown a knack for exploiting opportunities—for highlighting and mobilising people around structural problems like elite corruption and inequality. By removing Navalny, the Kremlin may succeed in weakening the focus of discontent in Russian society. But the more profound reasons responsible for citizens' grievances—stagnant wages, rising prices, venal officials—would remain.

Will the West save Navalny?

No.

Even if the West wanted to, it wouldn't be able to. Navalny's fate will be decided in Russia.

That does not mean that Western governments are powerless. But they should be realistic about the capacity to influence decision-making in Russia—through sanctions or otherwise. That is particularly true regarding somebody like Navalny, who has already been portrayed as a puppet of the West. Some have even doubted that there is enough political will in the West to enact new sanctions. And Navalny has been among them:

> Nobody is going to solve our problems ... Germany, the UK, or the US will never help us, or even think hard about how to save Russians from tyranny. We need to stop thinking about that, we need to stop hoping that foreign countries will help us. It's bullshit, foreign countries care about themselves.[39]

Navalny and his team have, nonetheless, called for international sanctions to be placed on particular Russian individuals: 'Go to YouTube, type "Alexei Navalny" and take all the subjects of our [FBK] investigations', Navalny said in October 2020.[40] And, when Navalny was detained in January 2021, his close associate Vladimir Ashurkov called for Western governments to sanction several prominent businessmen and political figures, not just the 'operatives' but the 'people with the money'.[41]

And this isn't the first time Navalny has called for such measures. He approved when the United States proposed sanctions following the death of Sergei Magnitsky: 'If this happens, it will be a massive blow [to the ruling elite] ... How are they going to be able to go to their Miami condos?', Navalny wondered.[42]

Overall, Navalny has been consistent in his attitude towards international sanctions. Yes to personal sanctions against corrupt officials. No to economic sanctions against Russia as a whole, which might hurt the Russian people more broadly.

One example of the latter was much discussed after Navalny's August 2020 poisoning. Some argued that Germany should cancel the Nord Stream 2 project—a gas pipeline project running from Russia to Germany, across the Baltic Sea. This was Navalny's response: 'That's Germany's business. Decide for yourself! Sanctions against Russia as a whole will not help.'[43] In fact, they might even 'help to consolidate the regime'.[44]

Do Navalny's calls for personal sanctions amount to an appeal for foreign powers to 'interfere in Russia's internal affairs', as Russian officials have argued? For Navalny, absolutely not. 'You shouldn't confuse Russia's interests and the fear of officials for their corrupt savings in Western banks.'[45] Sanctions against officials in the wake of Magnitsky's death, he wrote, were 'completely pro-Russian'.[46] Navalny also pointed out how Western countries were, in fact, enabling Russian corruption: 'Money laundering is a crime according to [Western] laws. Our crooks steal in Russia, and then launder in Europe; this can't be ignored.'[47] But Navalny hoped that, some day, 'all those responsible would be punished in Russia', without the need for international intervention.[48]

Is Navalny Russia's future?

Polling data might suggest not. When asked in early 2021, only 19 per cent of Russians said that they approved of Navalny's activities.[49] Any naïve assumption that Navalny is supported by the majority of Russians—that he would easily beat Putin if allowed to run against him—is wrong.

But these figures need to be taken for what they are: the results Navalny gets in a system in which he is ignored or vilified as an agent of foreign powers. When asked in late 2020, 49 per cent of Russians said that they thought Navalny's poisoning was made up or carried out by Western secret services.[50]

It's unclear what Navalny's approval figures would be if the restrictions he has faced in Russia were lifted. But the shift to such a state of affairs is precisely what he has campaigned for: to be a 'normal' politician in a system with a free media, rule of law, and free and fair elections.[51] However, that prospect does not seem to be on the horizon—in the short term, at least.

The societal structure of Navalny's support might give a glimpse into the future. Among eighteen- to twenty-four-year-olds, his approval rating is much higher than in other age groups, at 38 per cent. Any idea that all young people support Navalny is wrong. But, if this younger cohort remains more sympathetic to Navalny as its members grow up, then Navalny—or politicians with a similar platform and profile—may face a population more receptive to their message.[52]

Navalny and his team have sought to provide a positive view of what Russia could look like. According to Navalny, the 'wonderful Russia of the future', as he often says, will be prosperous, democratic, and forward-looking. And this Russia will not only be free:

> We have to fight not only against the lack of freedom in Russia, but also against the lack of happiness ... We have everything, but we're an unhappy country. Read Russian literature ... and it's just unhappiness and suffering ... We're in a circle of unhappiness and we can't get out of it. But, of course, we want to—and I propose to change the slogan. Russia must not only be free, it must be happy, too. Russia will be happy.[53]

And Navalny's supporters stress this positive vision when explaining their support for him. They point to Navalny being an 'alternative', as well as a courageous and inspiring figure.

Whether he would be able to deliver on this promise, however, remains an open question—especially when looking at the long list of reformers and revolutionaries who have dashed people's hopes in Russia and around the world.

Navalny is conscious that he is a symbol. And it's a crucial reason why he returned to Russia, even though he was well aware that he could end up in prison. When countless others put their future on the line, he could not remain outside of his homeland: 'In people's minds, if you left the country, that means you gave up.'[54] He had to lead by example, from the front.

But Navalny's significance is more than the actions of one person. His impact is also a result of his movement. Through anti-corruption activism, political campaigning, and protest organising, he has motivated thousands to take action—to overcome their fear that things cannot be changed or that change would result in chaos, much like in the 1990s. Even for some of those who don't support Navalny personally, they have joined protests to express their anger and frustration.

Navalny's current fate is in the hands of an elite he has consistently exposed and criticised. But, regardless of Navalny's own future—whether he will return to politics, remain behind bars, or worse—the people he has brought into activism will continue to rally for change, although facing ever more repression.

Closing down the FBK and Navalny's regional network means closing down Russia's main opposition platform. No political organisation as influential as these has been shut down since the fall of the Soviet Union. And this is the logical next step in an escalation that has been going on for many years.

Navalny and the FBK had always found a space from which to fight Russia's creeping authoritarianism—to switch arenas and adapt as much as they could. But the Kremlin has now deprived them of all obvious options. It is no exaggeration to say that, with this move, Russia's political regime has taken a decisive step towards full-fledged dictatorship.

Is Navalny Russia's future? The Kremlin clearly doesn't want him to be. But Navalny, his team, and his movement have been fighting for another possibility: that it's for the Russian people themselves to decide.

EPILOGUE

'THOSE WHO WANT TO FIGHT WAR MUST ONLY FIGHT DESPOTISM'

Pokrov, Vladimir Region—Penal Colony No. 2, 15 March 2022.

Navalny is on trial, yet again. He stands accused of embezzling money from the Anti-Corruption Foundation and of contempt of court—and faces fifteen more years behind bars.[1] The setting is even grimmer than his previous trials: Navalny is now being tried directly in jail, rather than in a regular courtroom. Journalists aren't even allowed in—they have to watch on a TV screen from an adjacent room.[2]

Navalny's 'closing statements'—referred to as 'last words' in the Russian judicial system—have become events in their own right. They've also been frequent, as Navalny himself has noted: 'We've had so many final statements it's almost funny. People are starting to roll their eyes: if these are really his last words, why do we keep hearing from him?'[3]

Beyond the prison walls of Pokrov IK-2, the world is an even grimmer place. On 24 February 2022, Russia launched a full-scale invasion of Ukraine—a war that not only threatens Ukraine but the very future of Navalny's country. As he said during the trial,

> the consequence of this war will be a breakdown, the collapse of our country. It sounds a little wild. But the phrase "Russo-Ukrainian War"

also sounds pretty wild. I myself said in this very courtroom when the trial began that everyone who thinks there will be a war is crazy. All the talk about our country collapsing is starting to sound more and more likely. They're just a group of sick, crazy old men. They don't have sympathy for anyone or anything. And our country is the very last thing they care about. Their only motherland is their Swiss bank accounts. And whatever they say about patriotism is a myth—as well as an enormous threat to us all.[4]

Navalny proceeded to tell the audience a 'great quote' by Tolstoy—but the live broadcast to journalists was cut. The quote—later posted on social media—read: '"War is a product of despotism. Those who want to fight war must only fight despotism."'[5]

Beyond politics, there was personal tragedy for Navalny in the war. It was reported that a distant relative—Ilya Ivanovich Navalny—had been killed in the town of Bucha (close to Kyiv) by Russian soldiers early on in the invasion.[6] The man was born in the same village as Alexei Navalny's father—a place evacuated after the nuclear accident at Chernobyl. For Navalny, this was yet another victim of a 'war ... unleashed by a raving maniac obsessed with some nonsense about geopolitics, history and the structure of the world.'[7]

Even more personal tragedy was to follow. On 23 March 2022, the journalist Oksana Baulina—a long-time colleague of Navalny—was killed during shelling in Kyiv.[8] Reporting in Ukraine for the online outlet The Insider, Baulina had earlier helped to launch Navalny's YouTube channel and livestreams. And, for him, she was another example of those brave Russians who had sacrificed a shiny career to fight for their values.

Back in Pokrov, Navalny made it clear what he thought about court proceedings: 'I hate your authority and despise your judicial system. Because it's impossible not to hate. Isn't it humiliating for you to pretend you're judges and prosecutors, when in reality, you're just cogs whose sole purpose is to repeat something you were told over the phone?'[9] Members of Navalny's team offered evidence that the judge received several calls from the Presidential Administration during trial proceedings.[10]

A week after Navalny's 'last words', the judge finally handed down the sentence: nine more years behind bars—and in a maximum security prison with harsher conditions than in Pokrov.[11] But, true to character, Navalny didn't miss an opportunity to sound optimistic in a Twitter post—and with a sharp reference to pop culture:

> 9 years. Well, as the characters of my favorite TV series "The Wire" used to say: "You only do two days. That's the day you go in and the day you come out" I even had a T-shirt with this slogan, but the prison authorities confiscated it, considering the print extremist.[12]

In a sense, the precise number of years doesn't really matter at this stage. Back in September 2021, when his lawyer notified him that yet another case was being brought against him, Navalny told his followers not to worry: he'd calculated that he'd 'be free by no later than spring 2051'—followed by a winking emoji.[13]

But what had life been like for Navalny in prison before this latest trial? We now go back to where we left off in the previous chapter, asking whether it was a mistake for Navalny to return to his homeland. We then look at how his team and movement fared in the face of unprecedented repression from the Russian authorities. And, finally, we ask: if Navalny is not Russia's future—in the short term, at least—then who will determine the country's fate?

The prisoner

From Pokrov to the European Parliament

After the dramatic hunger strike of 2021, life in jail seemed to settle down. For all its harshness, Navalny's penal colony in

Pokrov wasn't some place where 'musclemen with tattoos and steel teeth have knife fights to settle who'll get the best bunk beds by the window', as Navalny joked.[14] He continued to register the ups and downs of life in a Russian prison on Instagram—albeit through his lawyers.

Among the ups: from October 2021, he was no longer deemed an 'escape risk'—and that was 'good news', as he would no longer have to check in with a camera every two hours to prove that he hadn't escaped.[15]

Navalny also picked up new skills. In Russian labour colonies, inmates are supposed to learn a trade as part of mandatory work—and he learned how to sew, with 'excellent teachers, two patient women', which reminded him of his school days. 'Sometimes they say to me something like "Alexei Anatolievich, stop looking out the window, there's nothing interesting going on over there."'[16] He could register how inflation bit from the prices of the (limited and expensive) goods he could buy in the prison shop—meat, fish, corn, beans (all of these canned), cheese, and milk. Always thinking like a politician, Navalny questioned whether the head of the Central Bank and, of course, Putin could survive on a pension with this level of inflation.[17]

When New Year's Eve came—Russia's most important family holiday—Navalny noted the 'generous package' inmates were offered: 'mandarins, cake, and even Coca-Cola'. When a prisoner dressed as Ded Moroz—the Russian Santa Claus—asked if someone could read a poem, 71-year-old prisoner Valery read a few verses, asking Ded Moroz for parole.[18]

But prison was still prison. Navalny was relentlessly strip-searched.[19] And, as he noted in an interview with *The New York Times*, he was compelled to watch endless hours of propaganda films and state TV.[20] The Pokrov penal colony specialises, he said, in 'psychological violence'.[21] The emotional toll hit hardest on the 'birthdays of close relatives, especially children', because, as Navalny noted, 'what stupid wish can I send my son for his 14th birthday: write him a letter. What kind of memories will he have of communicating with his father?' In this perhaps more than anything else Navalny saw the whole meaning behind his time in prison: 'We need to build the wonderful Russia of the future that they will inherit.'[22]

But was a Russian penal colony really the best place for him to achieve that goal? Some asked whether he had made a serious misjudgement when returning to Russia in January 2021.

Was it a mistake to return to Russia?

In an interview with *Time* magazine in January 2022—a year after his return—Navalny was adamant that his decision was the right one: 'The question wasn't even on the agenda. From the moment I opened my eyes, I knew I had to return.' Pressed by the journalist, Simon Shuster, Navalny claimed that 'even if a sober analysis were to show that all of this has made things worse for me, and not for the Putin regime, I would still have returned. I just knew that's what I had to do.'[23]

We can't argue with Navalny's moral certainty. We can, however, try to assess whether his return to Russia and imprisonment have left his movement—and the opposition in general—better or worse off.

At first glance, the answer seems clear. Now that Navalny is in prison, the Russian opposition has been deprived of a leading, charismatic voice. He can still communicate with the public, but only through his lawyers. And communications with his team are severely hindered—as is his ability to keep up with what's happening in Russia and the world.

The answer might also seem obvious after the destruction of the movement and the intensified crackdown on critical voices following the invasion of Ukraine. But these developments were not in people's minds at the start of 2021. Navalny may well have thought it 'highly likely' that he would be imprisoned on his return to Moscow—but he likely did not expect everything else.[24] It seems inappropriate, then, to frame what occurred as the result of 'errors' on Navalny's part—and particularly if this takes attention away from the Kremlin's role in shaping his fate.

The severity of repression against Navalny, his team, and his movement—as well as independent media—throughout 2021 was, in a sense, puzzling. Was Putin so afraid of Navalny that he had to order the complete shutdown of his organisations and drive his staff into exile? Not being able to look inside Putin's mind, we instead looked at the system's actions and concluded that, yes, Putin takes Navalny extremely seriously. But the system's actions seemed preventive. In case of a breakdown of trust in the political leader—for instance, during an economic crisis—an organised opposition could channel grievances and help undermine a seemingly stable political order. Putin was acting, therefore, not because Navalny was immediately dangerous, but because he and his organisation could pose a real threat in the future.

After Russia's invasion of Ukraine, we are now in a better position to judge the steps taken by the system in 2021. It is plausible that the repression against Navalny and others was motivated by the prospect of a planned war. In the event of an attack on Ukraine, those in the Kremlin might have thought they would face less resistance within Russia if Navalny were not free and his organisations no longer able to function. It would be better to eradicate any possible organised resistance beforehand. Navalny could not be an anti-war leader behind bars—or dead. This also suggests that, even if Navalny had *not* returned to Russia in January 2021, his movement, the opposition more broadly, and independent media would still have been repressed by the authorities in the run-up to the invasion of Ukraine.

Navalny's return to Russia was an act of extraordinary defiance by a brave man. Aware of the potential costs to himself, he also knew the Kremlin was in a very difficult position—by locking him up, Russia's political leadership would lay bare its authoritarian nature. Navalny was also aware of the harm that staying abroad might cause him. The Kremlin would use this in its ongoing portrayal of him as an agent of the West. And he would likely be branded a hypocrite for asking people in Russia to take risks while he led a cosy life abroad. The decision to return was consistent with his character, his statements in the past about the limited influence of Russian politicians in exile, and his sense of the unique opportunity to challenge the Kremlin with the world watching.

Anyway, it may simply be too soon to reach a definitive answer. As noted by Vladimir Ashurkov, 'we are in the middle of this. It's not the end of Putin's story, of Russia's story. So, the situation is unfolding ... you can't truly say from where we are today whether it was a mistake to return.'[25]

It's also difficult to conclude that Navalny's return was an error when thinking of the broader symbolism. Much as Vladimir Putin has become the archetypal modern-day autocrat, so Navalny has become a symbol of defiance in the face of dictatorship. He was nominated for the Nobel Peace Prize, was awarded the Sakharov Prize for Freedom of Thought by the European Parliament, and was the subject of a high-profile documentary produced by HBO and CNN.[26] Navalny has turned into a global figure.

But his impact on the world has not, of course, been the work of one man. Navalny's team continued the movement's mission with him behind bars—yet, the pressure exerted against them by the authorities only increased, forcing them to adapt.

The team

The Vilnius office

The location is a leafy residential street in the Lithuanian capital. The office interiors are, in the words of the writer and journalist

Vladislav Davidzon, 'lean, minimalist, and sparsely occupied by young Russians dressed in white T-shirts or Moscow hipster attire'—figures that 'would not look out of place in a Palo Alto or London startup'.[27]

This is the centre of the Navalny movement in exile. Headed by Navalny's chief of staff, Leonid Volkov—who himself left Russia in July 2019, under pressure from law enforcement—the office was opened before the 2021 crackdown against the movement. But its importance grew as the authorities tightened the screws in Russia.[28]

'You have not emigrated—you have been forced to temporarily change the location of our office.'[29] These were Navalny's words in an October 2021 letter to his team—his 'friends', as he put it. With the Kremlin making the movement's activities in Russia impossible, there was no choice but to move operations abroad. The Anti-Corruption Foundation—although dissolved in Russia—was registered in the US as a 'private foundation'. The goal of achieving a 'Russia without Putin' was now best fought from outside of the country—a clear change to the team's previous strategy.

Navalny's letter was written shortly after the September 2021 legislative elections. These elections—and the Smart Voting project that the team had devised to disrupt them—had been a clear focus for the preceding six months.[30] The project aimed to convince opposition voters that it was worth taking part in elections, even when the Kremlin was both able and willing to tilt the electoral playing field to such a degree. But, although Navalny's team invested heavily in Smart Voting, the Kremlin was ready with new moves to counter them.

'David versus Goliath'

The authorities took the threat of Smart Voting very seriously—if the many steps taken to frustrate the project are anything to go by. The assault against Navalny's organisations not only thwarted their activities, but also, for instance, prevented Lyubov Sobol from running for a State Duma seat.[31] Various measures were taken to limit people's access to Smart Voting information—that is, information on the candidates that Navalny's team thought were best placed to challenge the United Russia candidate. Russia's communications regulator blocked the project's website; a Moscow court ordered Yandex and Google to remove content relating to the tactical voting scheme from search engine results; and Apple and Google buckled under pressure to remove the Smart Voting app from their app stores—much to the anger of Navalny, who called the companies Putin's 'accomplices'.[32]

And this censorship appeared to work: a September 2021 survey by the Levada Center found that 65 per cent of Russians had not heard of Smart Voting—and only 8 per cent had both heard of it and supported it.[33]

In spite of this, there were early signs that the project was effective, particularly in Moscow: paper ballots suggested that opposition candidates might win seats. But, with the incorporation of online votes—the results of which were suspiciously delayed in being announced—these projected wins vanished.[34] The authorities secured all fifteen State Duma seats from Moscow—and re-secured an overall constitutional majority in the legislature.[35]

Leonid Volkov, nevertheless, called Smart Voting a 'success' in a 'David versus Goliath' struggle.[36] He argued that the authorities' need to resort to egregious fraud exposed the nature of elections and of the regime. Similarly, Navalny called the result a 'triumph'—but also admitted that it wasn't possible to 'call the whole result a "victory"', since it had been 'bluntly stolen' from them.[37] He said that the Putin regime had been 'reborn' during the election campaign with the repressive steps taken against Smart Voting—but that this new version is 'incompatible with growth in any form' and that 'the Russian people will have to share this huge price with Putin and his crooks.' All the same,

Navalny tried to put a positive spin on things—he claimed that 'we have completed the task of mobilising people. We (sorry for the caps lock) CREATED A MAJORITY.'[38]

The reality was more complex, however. If the authorities were both able and willing to manipulate voting results after ballots had been cast, then Navalny's team would have an even harder time convincing people it was worth voting in the first place. There was a sense of disappointment—and despondency—in the opposition following the September elections.[39] What would Navalny's team do now?

The 'informational dissidents'

The term 'informational autocracy' refers to a particular type of non-democracy.[40] Unlike classical dictatorships—which rule by repression and fear—'informational autocracies' focus more on propaganda than purges. The approach of these regimes is to persuade citizens of the leadership's competence and legitimacy, rather than to beat them into submission.

In Russia's 'informational autocracy', Navalny and his team acted as 'informational dissidents'[41]—focussed on skewering the Kremlin's lies and exposing the true nature of the Russian political system. The most visible aspect of this work involved anti-corruption investigations. But, in the wake of the 2022 invasion of Ukraine, the focus shifted to combating information from the Kremlin about the war. This is how Navalny's team put it in a GoFundMe campaign launched in April 2022:

> Propaganda kills—in the truest sense of the word. Opening the news and looking at the pictures of ruined Ukrainian cities would be enough to realize this. The problem is that most people in Russia are denied the chance to see this news, and even if they do, they believe it to be fake. The sooner Russians wake up and recognize the horrific reality, the sooner the war will end.[42]

As the assault on independent media intensified following the invasion of Ukraine, Navalny's team proposed to 'launch [their] own news media channel, one that cannot be shut down by the Kremlin, and reach out to the millions who are still unaware of what Putin is doing on their behalf'.[43] The existing YouTube channel 'Popular Politics', which is run by the team, describes itself in Russian as the 'channel on which the truth is spoken about the war'.[44]

The goal to create a 'fully professionalized independent investigative reporting and media team' makes practical sense, given the expertise developed in the FBK and on YouTube.[45] And the new project wouldn't stop the team from continuing to release anti-corruption investigations. One looked into what the team called 'Putin's new yacht'—the 75,000,000,000-rouble 'Scheherazade' (around £530 million at the time).[46] Another explored what the FBK called the 'conductor of Putin's war'— an investigation that centred on Valery Gergiev, artistic director of the Mariinsky Theatre in St Petersburg.[47]

The 'informational dissidents' have broadened their target audience. Although continuing to inform Russians about high-level corruption—and, adding to this, information about the war—the second key audience now consists of foreign elites and citizens. The team has, for instance, used its knowledge about elite dynamics in Russia to put together a list of around 6,000 people—of 'bribetakers and warmongers'—that it recommends foreign governments to sanction.[48] The goal, according to Sergei Guriev, is 'to inform Western elites which elements of Putin's team are more instrumental to continue the war, to continue running this state'.[49]

Navalny's videos had already won an international viewership. But the crackdown in Russia and the war on Ukraine gave further impetus to the team's activities based and aimed *outside* Russia, which reflects a broader change. According to Guriev,

[t]he game is now different, because the regime transformed itself from a spin dictatorship into a fear dictatorship ... It's not just informational dissidents who can fight Putin, but also Ukrainian soldiers on the ground ... as well as international sanctions that can undermine Putin's support within Russia and within the elites ... it's a war that's fought on many fronts.[50]

But Guriev doesn't think the end is in sight: 'It's still far from being accomplished, it's still far from being established that Putin is doomed and will be gone very soon. So, in that sense, I think much more needs to be done.'[51]

But who will do that?

The movement

The end of an exception

'Do you expect any difficulties because of your work for Navalny?' This question was put to Navalny's staff in the regions in autumn 2017, when his presidential campaign was at its peak.[52]

But Yuri from Yekaterinburg didn't lose sleep over it. A lawyer by training, he had worked at the regional branch of the Investigative Committee for two years. Were he still a state employee, he said, then his part-time work for Navalny could have landed him in trouble. But, a few years earlier, he had opened a private practice.

Viktor—the first coordinator of Navalny's Yekaterinburg campaign office and Yuri's boss—framed his answer very similarly. Should he return to a managerial position in business after his stint as coordinator of the campaign office, he didn't expect any serious problems:

When you make your political views clear and open, of course your [business] circle narrows down ... [But that] doesn't bother me much. Navalny has common sense on his side, and it may even be a good thing that those without common sense will be weeded out.

But, when contacted again in March 2022, Yuri answers from New York and Viktor from Tbilisi. In February, they had both received credible hints that criminal cases might soon be opened against them. Viktor packed up and left for Georgia, while Yuri and his family flew to Mexico, requesting political asylum at the US border.

In Yekaterinburg, people had long believed that they had a special relationship with the local authorities—that their city was an exception. Yes, the region was part of the emerging authoritarian system, delivering votes to Putin and his party. But police acted less aggressively—and people felt freer than elsewhere.

This changed in 2021. The wave of repression rolling through the country after Navalny's return did not spare the city, levelling decades-old regional differences and striking down unwritten rules of conduct between authorities and local activists.

A movement decimated

There are countless stories like those of Yuri and Viktor. In August 2021, *RBK* published an article on what had happened to the coordinators of Navalny's regional headquarters.[53] Eight of thirty-seven had already emigrated, eleven more were under investigation, and three were in prison or under house arrest—including Andrei Borovikov from Arkhangelsk, who was sentenced to two and a half years for 'distributing pornography'. The details of the offence? Reposting a YouTube video from the German band Rammstein. Of those fifteen who claimed to have continued their political activism, several more have emigrated since.[54] And more former coordinators have been locked up—among them Liliya Chanysheva from Ufa, who was the first person from Navalny's movement charged with creating an 'extremist association'. She was arrested on 9 November 2021 and has been in custody ever since.[55]

Repression accelerated yet again in the wake of the Russian invasion of Ukraine. And this included further encroachments on the space for independent information. Only a week into the war, Russia's parliament passed the 'law on fakes', as it quickly came to be known. This legislation made 'discrediting' Russia's armed forces and the dissemination of 'knowingly false information' about its activities punishable with up to fifteen years in prison.[56] On top of a ban on the use of particular words—like 'war' and 'invasion'—the legislation aimed to have a chilling effect on dissenting voices challenging the authorities' official propaganda about the 'special operation'.

In addition, the country's communications regulator, Roskomnadzor, blocked websites of prominent online media, including Ekho Moskvy, the online TV channel Dozhd, and the web platform Mediazona. *Novaya Gazeta*—the oldest oppositional newspaper in the country, and led by Dmitry Muratov, the 2021 Nobel Peace Prize laureate—suspended its operations on 28 March 2022 after a second warning from Roskomnadzor.[57]

All of these media outlets had not only been important sources for independent news, as dozens of quotes in this book show. Some of them—like Ekho Moskvy and Dozhd—had been free spaces for Russia's liberal opposition—spaces where this increasingly marginalised group could meet and discuss recent infringements on democracy and to form their counterstrategies. They were also platforms where Navalny and his team could present themselves to the public—and where repression against the movement was regularly covered.

But, even if these platforms had remained open, ongoing repression meant there would be little opposition action to cover. Soon after the war broke out, Volkov and Zhdanov released a video claiming that, in the future, children would ask their parents what they did to stop this war.[58] They called for 'civil disobedience', including disobeying military orders and trying to convince friends and family members of the war's criminality. Volkov and Zhdanov also urged people to participate in protests—although they did not organise specific events.

A Navalny movement—understood as a network of politically active people who openly associate themselves with him—no longer exists in Russia. This doesn't mean that it will not re-emerge, but it does mean that, if we look for resistance against Russian authoritarianism and its war efforts, we must look beyond Navalny.

From street protest to street art

Thousands of people came to the streets immediately after they heard the news of the February invasion. After the destruction of Navalny's organisations and the disbanding of his movement, the protests were uncoordinated—but they were real. And authorities cracked down immediately. On the day of Russia's attack on Ukraine, the activist and Yabloko politician Marina Litvinovich was arrested in front of her house in Moscow after she had called for protests.[59] Over the next four weeks, OVD-Info counted over 15,000 detentions, some of them likely involving bystanders—thousands more than a year earlier during the protests following Navalny's return to Russia.[60] On 6 March, police detained over 5,000 people, making it the largest number of detentions on a single day in Russia's post-Soviet history.[61]

People held out at first, in exceptional acts of bravery. But anti-war demonstrations gradually died down. When the anonymous protest group Vesna ('Spring') called for sit-ins on 2 April across the country, hardly anyone showed up.[62]

It might be easy to view this as evidence that the war finds overwhelming support or tacit acceptance in the population. And the absence of widespread activity on the streets seems to dovetail with polls that report high popular support for Putin and for

Russia's 'special operation'.[63] But the absence of protest does not signal the absence of protest potential; grievances can remain hidden. When asking why more Russians are not on the street to protest the war, we need to consider the regime's actions of the past twenty years: co-opting or outlawing organised opposition, curtailing the independence of big business, appropriating influential media, marginalising independent voices—and systematically demoralising the citizenry through countless reminders that activism and political engagement are futile at best and dangerous at worst.

The absence of a coherent, public protest movement against the invasion of Ukraine is, then, the predictable result of all the constraints that Navalny and many others have been fighting for decades rather than a clear sign that Russians approve of the war.

But some Russians still resist. Single pickets—the only form of public protest that needs no prior agreement with authorities—have, for example, burgeoned during the war. In the beginning, people's signs often simply read 'No to war' (*Net voyne*). But, since the adoption of the 'law on fakes', the messaging has become creative. For example, activists were detained with signs reading '*** *****' and 'two words', alluding to—but not spelling out—the 'no [to] war' slogan.[64] As in Rostov in 2011, others were detained for holding blank sheets of paper.[65] And, in Ivanovo in central Russia, police opened a case against a local resident for distributing free copies of George Orwell's *1984*.[66] Overall, by mid-June 2022, OVD-Info had counted 171 criminal cases related to individual anti-war actions.[67]

And yet, in spite of this repression, each day people spray anti-war messages on pavements, bus stops, and brick walls. There is the now-established slogan *Net voyne*, but there are all sorts of other messages, like 'shame', 'love' or 'don't feed the war with your taxes', and various graffiti drawings of bombs, hearts, flowers, and the classic peace sign.[68] Since it can be anonymous and, therefore, less dangerous, such street art has replaced street protest for many. These spray-painted messages may console those who feel alone with their disagreement—and help them wait for better times.

* * *

While we cannot predict the future, we can take stock of the issues that have fuelled citizens' grievances—corruption, inequality, political domination, economic stagnation. With a costly, protracted war led by an increasingly brutal dictatorship, these issues—which pre-date the invasion—are here to stay and will likely fuel the desire for change. But for that change to materialise—be it anti-war and pro-democracy or something entirely different—there needs to be someone who can push for it. With Navalny in prison, his team abroad, and the movement in Russia decimated, who would that be?

Russia's future

Elites and coups

Most political and economic elites in Russia met the beginning of the invasion with incredulity and horror. Incredulity because the vast majority of senior officials were not included in pre-invasion planning—and thought the very idea of a full-scale invasion of Ukraine was ludicrous. Horror because of the consequences the war might have for the country—and their rule over it. Journalist Farida Rustamova reported that one of her interlocutors described officials' reactions in the following way: 'They're carefully enunciating the word clusterf*ck.'[69] In the words of the same source, 'the mood in the corridors of power is not at all happy. Many are in a state of near-paralysis.'

However shocked they might have been, this did not translate into any significant defections or sustained public stands against the 'special operation' from members of the elite—at least in the first months of the war. And, after initial bewilderment, the elite appeared to close ranks. The scale of the sanctions, plus relentless propaganda, had, it seemed, convinced many that a 'point of no-return' had now been reached. Victory had to be achieved. And, in any case, many surmised that, in current circumstances, resigning would be akin to treason.[70] Rustamova concluded that 'Putin's dream of a consolidation among the Russian elite has come true. These people understand that their lives are now tied only to Russia, and that that's where they'll need to build them.'[71]

But elite thinking continued to evolve. After three months of war, and many setbacks on the ground, journalist Andrey Pertsev reported that Putin had managed to make almost everyone in the Russian elite unhappy, if only in their own way. 'Hawks' were frustrated that general mobilisation hadn't been proclaimed and that an even more massive military effort hadn't been undertaken. 'Doves' were frustrated by the lack of progress in negotiations and the scale of the economic damage.[72]

Does this mean that a coup—or, at least, the appearance of visible cracks in the regime—may occur? Even though rumours of a coup reached fever pitch as reports of Russian military setbacks mounted, such rumours are the stuff of authoritarian politics.[73] Sources 'close to the Kremlin' may tell a reporter—anonymously, of course—of the whispers they hear in the corridors of power. But, in a system rife with secrecy, coercion, and fear, gossip can quickly be blown out of proportion; differences of opinion are not signs of plotting in the palace. It makes more sense to focus on whether members of the elite have incentives to challenge the existing leadership—and for now, at least, there appear to be few.

Opposition, anywhere?

Meanwhile, political support for any protest movement appeared only a distant possibility in the first months after the invasion.

Several deputies from the parliamentary opposition parties, particularly in the Communist Party (KPRF), voiced dissent. For instance, the politician Yevgeny Stupin—who was elected to Moscow City Council in 2019 with the help of Navalny's Smart Voting—spoke up for the rights of detained and beaten anti-war protesters.[74] Together with about 500 other KPRF members and activists close to the party, he even signed a call in mid-March for the party leadership to oppose the war.[75] And, on 1 May 2022, 57 members jointly left the party in the northern city of Surgut to protest against the party leadership's unconditional support of the Kremlin during the war.[76] These events suggest that the party is home to a group of possible dissenters—a group that grew after Navalny's movement was destroyed, leaving the Communist Party as the largest opposition force.

But these examples appeared to be exceptions. The parliamentary parties as a whole, including the KPRF, tried to outdo each other in signalling their fealty to the regime in a show of loyalty dubbed the 'Donbas consensus', echoing the 'Crimean consensus' seen in 2014. In June, the deputy party leader of the Communist Party called for the expulsion of people like Stupin and his supporters for their 'anti-Russian, anti-party, even anti-human positions.'[77] There were clear barriers to explicit anti-war action by the parliamentary opposition.

The prospect of protest

But might the authoritarian system be shaken by protest nonetheless? After all, the West has unleashed unprecedented sanctions on the Russian economy. This resulted in billions of dollars in capital flight and hundreds of thousands of jobs at risk with the exit of many foreign firms from the Russian market. According to the Russian Central Bank, Russia faces an economic crisis on the scale of the 1990s.[78]

In fact, in April and May, there were reports of strikes due to unpaid or lower wages—for instance, in a construction company in Tatarstan and at a delivery service in Moscow.[79] While the authorities will do everything to subdue open political dissent, they will have a harder time justifying repression of social protest during an economic crisis. This, in turn, might prompt political actors like the Communist Party to lend a voice to protesting citizens.

But much of this might be wishful thinking. For social protest to directly demand an end to Russia's war efforts, the West would have to make clear that ending the war will lead to an easing of sanctions. And yet, it is unclear that the Russian economy would immediately rebound if sanctions were scrapped. For these reasons, it's unlikely that social protest coalitions would directly demand an end to the war—particularly given the high risk of repression such a move would entail.

Rocking the boat

'Stability' has been the mantra of Putin's rule. After the 'chaos' of the 'wild 1990s'—favourite talking points on state TV—everything was supposed to be stable in Russia: from prices (low inflation) to politics (no revolution). And, to some extent, it was. Putin used stability 'to justify everything: from censorship and crackdowns on demonstrations to the rigging of elections', as Navalny said.[80] And it appeared that a major part of the population reached an agreement of sorts with the system—an implicit social contract in which the promise of stability was exchanged for citizens' political voices.

But this posed a clear problem for the opposition. Navalny and other opposition leaders always seemed to hit the 'stability wall'—that many people thought it was better to stick with a far-from-perfect Putin than to rock the boat. It was a clear challenge, then, to mobilise people to call for change if Putin's system promised—and sometimes provided—stability.

How might Russia's invasion of Ukraine affect this? The February invasion was, to be sure, not the first instance of military aggression under Putin. The Second Chechen War, the war with Georgia in 2008, the annexation of Crimea and the conflict in Donbas from 2014, and the Russian military's involvement in Syria have shown Russia's willingness and capacity for conflict under Putin's leadership. But the invasion of Ukraine is on another level. The scale of the 'special operation' in Ukraine—that is, the war on Ukraine—is unprecedented, as is the scale of Western sanctions. What does this mean for the very legitimacy of the authoritarian system built by Putin—for the future of Russia?

In the short term, it appeared that many Russians were ready to 'rally around the flag'—or, rather, 'rally around the Z', the mysterious symbol that stands for the 'special operation'. They have decided to stick with 'my country, right or wrong'—and, for those wavering, police batons and unhinged, jingoistic propaganda may convince them to stay in line.

But, in the longer term, a major source of legitimacy for the Putin regime will have been lost, possibly for a very long time. Ultimately, the durability of the regime depends on its ability to deliver goods to the population. The more difficult this becomes, the harder the authorities will have to work on reinventing themselves once more in an effort to shore up their legitimacy. Russia's political leadership may double down on trying to justify sacrifices—of fallen soldiers and of economic hardship—in terms of restoring Russian greatness. But it is not clear how long this narrative can last to prop up the system—and, deprived of this pillar of legitimacy, calls for change may well increase.

Conclusion

Melekhovo, Vladimir Region—Penal Colony No. 6, 15 June 2022.

'Space travel continues—I moved from ship to ship. Well, that is, hi everyone from the maximum security zone.'[81] Navalny is in quarantine, having just been transferred from Pokrov IK-2 to the maximum security penal colony Melekhovo IK-6—about two hours further east by car.

Navalny's post on Instagram announcing his arrival is a relief to many. The day before, his spokesperson, Kira Yarmysh, made an alarming announcement. When Navalny's lawyer came to see him in Pokrov, the prison guards stated, 'There is no such prisoner' here.[82] This was a repeat performance by Russia's prison authorities of what happened to Navalny in March 2021, when he also temporarily disappeared, out of contact with his family and his team.

In his 15 June Instagram post, Navalny put a positive spin on things, as ever—albeit with dark humour. He noted the problems in shifting his many books, saying that, 'yesterday, for the first time in my life, I dragged these bags and thought that a bonfire of books isn't necessarily something bad'. He also remarked on an announcement he'd seen in quarantine with information about the skills that could be learned in prison, along with the time it would take for training. The course on 'poultry carcass deboning' would take three months—the same amount of time as the course on sewing, a skill he'd learnt in Pokrov. 'I'm very indignant', he said.

In contrast to Navalny's post, however, media reporting on Melekhovo IK-6 painted a terrifying picture. Inmates have spoken of widespread abuse—of torture, rape, and suspicious deaths.[83] And Navalny soon found out—as he expected—that he'd be locked up with people convicted of serious crimes: 'Almost all of them are murderers. Their sentences are huge. Here my 9 years is the shortest sentence, and I'm like a pre-schooler. The average term here is 13–15 years. Some got 19 or 20. These are double murderers.' He painted a mixed picture of this crowd: 'It's all very interesting. And very scary too'.[84]

But Navalny found yet another way to lighten his plight—this time, by quietly reciting Shakespeare when carrying out his mandatory work. '[Y]ou know me, I'm an optimist and look for the bright side even in my dark existence ... While sewing, I've memorised Hamlet's monologue in English.'[85] His fellow inmates mistook this for 'summoning a demon'—but, as Navalny noted, that 'would be a violation of the [prison's] internal regulations'.[86]

* * *

Is Navalny Russia's future? It's difficult not to offer a bleaker assessment than we gave in the preceding chapter, one year ago. With new charges that could keep him imprisoned for up to fifteen years on top of the additional nine years handed down in March 2022, it's clear that the Kremlin wants his future to be behind bars.[87]

But the end of this book is not the end of Alexei Navalny's story. The uncertainty created by Russia's war on Ukraine may well be the beginning of the end for Putin's leadership—and open up opportunities for political change. What a post-Putin Russia would look like is far from certain—but Navalny, his team, and those activists and supporters who have formed his movement will continue their struggle to shape the 'wonderful Russia of the future'.

NOTES

1. WHO IS ALEXEI NAVALNY?

1. 'Kremlin Critic Navalny Boards Plane for Russia', AP (YouTube channel), 22 January 2021, https://www.youtube.com/watch?v=s923nKAYXxc. In the main text and substantive text included in the endnotes, we follow a simplified transliteration method based on the BGN-PCGN (United States Board on Geographic Names and Permanent Committee on Geographical Names for British Official Use) system—for example, 'Yulia Navalnaya' rather than 'Yuliya Naval'naya'. We use people's spelling preferences whenever we are aware of them. In the references, we follow the BGN-PCGN system. For the sake of legibility, we use the simplified transliteration 'Alexei Navalny' when he appears as the author of referenced material and when mentioning publications bearing his name—for example, 'Navalny (blog)' rather than 'Naval'nyy (blog)'.

2. 'Navalny's Anti-Corruption Foundation Releases New Investigation He Filmed before His Poisoning', Meduza, 3 September 2020, https://meduza.io/en/news/2020/09/03/navalny-s-anti-corruption-foundation-releases-new-investigation-he-filmed-before-his-poisoning

3. Alexei Navalny later recalled that he was not, in fact, in pain, 'but it felt like the end'. Andrey Kozenko, 'Navalny Poisoning: Kremlin Critic Recalls Near-Death Novichok Torment', BBC News, 7 October 2020, https://www.bbc.co.uk/news/world-europe-54434082

4. 'Alexei Navalny: Two Hours That Saved Russian Opposition Leader's Life', BBC News, 4 September 2020, https://www.bbc.co.uk/news/world-europe-54012278

5. 'Russia's Navalny Thanks "Unknown Friends" for Saving His Life', Reuters, 25 September 2020, https://www.reuters.com/article/us-russia-politics-navalny-idUSKCN26G1X0

6. Andrew Higgins, 'Aleksei Navalny Hospitalized in Russia in Suspected Poisoning', *The New York Times*, 20 August 2020, https://www.nytimes.com/2020/08/20/world/europe/navalny-poison-russia.html

7. Max Seddon, 'Pussy Riot Activist Likely Poisoned, Say Doctors', *Financial Times*, 18 September 2018, https://www.ft.com/content/ca3c7614-bb2d-11e8-94b2-17176fbf93f5; 'Russian Critic Vladimir Kara-Murza Suffers Sudden Organ Failure', BBC News, 2 February 2017, https://www.bbc.com/news/world-europe-38844292

8. Joshua Yaffa, 'What Navalny's Poisoning Really Says about the Current State of Putin's Russia', *The New Yorker*, 21 August 2020, https://www.newyorker.com/news/dispatch/what-navalnys-poisoning-really-says-about-the-current-state-of-putins-russia

9. A law enforcement source mentioned this diagnosis to state news agency TASS and added that this poisoning was 'not considered criminal yet'. 'Istochnik: Versiya namerennogo otravleniya Naval'nogo poka ne rassmatrivayetsya', TASS, 20 August 2020, https://tass.ru/proisshestviya/9245003

10. Anton Zverev, 'Russia First Treated Navalny for Suspected Poisoning then U-turned: Doctor', Reuters, 6 September 2020, https://www.reuters.com/article/us-russia-politics-navalny-health-idUSKBN25X0MA. Accounts differ regarding when Navalny was first given atropine, either by paramedics or in hospital—see 'Russia's Navalny Thanks "Unknown Friends" for Saving his Life'.

11. Amy Mackinnon, 'Why Putin Might Be Hoping Navalny Survives His Poisoning', *Foreign Policy*, 20 August 2020, https://foreignpolicy.com/2020/08/20/why-putin-might-be-hoping-navalny-survives-his-poisoning/

12. Patrick Revell, '"Poisoned" Russian Opposition Leader Navalny Lands in Berlin for Emergency Treatment', ABC News, 22 August 2020, https://abcnews.go.com/International/poisoned-russian-opposition-leader-navalny-lands-berlin-emergency/story?id=72541848

13. 'Alexei Navalny: "Poisoned" Russian Opposition Leader in a Coma',

BBC News, 20 August 2020, https://www.bbc.co.uk/news/world-europe-53844958

14. 'Kto i kak spasal Naval'nogo v pervyye dva chasa: Khronika', BBC News Russian, 2 September 2020, https://www.bbc.com/russian/features-54002575

15. This justification from the hospital authorities was stated by Kira Yarmysh. 'Alexei Navalny: "Poisoned" Russian Opposition Leader in a Coma'.

16. It is unclear whether this substance was found 'on Navalny' or 'on his belongings'. Kira Yarmysh, Twitter post, 21 August 2020, https://twitter.com/Kira_Yarmysh/status/1296681869099008000

17. Melissa Eddy and Andrew Kramer, 'Aleksei Navalny, Top Putin Critic, Is Flown to Germany after Suspected Poisoning', *The New York Times*, 21 August 2020, https://www.nytimes.com/2020/08/21/world/europe/russia-navalny-poison-hospital.html

18. 'Otslezhen ves' marshrut Naval'nogo pered otravleniyem: On kupalsya', *Moskovskiy Komsomolets*, 21 August 2020, https://www.mk.ru/incident/2020/08/21/otslezhen-ves-marshrut-navalnogo-pered-otravleniem-on-kupalsya.html

19. Tat'yana Stanovaya, Telegram post, 23 August 2020, https://t.me/stanovaya/559

20. Anton Zverev, 'Russia First Treated Navalny for Suspected Poisoning then U-turned'.

21. 'Russian Doctors Allow Alexei Navalny's Transfer to Germany', Deutsche Welle, 21 August 2020, https://www.dw.com/en/alexei-navalny-poisoning-omsk-berlin/a-54645234

22. Ibid.

23. Ibid.

24. Alexei Navalny, Twitter post, 21 August 2020, https://twitter.com/navalny/status/1296769338683338754. Navalny's team also appealed to the European Court of Human Rights for an 'interim measure'—an exceptional, urgent procedure for intervention when there is 'an imminent risk of irreparable harm' to an individual involved in 'proceedings before the Court'. 'Interim measures', Press Unit of the European Court of Human Rights, April 2021, https://www.echr.coe.

int/documents/fs_interim_measures_eng.pdf. The Court granted the request on the same day.

25. Miriam Berger, 'What Is Novichok, the Nerve Agent Linked to the Alexei Navalny Poisoning?', *The Washington Post*, 24 September 2020, https://www.washingtonpost.com/world/2020/08/26/what-are-chemicals-doctors-say-may-have-been-used-poison-alexei-navalny/

26. David Caldicott, 'What Is the Chemical Agent That Was Reportedly Used to Poison Russian Politician Alexei Navalny?', The Conversation, 25 August 2020, https://theconversation.com/what-is-the-chemical-agent-that-was-reportedly-used-to-poison-russian-politician-alexei-navalny-145013

27. Dmitry Polyanskiy, Twitter post, 24 August 2020, https://twitter.com/Dpol_un/status/1297933782230749185

28. 'Volodin uvidel v otravlenii Naval'nogo splanirovannuyu aktsiyu protiv Rossii', *RBK*, 3 September 2020, https://www.rbc.ru/rbcfreenews/5f50e6559a794702bcf7a7e6; 'Vyacheslav Volodin: situatsiya vokrug Naval'nogo—splanirovannaya aktsiya protiv Rossii', State Duma, 3 September 2020, http://duma.gov.ru/news/49408/

29. Andrey Zakharov and Sonya Groysman, 'Yadovityy marshrut: Reportazh o tom, chto vlasti mogli uznat' ob otravlenii Alekseya Naval'nogo, esli by zakhoteli', Proekt, 10 September 2020, https://www.proekt.media/report/otravlenie-navalnogo-tomsk/

30. 'Vozmozhnyye mesta otravleniya Naval'nogo v Tomske svyazany s vlastyami i silovikami', Tayga.info, 26 August 2020, https://tayga.info/158700

31. Although Novichok refers to a group of nerve agents, for simplicity's sake, we will sometimes refer simply to Novichok in the singular in the text.

32. Oliver Carroll and Benjamin Kentish, 'Putin Personally Ordered Attack on Spy, Says UK', *The Irish Independent*, 17 March 2018, https://www.independent.ie/world-news/europe/putin-personally-ordered-attack-on-spy-says-uk-36714143.html

33. Jon Shelton, 'Angela Merkel Says Novichok Poisoning of Russia's Navalny Was Attempted Murder', Deutsche Welle, 2 September 2020, https://www.dw.com/en/navalny-novichok-germany-russia/a-54794283

34. 'Chto otvetil Kreml' na zayavleniye Germanii ob otravlenii Naval'nogo "Novichkom"', BBC News Russian, 3 September 2020, https://www.bbc.com/russian/news-54010560

35. Aleksandr Kots and Ivan Pankin, 'Koma Alekseya Naval'nogo byla nastoyashchey: A "otravleniye—uzhe bol'shaya igra!', *Komsomol'skaya Pravda*, 26 February 2021, https://www.kp.ru/daily/27243/4371039/

36. Sergey Sokolov, 'Advokat "Novichka"', *Novaya Gazeta*, 3 September 2020, https://novayagazeta.ru/articles/2020/09/03/86947-advokat-novichka

37. 'Leonid Rink: Posle "Novichka" Naval'nyy ne doshel by do samoleta', RIA Novosti, 25 September 2020, https://ria.ru/20200925/novichok-1577748393.html

38. The chemist made his claims in an interview for the independent online TV channel Dozhd. Sergey Romashenko, 'Razrabotchik "Novichka" izvinilsya pered Alekseyem Naval'nym', 20 September 2020, https://www.dw.com/ru/razrabotchik-novichka-izvinilsja-pered-alekseem-navalnym/a-54992310

39. 'Lugovoy uveren, chto Naval'nogo mogli otravit' "Novichkom" tol'ko v Germanii', TASS, 2 September 2020, https://tass.ru/politika/9354929

40. Sabine Siebold et al., 'Special Report: In Germany's Black Forest, Putin Critic Navalny Gathered Strength and Resolve', Reuters, 25 February 2021, https://www.reuters.com/article/russia-politics-navalny-germany-specialr-idUSKBN2AP1BH

41. 'FSB Team of Chemical Weapon Experts Implicated in Alexey Navalny Novichok Poisoning', Bellingcat, 14 December 2020, https://www.bellingcat.com/news/uk-and-europe/2020/12/14/fsb-team-of-chemical-weapon-experts-implicated-in-alexey-navalny-novichok-poisoning/

42. 'Telefonnyy razgovor Naval'nogo s odnim iz ego ubiyts: Polnaya versiya', Navalny LIVE (YouTube channel), 21 December 2020, https://www.youtube.com/watch?v=HlJbwUhIBxE

43. Ibid. Luke Harding, '"Do You Remember the Underwear's Colour?" Navalny's Call with Duped Spy', *The Guardian*, 21 December 2020, https://www.theguardian.com/world/2020/dec/21/what-does-alexei-navalny-say-the-duped-russian-spy-admitted-about-his-poisoning

44. '"Komu on nuzhen-to? Esli by khoteli, doveli by do kontsa": Putin—

ob otravlenii Naval'nogo', *Meduza*, 17 December 2020, https://meduza.
io/news/2020/12/17/komu-on-nuzhen-to-esli-by-hoteli-doveli-by-do-
kontsa-putin-ob-otravlenii-navalnogo

45. Siebold et al., 'Special Report'.

46. Ibid.

47. Alexei Navalny, Instagram post, 13 January 2021, https://www.insta-
gram.com/p/CJ-lt0YoT2s/

48. 'Russia: Aleksei Navalny Becomes Prisoner of Conscience after Arrest
on Arrival in Moscow', Amnesty International, 17 January 2021,
https://www.amnesty.org/en/latest/news/2021/01/russia-aleksei-
navalny-becomes-prisoner-of-conscience-after-arrest-on-arrival-in-
moscow/

49. 'Amnesty International Statement on Aleksei Navalny', Amnesty
International, 25 February 2021, https://www.amnesty.org/en/latest/
news/2021/02/aleksei-navalny-prisoner-of-conscience/. The NGO later
apologised for the decision and 'decided to re-designate Alexei Navalny
as a "Prisoner of Conscience"'. 'Statement on Alexei Navalny's status
as Prisoner of Conscience', Amnesty International, 7 May 2021, https://
www.amnesty.org/en/latest/news/2021/05/statement-on-alexei-naval-
nys-status-as-prisoner-of-conscience/

50. Konstantin Voronkov, *Aleksey Naval'nyy: Groza zhulikov i vorov*
(Moscow: Eksmo, 2012). This book, written by an avowed Navalny
supporter, is built on many in-depth interviews with Navalny himself.
It remains one of the only first-hand accounts of Navalny's youth and
early career.

51. 'Pravila zhizni Alekseya Naval'nogo', *Esquire* (Russian edition),
29 November 2011, https://esquire.ru/rules/26-alexey-navalny/

52. Voronkov, *Aleksey Naval'nyy*, 16.

53. Ibid., 22.

54. Ibid., 22–4. Olesya Gerasimenko, '"Pyatnadtsat' minut bor'by s rezhimom v den'"', *The New Times*, 25 October 2010, https://newtimes.ru/
articles/detail/29360

55. Olesya Gerasimenko, '"Pyatnadtsat' minut bor'by s rezhimom v den'"'.

56. Voronkov, *Aleksey Naval'nyy*, 28.

57. Irina Mokrousova and Irina Reznik, 'Chem zarabatyvayet na zhizn'

Aleksey Naval'nyy', *Vedomosti*, 13 February 2012, https://www.vedo-mosti.ru/library/articles/2012/02/13/pesnya_o_blogere

58. Julia Ioffe, 'Net Impact: One Man's Cyber-Crusade against Russian Corruption', *The New Yorker*, 28 March 2011, https://www.newyorker.com/magazine/2011/04/04/net-impact

59. Ibid.; Mokrousova and Reznik, 'Chem zarabatyvayet na zhizn' Aleksey Naval'nyy'; Voronkov, *Aleksey Naval'nyy*. Throughout the text, we convert roubles into pounds sterling. If an amount is given in US dollars or Euros in a source, we present the amount in the original currency.

60. Keith Gessen, 'What Is Navalny?', *n+1*, 26 July 2013, https://nplusonemag.com/online-only/online-only/what-is-navalny/

61. Yuriy Dud', 'Naval'nyye—interv'yu posle otravleniya', vDud' (YouTube channel), 6 October 2020, https://youtu.be/vps43rXgaZc

62. Dmitriy Sokolov, 'Ot kurortnogo romana k spasitel'noy lyubvi: Chto svyazalo Yuliyu i Alekseya Naval'nykh', *Sobesednik*, 5 December 2020, https://sobesednik.ru/politika/20201130-lyubov-vyvela-navalnogo-iz-kom

63. Dasha Veledeyeva, 'Yuliya Naval'naya: "Esli segodnya vse klassno, to ya uzhe schastliva; Potomu chto zavtra sovershenno tochno mozhet vse izmenit'sya, i ya budu sil'no razocharovana"', *Harper's Bazaar* (Russian edition), 17 February 2021, https://bazaar.ru/heroes/harpers-bazaar/yuliya-navalnaya-svoyu-glavnuyu-zadachu-ya-vizhu-v-tom-chtoby-u-nas-v-seme-nichego-ne-izmenilos-deti-byli-detmi-a-dom-domom/

64. Kseniya Sobchak, 'Naval'nyy o tom, pochemu ego otpustili, sud'be Kapkova i legalizatsii gey-brakov–3', Dozhd' (YouTube channel), 22 July 2013, https://youtu.be/N9Ru0EyJxcQ; '"Nevidimoye men'shinstvo": K probleme gomofobii v Rossii', Levada Center, 5 May 2015, https://www.levada.ru/2015/05/05/nevidimoe-menshinstvo-k-probleme-gomofobii-v-rossii/

65. Alexei Navalny, 'Bol'shoy privet Putinu i ego povaru (+ moya deklaratsiya po pros'be sotrudnitsy RT)', Navalny.com (blog), 28 July 2020, https://navalny.com/p/6408/

66. Yevgeniya Al'bats, Twitter post, 2 February 2021, https://twitter.com/albats/status/1356726777289220097

67. David Hoffman, *The Oligarchs: Wealth and Power in the New Russia* (New York: Public Affairs, 2011).

68. Ilya Matveev, 'Measuring Income Inequality in Russia: A Note on Data Sources', *Russian Analytical Digest* 263 (2021): 5–7.

69. The reported figures are from a poll conducted by the independent Levada Center in January 2021. Dina Smeltz et al., 'In Russia, Navalny Inspires Respect for Some, Indifference for Most', The Chicago Council on Global Affairs, 22 February 2021, https://www.thechicagocouncil.org/research/public-opinion-survey/russia-navalny-inspires-respect-some-indifference-most

70. See the information provided on 17 January 2021 by 'Belyy Shchetchik', an organisation that specialises in counting protest participants: https://ru-ru.facebook.com/WhiteCounter/posts/3924460010898988

71. Polina Ivanova, '"Are you detaining me?" Navalny Flies Home, and Straight into Trouble', Reuters, 17 January 2021, https://www.reuters.com/world/europe/are-you-detaining-me-navalny-flies-home-straight-into-trouble-2021–01–17/

72. 'Sud v otdelenii politsii Khimok arestoval Alekseya Naval'nogo na 30 sutok', Deutsche Welle, 18 January 2021, https://www.dw.com/ru/sud-v-otdelenii-policii-himok-arestoval-alekseja-navalnogo/a-562 61258

73. 'Naval'nyy obratilsya k presse v aeroportu Sheremet'yevo', Current Time, 17 January 2021, https://www.facebook.com/watch/?v=457454628 610724

2. THE ANTI-CORRUPTION ACTIVIST

1. Alexei Navalny, 'Dvorets dlya Putina: Istoriya samoy bol'shoy vzyatki', Navalny.com, 2021, https://palace.navalny.com/

2. Alexei Navalny, 'Dvorets dlya Putina: Istoriya samoy bol'shoy vzyatki', Alexei Navalny (YouTube channel), 19 January 2021, https://youtu.be/ipAnwilMncI

3. 'Fil'm "Dvorets dlya Putina" na yut'yube posmotreli 100 millionov raz', Meduza, 28 January 2021, https://meduza.io/news/2021/01/28/film-dvorets-dlya-putina-na-yutyube-posmotreli-100-millionov-raz

4. 'Fil'm "Dvorets dlya Putina"', Levada Center, 8 February 2021, https://www.levada.ru/2021/02/08/film-dvorets-dlya-putina/

5. The direct translation of the Russian main title is 'A Palace for Putin',

which more clearly conveys the ambiguity of whether Putin owns or merely benefits from the estate.

6. Yevgeniy Kalyukov, 'Putin otvetil na vopros studenta o "dvortse" v Gelendzhike', *RBK*, 25 January 2021, https://www.rbc.ru/politics/25/01/2021/600eb14a9a794706660a6669

7. Timur Batyrov, '"Mesto shikarnoye": Arkadiy Rotenberg nazval sebya benefitsiarom "dvortsa" pod Gelendzhikom', *Forbes* (Russian edition), 30 January 2021, https://www.forbes.ru/newsroom/milliardery/419927-mesto-shikarnoe-arkadiy-rotenberg-nazval-sebya-beneficiarom-dvorca-pod

8. Yelena Mazneva and Irina Malkova, 'Bogdanov ne znayet khozyayev "Surguta"', *Vedomosti*, 30 April 2008, https://www.vedomosti.ru/library/articles/2008/04/30/bogdanov-ne-znaet-hozyaev-surguta

9. Mazneva and Malkova, 'Bogdanov ne znayet khozyayev "Surguta"'; Carl Schreck, 'Russia's Erin Brockovich: Taking On Corporate Greed', *Time*, 9 March 2010, http://content.time.com/time/world/article/0,8599,1970475,00.html; Nataliya Vasilyeva, 'Activist Takes On Secretive Russian Firms', *The Seattle Times*, 1 April 2010, https://www.seattletimes.com/business/activist-takes-on-secretive-russian-firms/

10. Olga Khvostunova, 'Who is Mr. Navalny?', Institute of Modern Russia, 18 January 2012, https://imrussia.org/en/politics/183-who-is-mr-navalny

11. 'Pravila zhizni Alekseya Naval'nogo', *Esquire* (Russian edition), 29 November 2011, https://web.archive.org/web/20111130054351/http://esquire.ru/wil/alexey-navalny

12. Gregory Asmolov, 'Aleksey Naval'nyy: "Ya pytayus' dokazat', chto borot'sya s rezhimom—eto veselo"', Global Voices, 28 October 2010, https://ru.globalvoices.org/2010/10/29/2703/

13. Lyudmila Vasina, 'Aleksey Naval'nyy protiv goskorporatsiy', RFE/RL, 30 December 2009, https://www.svoboda.org/a/1917766.html

14. Artem Galustyan, 'Istoriya odnogo Naval'nogo', *Kommersant*, 21 August 2019, https://www.kommersant.ru/doc/2235276

15. Alexei Navalny, 'Blagotvoritel'nost' v RF', Navalny (blog), 6 August 2008, https://navalny.livejournal.com/272534.html. This number of comments is correct as of 23 April 2021.

16. Alexei Navalny, 'Kak pilyat v Gazprome', Navalny (blog), 24 December 2008, https://navalny.livejournal.com/342311.html. This number of comments is correct as of 23 April 2021.

17. Alexei Navalny, 'Kak pilyat v VTB', Navalny (blog), 30 November 2009, https://navalny.livejournal.com/411199.html. This number of comments is correct as of 23 April 2021.

18. Alexei Navalny, 'Kak pilyat v Transnefti', Navalny (blog), 16 November 2010, https://navalny.livejournal.com/526563.html. This number of comments is correct as of 23 April 2021.

19. Vera Yurchenko, 'Chelovek iz interneta', *Novaya Gazeta*, 15 February 2018, https://www.novayagazeta.ru/articles/2018/02/15/75520-chelovek-iz-interneta

20. 'Gde marzha?', *Forbes* (Russian edition), 3 September 2008, https://www.forbes.ru/forbes/issue/2008–09/10510-gde-marzha

21. '"Transneft"': Bloger Naval'nyy sluzhit interesam protivnikov VSTO', *Vedomosti*, 13 January 2011, https://www.vedomosti.ru/business/news/2011/01/13/bloger_navalnyj_sluzhit_interesam_protivnikov_vsto_glava

22. 'Putin: Svedeniya o khishcheniyakh v "Transnefti" nado proverit', BBC News Russian, 29 December 2010, https://www.bbc.com/russian/business/2010/12/101229_putin_transneft_investigation

23. 'Putin otbil ataku Naval"nogo na Transneft"', Reuters, 29 September 2011, https://www.reuters.com/article/orutp-russia-transneft-putin-idRURXE78R16S20110929

24. Khvostunova, 'Who Is Mr. Navalny?'

25. Alexei Navalny, 'Yabadabadu!', Navalny (blog), 14 February 2011, https://navalny.livejournal.com/553388.html

26. Vasina, 'Aleksey Naval'nyy protiv goskorporatsiy'.

27. 'Trevozhashchiye problemy', Levada Center, 10 September 2020, https://www.levada.ru/2020/09/10/trevozhashhie-problemy-3/

28. Thomas Remington, 'Russian Economic Inequality in Comparative Perspective', *Comparative Politics* 50, no. 3 (2018): 395–416.

29. In this chapter, we draw on original accounts from activists working in Navalny's campaign offices. The interviews were conducted between 2017 and 2021.

30. Ellen Barry, 'Rousing Russia with a Phrase', *The New York Times*, 9 December 2011, https://www.nytimes.com/2011/12/10/world/europe/the-saturday-profile-blogger-aleksei-navalny-rouses-russia.html

31. 'Forbes i Aleksey Naval'nyy organizovali "Tsentr zashchity aktsionerov"', Lenta, 15 December 2009, https://lenta.ru/news/2009/12/15/navalny/

32. Alexei Navalny, 'Chastnoye litso', Navalny (blog), 30 December 2009, https://navalny.livejournal.com/417512.html

33. Yuliya Kalinina, 'Blog nakazhet', *Moskovskiy Komsomolets*, 9 June 2011, https://www.mk.ru/politics/2011/06/09/596335-blog-nakazhet.html

34. 'Gde marzha?'

35. Henry Foy, '"We Need to Talk about Igor": The Rise of Russia's Most Powerful Oligarch', *Financial Times*, 1 March 2018, https://www.ft.com/content/dc7d48f8-1c13-11e8-aaca-4574d7dabfb6

36. Kalinina, 'Blog nakazhet'.

37. 'Case of Magnitskiy and Others v. Russia: Judgment', European Court of Human Rights (ECtHR), 27 August 2019, http://hudoc.echr.coe.int/eng?i=001–195527

38. Charles Clover, 'Hermitage Closes Embattled Russian Fund', *Financial Times*, 26 March 2013, https://www.ft.com/content/13e35c46–9637–11e2–9ab2–00144feabdc0

39. 'Magnitsky Wins Russian Rights Battle 10 Years after His Death', BBC News, 27 August 2019, https://www.bbc.com/news/world-europe-49481471

40. Ibid.

41. Benjamin Bidder, 'Questions Cloud Story Behind U.S. Sanctions', *Der Spiegel*, 26 November 2019, https://www.spiegel.de/international/world/the-case-of-sergei-magnitsky-anti-corruption-champion-or-corrupt-anti-hero-a-1297796.html; 'Response to Der Spiegel Story on Magnitsky Case', Russian Untouchables, December 2019, http://russian-untouchables.com/rus/docs/Response%20to%20Der%20Spiegel%20Article%20on%20Magnitsky%20Case%20-%20Copy%20sm.pdf; 'Why DER SPIEGEL Stands Behind its Magnitsky Reporting', *Der Spiegel*, 17 December 2019, https://www.spiegel.de/international/world/spiegel-responds-to-browder-criticisms-of-magnitsky-story-a-1301716.html

42. 'Case of Magnitskiy and Others v. Russia: Judgment'.

43. The summary of the case presented here is based on the ECtHR's ruling in the Kirovles case. 'Case of Navalnyy and Ofitserov v. Russia: Judgment', ECtHR, 23 February 2016, http://hudoc.echr.coe.int/fre?i=001–161060

44. 'Delo Naval'nogo: Bol'she goda sledovateli iskali "zloy umysel" i ne nashli...', Gorod Kirov, 4 February 2011, https://gorodkirov.ru/content/article/delo-navalnogo-bolshe-goda-sledovateli-iskali-zloj-umyisel-i-ne-nashli-20110204–1329/

45. 'SK RF otmenil postanovleniye ob otkaze v vozbuzhdenii dela protiv Naval'nogo', Forbes (Russian edition), 8 February 2011, https://www.forbes.ru/news/63027-sk-rf-otmenil-postanovlenie-ob-otkaze-v-vozbuzhdenii-dela-protiv-navalnogo

46. 'Sledstvennyy komitet otkazalsya vozbuzhdat' delo protiv Naval'nogo', Lenta, 15 March 2011, https://lenta.ru/news/2011/03/15/nocase

47. 'Na Naval'nogo zaveli ugolovnoye delo', Lenta, 10 May 2011, https://lenta.ru/news/2011/05/10/navalny

48. Alexei Navalny, 'Kirovskiy les ukral kto-to drugoy', Navalny (blog), 28 May 2012, https://navalny.livejournal.com/707461.html; Michael Weiss, 'What the Aleksei Navalny Case Says about Life in Putin's Russia', The Atlantic, 22 April 2013, https://www.theatlantic.com/international/archive/2013/04/what-the-aleksei-navalny-case-says-about-life-in-putins-russia/275175/

49. Navalny, 'Kirovskiy les ukral kto-to drugoy'.

50. 'Ugolovnoye delo v otnoshenii Naval'nogo vozobnovleno', BBC News Russian, 29 May 2012, https://www.bbc.com/russian/russia/2012/05/120529_navalny_case_reopened

51. 'Case of Navalnyy and Ofitserov v. Russia: Judgment'.

52. Navalny, 'Kirovskiy les ukral kto-to drugoy'.

53. 'Professiya aktsioner', Ogonyok, 13 July 2009, https://www.kommersant.ru/doc/1197604

54. 'Gde marzha?'

55. 'Aleksey Naval'nyy, avtor proyekta Tsentr zashchity aktsionerov', Lenta, 22 December 2009, https://lenta.ru/conf/navalny/

56. Vasilyeva, 'Activist Takes On Secretive Russian Firms'.

57. 'Gde marzha?'

58. Schreck, 'Russia's Erin Brockovich'.

59. '"Transneft"': Bloger Naval'nyy sluzhit interesam protivnikov VSTO'.

60. Mikhail Zubov, '"Bor'ba kremlevskikh bashen": Zachem Naval'nyy reshil idti v prezidenty', *Moskovskiy Komsomolets*, 13 December 2016, https://www.mk.ru/politics/2016/12/13/borba-kremlevskikh-bashen-zachem-navalnyy-reshil-idti-v-prezidenty.html; 'Gde marzha?'

61. Julia Ioffe, 'Net Impact: One Man's Cyber-Crusade against Russian Corruption', *The New Yorker*, 28 March 2011, https://www.newyorker.com/magazine/2011/04/04/net-impact; 'Partiya talantlivykh oratorov', Lenta, 22 February 2011, https://lenta.ru/articles/2011/02/22/navalny/

62. Stanislav Kucher, '"Dostatochno legko ustanovit', chto za mnoy nikto ne stoit"', Kommersant FM, 28 May 2011, https://www.kommersant.ru/doc/1650215

63. Karen Dawisha, *Putin's Kleptocracy: Who Owns Russia?* (New York: Simon & Schuster, 2014).

64. Andrei Yakovlev, 'The Evolution of Business–State Interaction in Russia: From State Capture to Business Capture?', *Europe-Asia Studies* 58, no. 7 (2006): 1033–56.

65. 'Dialog Khodorkovskogo s Putinym nezadolgo do aresta', Nikolay Petrov (YouTube channel), 30 October 2015, https://www.youtube.com/watch?v=u6NKb79VN8U

66. Thane Gustafson, *Wheel of Fortune: The Battle for Oil and Power in Russia* (Cambridge, MA: Harvard University Press, 2012).

67. 'The Oligarch Who Came in from the Cold', *Forbes*, 18 March 2002, https://www.forbes.com/forbes/2002/0318/110.html

68. Daniel Treisman, 'Russia's Billionaires', *American Economic Review* 106, no. 5 (2016): 236–41.

69. Heiko Pleines, 'The Political Role of Business Magnates in Competitive Authoritarian Regimes', *Jahrbuch für Wirtschaftsgeschichte/Economic History Yearbook* 60, no. 2 (2019): 299–334.

70. 'Partiya talantlivykh oratorov: "Edinaya Rossiya" otvetila Alekseyu Naval'nomu kak smogla', Lenta, 22 February 2011, https://lenta.ru/articles/2011/02/22/navalny

71. Robert Orttung, 'Corruption in Russia', *Russian Analytical Digest* 144 (2014): 2–4.

72. Dada Lindell and Margarita Alekhina, 'V Rossii rekordno vyroslo chislo osuzhdennykh za krupnyye vzyatki', *RBK*, 30 April 2020, https://www.rbc.ru/society/30/04/2020/5e9daa0e9a794771cc07e9bd

73. Gilles Favarel-Garrigues, 'Les figures du justicier anti-corruption en Russie post-soviétique', in *Dénoncer la corruption: Chevaliers blancs, pamphlétaires et promoteurs de la transparence à l'époque contemporaine*, ed. Cesare Mattina et al. (Paris: Demopolis, 2018), 323–341, here 329.

74. Felix Light, 'Russia's Communists Are Split Over Support for Navalny', *The Moscow Times*, 12 February 2021, https://www.themoscowtimes.com/2021/02/12/russias-communists-are-split-over-support-for-navalny-a72917

75. Polina Nikolskaya and Darya Korsunskaya, 'Russian Ex-Minister Ulyukayev Jailed for Eight Years over $2 Million Bribe', Reuters, 15 December 2017, https://www.reuters.com/article/us-russia-ulyukayev-verdict-idUSKBN1E90SN

76. Vasina, 'Aleksey Naval'nyy protiv goskorporatsiy'.

77. Schreck, 'Russia's Erin Brockovich'.

78. Andrew Kramer, 'Russian Site Smokes Out Corruption', *The New York Times*, 27 March 2011, https://www.nytimes.com/2011/03/28/business/global/28investor.html

79. Schreck, 'Russia's Erin Brockovich'.

80. 'Professiya aktsioner'.

81. Alexei Navalny, 'Kraudsorsing', Navalny (blog), 17 June 2010, https://navalny.livejournal.com/476181.html

82. Nikolay Petrov, 'The Navalny Effect: RosPil.Net', Carnegie Moscow Center, 8 December 2010, https://carnegie.ru/2010/12/08/navalny-effect-rospil.net-pub-42105

83. Alena Ledeneva, *Can Russia Modernise? Sistema, Power Networks and Informal Governance* (Cambridge: Cambridge University Press, 2013), 277.

84. Gregory Asmolov, 'Russia: Blogger Navalny Tries to Prove That Fighting Regime Is Fun', Global Voices, 27 October 2010, https://globalvoices.org/2010/10/27/russia-blogger-alexey-navalny-on-fighting-regime/

85. The 'Unified Procurement Information System'—an online information

portal—was launched in 2006, providing access to information about state procurements. The website is available at: https://zakupki.gov.ru/epz/main/public/home.html

86. Ioffe, 'Net Impact'.

87. Alexei Navalny, 'Vse v nablyudateli', Navalny (blog), 24 January 2012, https://navalny.livejournal.com/666519.html

88. 'Yama' is Russian for 'pothole'. The project's website is available at: https://rosyama.ru/

89. Asmolov, 'Aleksey Naval'nyy: "Ya pytayus' dokazat', chto borot'sya s rezhimom—eto veselo"'.

90. Yurchenko, 'Chelovek iz interneta'.

91. The website can be accessed at: https://www.dissernet.org/

92. Asmolov, 'Aleksey Naval'nyy: "Ya pytayus' dokazat', chto borot'sya s rezhimom—eto veselo"'.

93. Alexei Navalny, 'Yuristy dlya RosPila', Navalny (blog), 14 February 2011, https://navalny.livejournal.com/552963.html

94. Alexei Navalny, 'Dva Ob"yavleniya', Navalny (blog), 28 February 2011, https://navalny.livejournal.com/558726.html

95. Lyubov' Sobol', 'Privet =)', SOBOLLUBOV (blog), 2 March 2011, https://sobollubov.livejournal.com/2299.html

96. Olesya Gerasimenko, '"Ya gotova utashchit' s soboy v mogilu reyting Sobyanina": Kak yurist fonda Naval'nogo stala novym simvolom protesta', BBC News Russian, 2 August 2019, https://www.bbc.com/russian/features-49165540

97. Aleksandra Dyn'ko, '"Ya ne gotova vsyu zhizn' prozhit' v takoy Rossii": Yurist FBK Lyubov' Sobol", Russkiy Monitor, 27 May 2015, https://rusmonitor.com/ya-ne-gotova-vsyu-zhizn-prozhit-v-takojj-rossii-yurist-fbk-lyubov-sobol.html

98. Il'ya Klishin, 'Tayna naval'nogo kabineta', Openspace, 2012, http://www.openspace.ru/article/468

99. Yuriy Dud', 'Naval'nyy: O revolyutsii, Kavkaze i Spartake', vDud' (YouTube channel), 18 April 2017, https://www.youtube.com/watch?v=Bf9zvyPachs

100. 'Chto eto za sayt?', RosPil, no date, https://web.archive.org/web/20111029060832/http://rospil.info:80/about

101. Mikhail Loginov, 'The Navalny Effect', openDemocracy, 7 June 2011, https://www.opendemocracy.net/en/odr/navalny-effect/

102. Ibid.

103. Ibid.

104. Irina Mokrousova and Irina Reznik, 'Chem zarabatyvayet na zhizn' Aleksey Naval'nyy', *Vedomosti*, 13 February 2012, https://www.vedomosti.ru/library/articles/2012/02/13/pesnya_o_blogere; Alexei Navalny, '"Na eti 2% i zhivu" (c)', Navalny (blog), 13 February 2012, https://navalny.livejournal.com/676773.html. The Unified State Register of Legal Entities shows that the organisation had been registered in September 2011, but its existence was not made public by Navalny until 2012.

105. Mokrousova and Reznik, 'Chem zarabatyvayet na zhizn' Aleksey Naval'nyy'.

106. 'Chto eto za sayt', RosPil, 2012, https://web.archive.org/web/201 20105013641/http:/rospil.info/about

107. Mokrousova and Reznik, 'Chem zarabatyvayet na zhizn' Aleksey Naval'nyy'.

108. Ol'ga Beshley, 'Neutomimyy optimist', *The New Times*, 6 June 2012, https://newtimes.ru/articles/detail/53086

109. '200 bogateyshikh biznesmenov Rossii: 2012', *Forbes* (Russian edition), no date, https://www.forbes.ru/rating/bogateishie-biznesmeny-rossii-2012/2012

110. Klishin, 'Tayna naval'nogo kabineta'.

111. Beshley, 'Neutomimyy optimist'.

112. Alexei Navalny, 'Ashurkov', Navalny (blog), 4 June 2012, https://navalny.livejournal.com/710095.html

113. Kseniya Sobchak, 'Fridman priznalsya, chto uvolil sponsora Naval'nogo po politicheskim prichinam', Dozhd', 12 April 2012, https://tvrain.ru/teleshow/sobchak_zhivem/fridman_priznalsya_chto_uvolil_sponsora_navalnogo_po_politicheskim_prichinam-228312/

114. Roman Badanin and Ivan Osipov, '"Ya ponimal, chto sotrudnichestvo s Naval'nym mozhet byt' ugrozoy dlya moyey raboty"', *Forbes* (Russian edition), 25 April 2012, https://www.forbes.ru/sobytiya/lyudi/81639-ya-ponimal-chto-sotrudnichestvo-s-navalnym-mozhet-predstavlyat-ugrozu-dlya-moei

115. Alexei Navalny, '16 smelykh', Navalny (blog), 30 May 2012, https://navalny.livejournal.com/708361.html; Mariya Zheleznova, Aleksey Rozhkov, and Polina Khimshiashvili, 'Kto sponsiruyet fond bor'by s korruptsiyey Naval'nogo', *Vedomosti*, 30 May 2012, https://www.vedomosti.ru/politics/articles/2012/05/30/16_druzej_navalnogo

116. Specifically, Dmitry Bykov, Boris Akunin, Leonid Parfyonov, Sergei Guriev, and Ekaterina Zhuravskaya.

117. Thomas Grove and Alissa de Carbonnel, 'Russian Protest Fund Manager Looks to Elite for Cash', Reuters, 31 May 2012, https://www.reuters.com/article/us-russia-protest-fund-idUSBRE84U1EP20120531

118. Alexei Navalny, 'Ashurkov', Navalny.com (blog), 30 July 2014, https://navalny.com/p/3704/

119. Courtney Weaver, 'UK Grants Asylum to Russian Dissident', *Financial Times*, 1 April 2015, https://www.ft.com/content/dbb50132-d890-11e4-ba53-00144feab7de

120. Alexei Navalny, 'Potupchik ne predlagat'', Navalny (blog), 6 February 2012, https://navalny.livejournal.com/673497.html

121. Klishin, 'Tayna naval'nogo kabineta'; 'An Interview with Anna Veduta, Russian Activist, Expert, and Feminist', Global Voices, 26 May 2017, https://globalvoices.org/2017/05/26/an-interview-with-anna-veduta-russian-activist-expert-and-feminist/

122. This report is available on the FBK's website as of April 2021. 'Otchet po platezham s 01.09.2012 do 31.11.2012 vklyuchitel'no', Anti-Corruption Foundation, no date, https://fbk.info/fbk-media/reports/report_2012_wfTzGyk.xlsx

123. Larisa Trubitsina, 'Georgiy Alburov: "Planiruyem samoye tesnoye sotrudnichestvo so vsemi nablyudatel'skimi soobshchestvami"', Dvizheniye Vmeste, 1 December 2012, https://web.archive.org/web/20160405073516/http://www.dvizhenievmeste.com/archives/28452

124. Viktor Feshchenko, 'Verkhom na khaype: Chto pod kapotom u media-mashiny Alekseya Naval'nogo', Sekret Firmy, no date, https://secret-mag.ru/navalnyi/

125. Anya Ayvazyan, '"Ya rad, chto my vse v itoge rabotayem na Alekseya"', Public Post, 3 April 2013, https://web.archive.org/web/20130619013459/http://publicpost.ru/theme/id/3571/ya_rad_chto_my_vse_v_itoge_rabotaem_na_alekseya/

126. 'Vladimir Pekhtin, Putin Ally, Quits over Foreign Homes', BBC News, 20 February 2013, https://www.bbc.co.uk/news/world-europe-215 25364

127. Feshchenko, 'Verkhom na khaype'; 'Otchet o rabote Fonda Bor'by s Korruptsiyey za 2014 god', Anti-Corruption Foundation, no date, https://fbk.info/fbk-media/reports/fbk_report_2014.pdf

128. Alexei Navalny, 'Mne sverkhu vidno vsyo, ty tak i znay', Navalny (blog), 12 August 2013, https://navalny.livejournal.com/835847.html

129. Yurchenko, 'Chelovek iz interneta'.

130. When Anton Nossik—one of these pioneers of the Runet—passed away in 2017, Navalny had warm words for a man he called one of his 'mentors'. Alexei Navalny, 'Anton', Navalny.com (blog), 9 July 2017, https://navalny.com/p/5445/

131. In 2014, Navalny moved his blog from the LiveJournal platform to his personal site: Navalny.com. Dmitriy Bykov, 'Aleksey Naval'nyy: Vlast' ustupit stol'ko, skol'ko my potrebuyem', *Sobesednik*, 5 December 2014, https://sobesednik.ru/dmitriy-bykov/20141203-aleksey-naval-nyy-sudbu-strany-vsegda-reshaet-odin-procent

132. Feshchenko, 'Verkhom na khaype'.

133. Ibid.

134. Ibid.

135. Alexei Navalny, 'Po kassovym sboram "Chayka" pobila "Zvezdnyye voyny"', Navalny.com (blog), 24 December 2015, https://navalny. com/p/4646/

136. Alexei Navalny, 'Kak my delali "Dimona": Otvety na voprosy i insaydy', Alexei Navalny (YouTube channel), 21 March 2017, https://youtu. be/2AWyNwLI9oM

137. Alexei Navalny, 'Don't call him "Dimon"', Alexei Navalny (YouTube channel), 2 March 2017, https://www.youtube.com/watch?v=qrwlk7_ GF9g&t=2s

138. Andreas Umland, 'A Second Gorbachev?', *Prospect*, 28 March 2008, https://www.prospectmagazine.co.uk/magazine/asecondgorbachev

139. Navalny, 'Don't call him "Dimon"'.

140. 'Medvedev vpervyye otreagiroval na rassledovaniye FBK', BBC News Russian, 4 April 2017, https://www.bbc.com/russian/news-39494183

141. Alexei Navalny, 'Nedelyu nazad vypustili rassledovaniye "On vam ne Dimon": Reaktsiya vlasti', Navalny.com (blog), 9 March 2017, https://navalny.com/p/5269/

142. Ibid.

143. Alexei Navalny, 'Raz molchat, nado vykhodit' na miting', Navalny.com (blog), 14 March 2017, https://navalny.com/p/5274/; 'Skol'ko lyudey vyshli na ulitsy 26 marta i skol'ko zaderzhali? Karta protesta', Meduza, 27 March 2017, https://meduza.io/feature/2017/03/27/skolko-lyudey-vyshli-na-ulitsy-26-marta-i-skolko-zaderzhali-karta-protesta

144. 'Dmitriy Zimin', *Forbes* (Russian edition), no date, https://www.forbes.ru/rating/100-bogateishih-biznesmenov-rossii/2006/zimin

145. '"Ne khochetsya, konechno, stanovit'sya vragom gosudarstva"', Znak, 10 December 2018, https://www.znak.com/2018–12–10/zachem_semya_millionerov_ziminyh_pomogaet_navalnomu_i_nezavisimym_media_intervyu

146. 'Biznesmen Boris Zimin ob"yasnil, pochemu pomog vyvezti Naval'nogo v Germaniyu', *Forbes* (Russian edition), 31 August 2020, https://www.forbes.ru/newsroom/obshchestvo/408105-biznesmen-boris-zimin-obyasnil-pochemu-pomog-vyvezti-navalnogo-v

147. Dud', 'Naval'nyy: O revolyutsii, Kavkaze i Spartake'.

148. Yelizaveta Osetinskaya, 'Chto budet s biznesom v Rossii Naval'nogo: Spor s politikom o roste ekonomiki, migrantakh i media', Russkiye Norm! (YouTube channel), 2020, https://youtu.be/nGT6wq-lPnE

149. Alexei Navalny, 'Bol'shoy privet Putinu i ego povaru (+ moya deklaratsiya po pros'be sotrudnitsy RT)', Navalny.com (blog), 28 July 2020, https://navalny.com/p/6408/

150. Yuriy Dud', 'Naval'nyye: Interv'yu posle otravleniya', vDud' (YouTube channel), 6 October 2020, https://youtu.be/vps43rXgaZc

151. Alexei Navalny, 'Voprosy agitatsii: Vozmozhno, eta kvartira mera v Mayami budet neplokho agitirovat' za menya', Navalny.com (blog), 21 December 2016, https://navalny.com/p/5173/. Emphasis in original.

152. According to some reports, the mayor did not deny the acquisition of the apartments, but claimed that they belonged to his ex-wife.

'Nizhegorodskaya prokuratura otkazalas' proveryat' Karnilina po zayavleniyu Naval'nogo', Zercalo, 21 February 2017, https://www.zercalo.org/news/15825-nizhegorodskaya-prokuratura-otkazalas-proveryat-ivana-karnilina-po-zayavleniyu-navalnogo#!/

153. The mayor resigned in May the following year—something Navalny attributed to the investigation. Roman Kryazhev, 'Ivan Karnilin uvel sebya na pensiyu', *Kommersant*, 24 May 2017, https://www.kommersant.ru/doc/3305426

154. Ben Smith, 'How Investigative Journalism Flourished in Hostile Russia', *The New York Times*, 21 February 2021, https://www.nytimes.com/2021/02/21/business/media/probiv-investigative-reporting-russia.html

155. Andrey Gatinskiy and Anna Rudyak, 'V fonde Naval'nogo izvinilis' za oshibki v rolike o Koval'chuke', *RBK*, 26 May 2017, https://www.rbc.ru/rbcfreenews/5927fea09a7947d1cbffd7bb

156. Kira Yarmysh, Facebook post, 26 May 2017, https://www.facebook.com/kira.yarmysh/posts/1498481863545341

157. Piotr Mironenko, Sergey Smirnov, and Irina Pankratova, 'Sotsseti vzorvalis' iz-za rassledovaniya Naval'nogo. Pochemu eto vazhno i chto s nim ne tak?', The Bell, 4 December 2019, https://thebell.io/sotsseti-vzorvalis-iz-za-rassledovaniya-navalnogo-pochemu-eto-vazhno-i-chto-s-nim-ne-tak

158. Nataliya Zotova, 'Bez Naval'nogo: Kak FBK rabotayet bez svoyego lidera', BBC News Russian, 11 September 2020, https://www.bbc.com/russian/features-54119390

159. In September 2020, the BBC reported that thirty people worked at the FBK. Ibid.

160. 'Otchet o rabote Fonda Bor'by s Korruptsiyey za 2013 god', Anti-Corruption Foundation, no date, https://fbk.info/fbk-media/reports/fbk_report_2013_ZfkDQXk.pdf

161. 'Finansovyy Otchet', Anti-Corruption Foundation, no date, https://report2019.fbk.info/media/report_2019_finance.pdf

162. Kira Dyuryagina, 'Lyubov' Sobol' nachala kampaniyu po vyboram v Gosdumu', *Kommersant*, 15 October 2020, https://www.kommersant.ru/doc/4531506

163. Olesya Gerasimenko, "'Ya gotova utashchit' s soboy v mogilu reyting Sobyanina'"; Denis Korotkov, 'Povar lyubit poostreye', *Novaya Gazeta*, 21 October 2018, https://novayagazeta.ru/articles/2018/10/22/78289-povar-lyubit-poostree; Andrew Higgins, "'I Am Always Asked if I Am Afraid": Activist Lawyer Takes On Putin's Russia', *The New York Times*, 6 September 2019, https://www.nytimes.com/2019/09/06/world/europe/russia-lyubov-sobol-protests.html

164. 'Russia's Dysfunctional Funeral Business Gets a Makeover', *The Economist*, 23 December 2017, https://www.economist.com/business/2017/12/23/russias-dysfunctional-funeral-business-gets-a-makeover

165. Yevgeniy Kalyukov, 'Naval'nyy soobshchil o vzyskanii ₽88 mln v pol'zu "Moskovskogo shkol'nika"', *RBK*, 28 October 2019, https://www.rbc.ru/society/28/10/2019/5db6e82e9a794767ea737163

166. 'Dvizheniye "Za prava cheloveka" namereno ignorirovat' zakon ob "inostrannykh agentakh"', *Vedomosti*, 21 July 2012, https://www.vedomosti.ru/politics/news/2012/07/21/dvizhenie_za_prava_cheloveka_namereno_ignorirovat_zakon_ob

167. Aleksey Kovalev, '"Meduza" nashla ispantsa, iz-za kotorogo FBK priznali "inostrannym agentom": On ne mozhet ob"yasnit', zachem pomogal rossiyskim bortsam s korruptsiyey', Meduza, 18 October 2019, https://meduza.io/feature/2019/10/18/meduza-nashla-ispantsa-iz-za-kotorogo-fbk-priznali-inostrannym-agentom-on-ne-mozhet-ob-yasnit-zachem-pomogal-rossiyskim-bortsam-s-korruptsiey

168. 'Russia Agents Raid Alexei Navalny Offices with Power Tools', BBC News, 26 December 2019, https://www.bbc.com/news/world-europe-50916198

169. Dver' FBK, Twitter post, 18 October 2019, https://twitter.com/fbk_door/status/1185248471902838785

170. Alexei Navalny, 'SOS: Likvidatsiya FBK', Navalny.com (blog), 20 July 2020, https://navalny.com/p/6400/

171. Georgiy Tadtayev and Mayya Bobenko, 'Prigozhin vykupil dolg Naval'nogo i FBK u "Moskovskogo shkol'nika"', *RBK*, 26 August 2020, https://www.rbc.ru/society/26/08/2020/5f46025b9a79473a6cebe1d7; 'Powerful "Putin's Chef" Prigozhin Cooks Up Murky Deals',

BBC News, 4 November 2019, https://www.bbc.com/news/world-europe-50264747; Mikhail Maglov, Nataliya Shagirova, and Dmitriy Treshchanin, 'Faktchek: Svyazana li imperiya Prigozhina so vsemi sluchayami dizenterii v Moskve', Current Time, 28 March 2019, https://www.currenttime.tv/a/fact-check-prigozhin-dysentery-empire/29846739.html; 'Russian Oligarch and Opposition Nemesis Buys Civil-Suit Debt Owed by Navalny and Company, Says He'll "Ruin" Him, If He Survives Poisoning', Meduza, 26 August 2020, https://meduza.io/en/news/2020/08/26/russian-oligarch-and-opposition-nemesis-buys-civil-suit-debt-owed-by-navalny-and-company-says-he-ll-ruin-him-if-he-survives-poisoning

172. Alexei Navalny, 'Tam, za 6-metrovym zaborom dachi Medvedeva', Navalny.com (blog), 15 September 2016, https://navalny.com/p/5059/

173. Alexei Navalny, 'Sekretnaya dacha Dmitriya Medvedeva', Alexei Navalny (YouTube channel), 15 September 2016, https://www.youtube.com/watch?v=nMVJxTcU8Kg

174. 'Russian Activist in Jail for Giant Duck Protest', BBC News, 26 February 2018, https://www.bbc.com/news/world-europe-43202127

3. THE POLITICIAN

1. Alexei Navalny, 'Pora vybirat': Aleksey Naval'nyy—kandidat v prezidenty Rossii', Alexei Navalny (YouTube channel), 13 December 2016, https://youtu.be/wkN8sSrUbdY

2. Ibid.

3. Aleksandr Gorbachev, '"Ya khochu ustanovit' novyye standarty politiki voobshche": Interv'yu Alekseya Naval'nogo o tom, zachem on idet v prezidenty', Meduza, 15 December 2016, https://meduza.io/feature/2016/12/15/ya-hochu-ustanovit-novye-standarty-politiki-voobsche

4. Aleksey Venediktov and Lesya Ryabtseva, 'Sbityy fokus', Ekho Moskvy, 15 October 2014, https://echo.msk.ru/programs/focus/1417522-echo.html

5. Alexei Navalny, 'Programma Alekseya Naval'nogo', NAVALNY 2018, 2017, https://web.archive.org/web/20171213143847/https://2018.navalny.com/platform/

6. Yuriy Dud', 'Naval'nyy: O revolyutsii, Kavkaze i Spartake', vDud' (YouTube channel), 18 April 2017, https://www.youtube.com/watch?v=Bf9zvyPachs

7. Graeme Robertson, 'Protest, Civil Society and Informal Politics', in *Developments in Russian Politics 9*, ed. Richard Sakwa, Henry Hale, and Stephen White (London: Red Globe, 2019), 80–93.

8. Olesya Gerasimenko, '"Pyatnadtsat' minut bor'by s rezhimom v den'"', *The New Times*, 25 October 2010, https://newtimes.ru/articles/detail/29360

9. Konstantin Voronkov, *Aleksey Naval'nyy: Groza zhulikov i vorov* (Moscow: Eksmo, 2012), 22.

10. Voronkov, *Aleksey Naval'nyy*, 28–31.

11. In Russian, the name was formed by the initials of the founders of the party: Yavlinsky, Yuri Boldyrev, and Vladimir Lukin.

12. Voronkov, *Aleksey Naval'nyy*, 37–8.

13. Gerasimenko, '"Pyatnadtsat' minut bor'by s rezhimom v den'"'.

14. Yuliya Kalinina, 'Blog nakazhet', *Moskovskiy Komsomolets*, 9 June 2011, https://www.mk.ru/politics/2011/06/09/596335-blog-nakazhet.html

15. Oleg Kashin, 'Nedovol'nykh zhil'tsov prinyali v partiyu', *Kommersant*, 10 June 2004, https://www.kommersant.ru/doc/482159

16. Gerasimenko, '"Pyatnadtsat' minut bor'by s rezhimom v den'"'.

17. Gaidar and Navalny had begun their collaboration with the DA! ('Democratic Alternative!') movement the year before. Yelena Loskutova, *Yunaya politika: Istoriya molodezhnykh politicheskikh organizatsiy sovremennoy Rossii* (Moscow: Tsentr 'Panorama', 2008), 71–79.

18. Ruslan Kadrmatov, 'Prishli za Tesakom', Lenta, 4 July 2007, https://lenta.ru/articles/2007/07/04/tesak/

19. 'Politicheskiye debaty v moskovskom klube zakonchilis' strel'boy', *Vedomosti*, 31 October 2007, https://www.vedomosti.ru/library/news/2007/10/31/politicheskie-debaty-v-moskovskom-klube-zakonchilis-strelboj

20. Alexei Navalny, 'Yale', Navalny (blog), 28 April 2010, https://navalny.livejournal.com/453781.html

21. Gerasimenko, '"Pyatnadtsat' minut bor'by s rezhimom v den'"'.

22. Véra Nikolski, *National-bolchévisme et néo-eurasisme dans la Russie con-*

temporaine: La carrière militante d'une idéologie (Paris: Mare et Martin, 2013).

23. Fabrizio Fenghi, 'The Eternal Adolescent Savenko: Eduard Limonov, the Hooligan of Russian Literature and Politics, Dies in Moscow at the Age of 77', NYU Jordan Center, 6 April 2020, https://jordanrussiacenter.org/news/the-eternal-adolescent-savenko/

24. Alexei Navalny, 'Postupayut vstrevozhennyye zvonki ot obshchestvennosti', Navalny (blog), 31 October 2006, https://navalny.livejournal.com/53991.html; 'Novaya politika: Kto takoy Naval'nyy?', *Afisha Daily*, 27 February 2012, https://daily.afisha.ru/archive/gorod/archive/new-politics-navalny/

25. Irina Mokrousova and Irina Reznik, 'Chem zarabatyvayet na zhizn' Aleksey Naval'nyy', *Vedomosti*, 13 February 2012, https://www.vedomosti.ru/library/articles/2012/02/13/pesnya_o_blogere

26. 'Manifest Natsional'nogo russkogo osvoboditel'nogo dvizheniya "NAROD"', Agentstvo Politicheskikh Novostey, 27 June 2007, https://www.apn.ru/publications/article17321.htm

27. Ibid.

28. Vladimir Putin, 'Stenogramma pryamogo tele- i radioefira ("Pryamaya liniya s Prezidentom Rossii")', Kremlin, 18 December 2003, http://kremlin.ru/events/president/transcripts/22256; Marlène Laruelle, 'Misinterpreting Nationalism: Why Russkii is Not a Sign of Ethnonationalism', PONARS, 27 January 2016, https://www.ponarseurasia.org/misinterpreting-nationalism-why-russkii-is-not-a-sign-of-ethnonationalism/

29. Alexei Navalny, 'Ofitsial'no', Navalny (blog), 26 June 2007, https://navalny.livejournal.com/139946.html

30. Il'ya Azar, '"Yabloko" otkatilos'', Gazeta.ru, 15 December 2007, https://web.archive.org/web/20071225122907/www.gazeta.ru/politics/elections2008/2007/12/21_a_2454702.shtml

31. 'Novaya politika: Kto takoy Naval'nyy?'.

32. For an overview of this phenomenon, see Martin Laryš and Miroslav Mareš, 'Right-Wing Extremist Violence in the Russian Federation,' *Europe-Asia Studies* 63, no. 1 (2011): 129–54.

33. Olesya Gerasimenko and Yelena Shmarayeva, 'Delo trinadtsati',

Kommersant Vlast, 25 July 2011, https://www.kommersant.ru/ doc/ 1681380

34. 'Konferentsiya "Novyy politicheskiy natsionalizm"', Agentstvo Politicheskikh Novostey, 9 June 2008, https://www.apn.ru/index. php?newsid=20057

35. Yekaterina Savina, 'Vmenyayemykh sobrali v odnom zale', *Kommersant*, 9 June 2008, https://www.kommersant.ru/doc/901541

36. Masha Gessen, 'The Evolution of Alexey Navalny's Nationalism', *The New Yorker*, 15 February 2021, https://www.newyorker.com/news/ our-columnists/the-evolution-of-alexey-navalnys-nationalism

37. Natalia Moen-Larsen, '"Normal Nationalism": Alexei Navalny, LiveJournal and "the Other"', *East European Politics* 30, no. 4 (2014): 548–67.

38. Gregory Asmolov, 'Russia: Blogger Navalny Tries to Prove That Fighting Regime Is Fun', Global Voices, 27 October 2010, https://glo-balvoices.org/2010/10/27/russia-blogger-alexey-navalny-on-fighting-regime/

39. Aleksandr Verkhovskiy, 'Sovremennoye diskursivnoye protivostoyaniye russkikh natsionalistov i federal'nykh vlastey', *Vestnik obshchestvennogo mneniya* 110, no. 4 (December 2011): 5–18.

40. Laryš and Mareš, 'Right-Wing Extremist Violence in the Russian Federation.'

41. 'Stan' natsionalistom!', Alexei Navalny (YouTube channel), 17 October 2007,: https://youtu.be/ICoc2VmGdfw

42. 'NAROD za legalizatsiyu oruzhiya', Alexei Navalny (YouTube channel), 19 September 2007, https://youtu.be/oVNJiO10SWw

43. Shaun Walker, 'Alexei Navalny on Putin's Russia: "All Autocratic Regimes Come to an End"', *The Guardian*, 29 April 2017, https:// www.theguardian.com/world/2017/apr/29/alexei-navalny-on-putins-russia-all-autocratic-regimes-come-to-an-end

44. Il'ya Azar, 'Ushchemlennyy russkiy', Lenta, 4 November 2011, https:// lenta.ru/articles/2011/11/04/navalny/

45. This information is provided on the consular information portal of the Ministry of Foreign Affairs, valid as of January 2021, https://www. kdmid.ru/

46. Kseniya Sobchak and Kseniya Sokolova, 'Problema babla i zla', *GQ* (Russian edition), 24 February 2011, https://web.archive.org/web/20110528054908/www.gq.ru/talk/sobchak-sokolova/1537

47. Azar, 'Ushchemlennyy russkiy'.

48. Alisa Volkova, '"Khvatit kormit' Kavkaz": Kak menyalsya natsionalizm Naval'nogo', Kavkaz.Realii, 1 February 2021, https://www.kavkazr.com/a/31075519.html

49. 'Ot nikh prosyat tol'ko odnogo: Razvesit' vezde plakaty Putina i dat' emu 99%; Za eto oni mogut delat' chto khotyat'', Ura.ru, 9 February 2012, https://ura.news/articles/1036257585

50. Julia Ioffe, 'Net Impact: One Man's Cyber-Crusade against Russian Corruption', *The New Yorker*, 28 March 2011, https://www.newyorker.com/magazine/2011/04/04/net-impact

51. Andrew Kramer, 'Russian Site Smokes Out Corruption', *The New York Times*, 27 March 2011, https://www.nytimes.com/2011/03/28/business/global/28investor.html

52. Leonid Volkov, 'I obo vsem ostal'nom', O vsyakoy vsyachine (blog), 6 July 2011, https://leonwolf.livejournal.com/284373.html

53. Tobias Rupprecht, 'Formula Pinochet: Chilean Lessons for Russian Liberal Reformers during the Soviet Collapse, 1970–2000', *Journal of Contemporary History* 51, no. 1 (2015): 165–86.

54. Voronkov, *Aleksey Naval'nyy*, 31.

55. Alexei Navalny, 'Chto delat' oppozitsii', Navalny (blog), 16 June 2010, https://navalny.livejournal.com/475935.html

56. Oleg Kashin, 'Nastoyashchiy lider tot, kto otkazyvayetsya prodat' ideyu i lyudey za kabinet s komnatoy otdykha', *Kommersant*, 19 October 2010, https://www.kommersant.ru/doc/1524739

57. Navalny, 'Chto delat' oppozitsii'.

58. Alexei Navalny, 'Doklad dvizheniya NAROD: Interesny vashi mneniya', Navalny (blog), 6 December 2007, https://navalny.livejournal.com/185724.html

59. Navalny, 'Chto delat' oppozitsii'.

60. Alexei Navalny, 'Za lyubuyu partiyu, protiv Edinoy Rossii', Navalny (blog), 6 July 2011, https://navalny.livejournal.com/603104.html

61. Alexei Navalny, 'Ladno, davayte ob"yavim konkurs EdRo-plakata',

Navalny (blog), 24 February 2011, https://navalny.livejournal.com/556796.html

62. For a study on the party in the 1990s, see Luke March, *The Communist Party in Post-Soviet Russia* (Manchester: Manchester University Press, 2002).

63. Isabel Gorst, 'Ultranationalist Leader Vladimir Zhirinovsky Orders Aides to Rape Pregnant Journalist', *The Irish Times*, 25 April 2014, https://www.irishtimes.com/news/world/europe/russia-s-ultranationalist-leader-vladimir-zhirinovsky-orders-aides-to-rape-pregnant-journalist-1.1773043

64. Navalny, 'Za lyubuyu partiyu, protiv Edinoy Rossii'.

65. Yevgeniya Al'bats et al., 'Dekabr' 2011-go', *The New Times*, 3 December 2012, https://newtimes.ru/articles/detail/60591

66. Ol'ga Kuz'menkova, '"Ot dushi togda oralos"', Gazeta.ru, 5 December 2012, https://www.gazeta.ru/politics/2012/12/04_a_4878797.shtml

67. Alexei Navalny, no title, Navalny (blog), 21 December 2011, https://navalny.livejournal.com/657702.html

68. 'Miting na prospekte Sakharova zavershilsya bez proisshestviy', Lenta, 24 December 2011, https://lenta.ru/news/2011/12/24/meeting/

69. 'Pryamaya rech: Vystupleniya na mitinge protesta v Moskve', Reuters, 24 December 2011, https://www.reuters.com/article/orutp-russia-rally-quotes-idRURXE7BN03C20111224

70. Alexei Navalny, 'Pro vchera', Navalny (blog), 25 December 2011, https://navalny.livejournal.com/2011/12/25/

71. Alexei Navalny, 'Vcherashniy efir pro "chto delat' dal'she"', Navalny (blog), 27 December 2011, https://navalny.livejournal.com/2011/12/27/

72. Tikhon Dzyad'ko, '12 druzey Naval'nogo: Kto gotov vkladyvat'sya v oppozitsionnogo politika?', Dozhd', 29 February 2012, https://tvrain.ru/teleshow/harddaysnight/12_druzey_navalnogo_kto_gotov_vkladyvatsya_v_oppozitsionnogo_politika-185702/

73. Alexei Navalny, 'Karusel'no-otkrepitel'nyy prezident', Navalny (blog), 5 March 2012, https://navalny.livejournal.com/690060.html

74. 'Boi fontannogo znacheniya', *The New Times*, 5 March 2012, https://newtimes.ru/articles/detail/50740

75. Ibid.

76. 'Orgkomitet bol'she ne nuzhen', Lenta, 9 April 2012, https://lenta.ru/articles/2012/04/09/navalny3/

77. Françoise Daucé, *Être opposant dans la Russie de Vladimir Poutine* (Paris: Le bord de l'eau, 2016).

78. Florian Toepfl, 'From Connective to Collective Action: Internet Elections as a Digital Tool to Centralize and Formalize Protest in Russia', *Information, Communication & Society* 21, no. 4 (2018): 531–47.

79. Mischa Gabowitsch, *Protest in Putin's Russia* (Cambridge: Polity Press, 2016).

80. Ben Judah, *Fragile Empire: How Russia Fell In and Out of Love with Vladimir Putin* (London: Yale University Press, 2013), 206–7.

81. Marlène Laruelle, 'Alexei Navalny and Challenges in Reconciling "Nationalism" and "Liberalism"', *Post-Soviet Affairs* 30, no. 4 (2014): 276–97, here 279.

82. Robert Orttung and Julian Waller, 'Navalny and the Moscow Mayoral Election', *Russian Analytical Digest* 136 (2013), 1–12, here 10.

83. Leonid Volkov, Twitter post, 4 June 2013, https://twitter.com/leonid-volkov/status/341908416018669568

84. Andrey Kozenko, 'Put' k sebe: Sergey Sobyanin ushel, chtoby vernut'sya', Lenta, 4 June 2013, https://lenta.ru/articles/2013/06/04/major/

85. Mikhail Rubin, with Olga Churakova and Roman Badanin, 'Enemy Number One: How the Regime has Struggled to Thwart Alexei Navalny', Proekt, 24 August 2020, https://www.proekt.media/en/narrative-en/kremlin-vs-navalny/

86. Orttung and Waller, 'Navalny and the Moscow Mayoral Election', 10.

87. 'Case of Navalnyy and Ofitserov v. Russia: Judgment', ECtHR, 23 February 2016, http://hudoc.echr.coe.int/fre?i=001–161060

88. Rubin, with Churakova and Badanin, 'Enemy Number One'.

89. Alena Ledeneva, 'Telephone Justice in Russia', Post-Soviet Affairs 24, no. 4 (2008): 324–350.

90. 'Podderzhka: My za Naval'nogo!', Navalny2013.ru, 2013, https://web.archive.org/web/20130815000000*/http://navalny2013.ru/support/

91. Il'ya Azar, '"My ne mozhem razorvat'sya vo vse storony": Interv'yu s kandidatom v mery Moskvy Sergeyem Mitrokhinym', Lenta, 15 August 2013, https://lenta.ru/articles/2013/08/15/mitrokhin/

92. Il'ya Azar, "'Pochemu my ne mozhem vyigrat'?" Glava shtaba Naval'nogo o sudakh v Kirove i dogovorennostyakh s Sobyaninym', Lenta, 23 July 2013, https://lenta.ru/articles/2013/07/23/volkov/

93. Ibid.

94. 'Alexei Naval'nyy: "My vozrodili politiku. I eto kruto"', *The New Times*, 25 August 2013, https://newtimes.ru/articles/detail/70195/

95. Patyulina used the English words for 'sexual harassment', and the parentheses in the quotation are hers. Il'ya Varlamov and Yekaterina Patyulina, 'Pochemu possorilis' Aleksey Naval'nyy i Maksim Kats', Varlamov (blog), 1 June 2016, https://varlamov.ru/1755254.html

96. Ibid.

97. Kevin Rothrock, 'What It's Like to Come Forward About Sexual Harassment in the Russian Opposition', Global Voices, 3 June 2016, https://globalvoices.org/2016/06/03/what-its-like-to-come-forward-about-sexual-harassment-in-the-russian-opposition/; Dud', 'Naval'nyy: O revolyutsii, Kavkaze i Spartake'.

98. Nadezhda Pomerantseva, "'Ya postradal ot rezhima, ne buduchi professional'nym politikom"', Gazeta.ru, 23 August 2013, https://www.gazeta.ru/politics/2013/08/23_a_5603225.shtml

99. Alexei Navalny, 'Programma kandidata v mery Moskvy', 2013, https://web.archive.org/web/20130717141410/https://navalny.ru/platform/Navalny_Program.pdf

100. Zhanna Ul'yanova, 'Personal'naya programma Naval'nogo', Gazeta.ru, 1 July 2013, https://www.gazeta.ru/politics/2013/07/01_a_5402685.shtml?updated

101. Aleksey Venediktov, 'Interv'yu: Migratsiya', Ekho Moskvy, 23 August 2013, https://echo.msk.ru/programs/beseda/1139878-echo/

102. Kalinina, 'Blog nakazhet'.

103. Ibid.

104. Leonid Volkov and Fyodor Krasheninnikov, 'Volkov, Krasheninnikov: Let's Go Party', *Vedomosti*, 18 April 2012, https://www.vedomosti.ru/opinion/articles/2012/04/18/lets_go_party

105. 'Elektronnaya partiya: "Lenta.ru" izuchila ustroystvo "partii Naval'nogo"', Lenta, 6 August 2012, https://lenta.ru/articles/2012/08/ 06/electronicperformers/

106. 'Programnye tezisy', Narodnyy Al'yans, 2012, https://web.archive.org/web/20120915132140/http://peoplesalliance.ru/us/programmnye_tezisy/

107. 'Elektronnaya partiya'.

108. Alexei Navalny, 'Itogi "vyborov"', Navalny.com (blog), 15 September 2014, https://navalny.com/p/3813/

109. Alexei Navalny, 'O vyborakh: Nasha taktika', Navalny.com (blog), 11 September 2014, https://navalny.com/p/3803/

110. Boris Nemtsov, 'Koalitsiya "Za evropeyskiy vybor" kak al'ternativa samoizolyatsii i agressii', Ekho Moskvy, 16 November 2014, https://echo.msk.ru/blog/nemtsov_boris/1438170-echo/

111. Natal'ya Korchenkova, 'RPR–PARNAS ob"yedinyayet soyuznikov v koalitsiyu', *Kommersant*, 17 November 2014, https://www.kommersant.ru/doc/2612394

112. 'Zayavleniye s"yezda "partii Progressa"', Partiya Progressa, 1 February 2015, https://web.archive.org/web/20150202155249/https://party-progress.org/news/24/

113. Mariya-Luiza Tirmaste et al., 'Mikhail Kas'yanov i Aleksey Naval'nyy poshli na novoye ob"yedineniye', *Kommersant*, 18 April 2015, http://www.kommersant.ru/doc/2712281

114. Alexei Navalny, 'Plany u nas konkretnyye: 6 izbiratel'nykh kampaniy v 3-kh regionakh', Navalny.com (blog), 22 April 2015, https://navalny.com/p/4211/

115. Geir Flikke, 'Canaries in a Coal Mine: The Uphill Struggle of Russia's Non-System Liberals', *Demokratizatsiya* 24, no. 3 (2016): 291–325.

116. Yuri Vendik, 'Vybory v Kostrome: Ozhivleniye iz-za PARNASa', BBC News Russian, 11 September 2015, https://www.bbc.com/russian/russia/2015/09/150911_kostroma_pre_elections_report

117. Grigoriy Belonuchkin and Dmitriy Belomestnov, *Est' takiye partii! 2016–2017: Putevoditel' izbiratelya* (Moscow: Panorama, 2017), 120–121.

118. Rubin, with Churakova and Badanin, 'Enemy Number One'.

119. Alexei Navalny, 'Ya, navernoye, dolzhen izvinit'sya', Navalny.com (blog), 5 May 2016, https://navalny.com/p/4860/

120. Yelizaveta Antonova, 'Naval'nyy protiv Kas'yanova', *RBK*, 27 April

2016, https://www.rbc.ru/newspaper/2016/04/28/5720d8a09a79478 8d48aafdf

121. Alexei Navalny, 'O rezul'tatakh "vyborov": Eto ne vashe porazheniye', Navalny.com (blog), 20 September 2016, https://navalny.com/p/5064/

122. Ibid.

123. Diana Bruk, 'The Best of Vladimir Zhirinovsky, the Clown Prince of Russian Politics', Vice, 10 August 2013, https://www.vice.com/en/article/xd5q47/the-best-of-vladimir-zhirinovsky-russias-craziest-politician

124. Taisiya Bekbulatova, 'Prekrasnyy art-proyekt, tresh, steb', Meduza, 21 November 2017, https://meduza.io/feature/2017/11/21/prekrasnyy-art-proekt-tresh-steb

125. 'Sobchak prokommentirovala plany Kremlya nayti Putinu sopernika dlya vyborov sredi zhenshchin', Vedomosti, 1 September 2017, https://www.vedomosti.ru/politics/news/2017/09/01/731964-copernikom

126. Alexei Navalny, '2018: Ya budu uchastvovat' v vyborakh i khochu stat' vashim golosom', Navalny.com (blog), 13 December 2016, https://navalny.com/p/5162/

127. Alexei Navalny, 'Bor'ba s korruptsiyey i est' moya ekonomicheskaya programma', *Vedomosti*, 1 March 2012, https://www.vedomosti.ru/opinion/articles/2012/03/01/ne_vrat_i_ne_vorovat

128. Alexei Navalny, 'Sobchak i vybory, vosstaniye migrantov, Lyaskin izbil sam sebya, zapugivaniye shkol'nika vo Vladivostoke', Navalny LIVE (YouTube channel), 21 September 2017, https://www.youtube.com/watch?v=ubDFhgc4qIo

129. Navalny, '2018: Ya budu uchastvovat' v vyborakh i khochu stat' vashim golosom'.

130. Navalny, 'Programma Alekseya Naval'nogo'.

131. Leonid Volkov, 'God kampanii: To, chego ne bylo, a teper' ono est'', Leonidvolkov.ru (blog), 12 December 2017, https://www.leonid-volkov.ru/p/255/

132. Alexei Navalny, '"Khvatit kormit' oligarkhov": Universal'nyy lozung', Navalny.com (blog), 19 December 2016, https://navalny.com/p/5169/

133. Navalny, 'Programma Alekseya Naval'nogo'.

134. See, for instance, the interview of Volkov with Zhanna Nemtsova:

‘Vybory v Gosdumu-2021 budut nochnym koshmarom dlya “Edinoy Rossii”: Leonid Volkov v “Nemtsova.Interv'yu”’, Deutsche Welle (YouTube channel), 20 November 2019, https://www.youtube.com/watch?v=Ca-gfNgmnmM

135. Navalny, ‘Programma Alekseya Naval'nogo’.

136. Kathrin Hille, ‘Alexei Navalny: A Genuine Alternative to Vladimir Putin?’, *Financial Times*, 7 August 2017, https://www.ft.com/content/16df421e-72c1-11e7-aca6-c6bd07df1a3c

137. Anton Zhelnov, ‘Aleksey Naval'nyy: “Elita tol'ko zhdet momenta, chtoby predat' Putina”’, Dozhd', 1 November 2016, https://tvrain.ru/teleshow/harddaysnight/navalny-420199/

138. Venediktov and Ryabtseva, ‘Sbityy fokus’.

139. ‘Debaty: Aleksey Naval'nyy vs. Igor' Girkin (Strelkov)’, Ekho Moskvy, 20 July 2017, http://echo.msk.ru/blog/echomsk/2022082-echo/

140. Ibid.

141. Navalny, ‘Programma Alekseya Naval'nogo’.

142. Alexei Navalny, ‘God kampanii. Bol'she o programme’, Navalny.com (blog), 13 December 2017, https://navalny.com/p/5662/

143. Leonid Volkov, ‘Final'nyy finansovyy otchet kampanii Naval'nogo’, Leonidvolkov.ru (blog), 25 April 2018, https://www.leonidvolkov.ru/p/289/

144. ‘Naval'nyy v Murmanske: “Vasha gubernator schitayet, chto ona krutaya tyotya!”’, Severpost, 18 September 2017, https://severpost.ru/read/58085/; Dmitriy Komarov, ‘Ya vas nauchu plokhomu’, Znak, 16 September 2017, https://www.znak.com/2017-09-16/aleksey_navalnyy_sobral_neskolko_tysyach_chelovek_na_miting_v_ekaterinburge

145. ‘Case of Navalnyy and Ofitserov v. Russia: Judgment’.

146. Margarita Alekhina, Natal'ya Galimova, and Il'ya Rozhdestvenskiy, ‘Naval'nyy poluchil pyat' let uslovno po “delu Kirovlesa”’, *RBK*, 8 February 2017, https://www.rbc.ru/society/08/02/2017/589890179a7947795fb26569

147. Anastasiya Agamalova, Anastasiya Kornya and Elena Mukhametshina, ‘TsIK otkazal Naval'nomu v uchastii v vyborakh prezidenta’, *Vedomosti*, 25 December 2017, https://www.vedomosti.ru/politics/articles/2017/12/25/746411-navalnomu-viborah-prezidenta

148. 'Pamfilova: Naval'nyy smozhet ballotirovat'sya posle 2028 goda', TASS, 17 October 2017, https://tass.ru/politika/4652240

149. Alexei Navalny, 'Ob"yavlyayem zabastovku izbirateley', Alexei Navalny (YouTube channel), 25 December 2017, https://www.youtube.com/watch?v=Tz50vEX0nwE

150. Alexei Navalny, 'Ob itogakh zabastovki i "vyborov"', Navalny.com (blog), 20 March 2018, https://navalny.com/p/5820/

151. Alexei Navalny, 'Kak ya proigral: I kakiye nado sdelat' vyvody', Navalny.com (blog), 25 March 2018, https://navalny.com/p/5824/

4. THE PROTESTER

1. Yelizaveta Fomina, 'Regiony Rossii v podderzhku Naval'nogo: massovyye zaderzhaniya i trebovaniya peremen', Deutsche Welle, 24 January 2021, https://www.dw.com/ru/protesty-v-rossii-massovye-zaderzhaniya-i-trebovaniya-peremen/a-56326186

2. Alexei Navalny, 'Dvorets dlya Putina: Istoriya samoy bol'shoy vzyatki', Alexei Navalny (YouTube channel), 19 January 2021, https://youtu.be/ipAnwilMncI. Navalny's call to action starts at 1:47:49.

3. The chapter relies on original accounts from many Russians in different cities across the country. Some of them were employed in Navalny's campaign offices, some were volunteer activists, some did not think of themselves as supporters, but all were politically active in one way or another. The interviews were conducted between 2017 and 2021.

4. 'Aleksey Naval'nyy: aresty s 2011 po 2021 gody (infografika)', Deutsche Welle, 19 January 2021, https://www.dw.com/ru/aleksej-navalnyj-aresty-za-protesty-infografika/a-45626448

5. Yuriy Dud', 'Naval'nyy: O revolyutsii, Kavkaze i Spartake', vDud' (YouTube channel), 18 April 2017, https://www.youtube.com/watch?v=Bf9zvyPachs

6. Andreas Schedler, 'Elections Without Democracy: The Menu of Manipulation', *Journal of Democracy* 13, no. 2 (2002): 36–50.

7. The veteran activists in Perm—as in many other places—had been involved in a campaign against an encroachment by the regional administration on the city's autonomy. In 2009, they had started a campaign to retain mayoral elections, which were gradually being replaced by appointed 'city managers' across the country.

8. For a full description of the conflict, see Jan Matti Dollbaum, 'When Does Diffusing Protest Lead to Local Organization Building? Evidence from a Comparative Subnational Study of Russia's "For Fair Elections" Movement', *Perspectives on Politics* (Forthcoming): 1–16. Published online in 2020: https://doi.org/10.1017/S1537592720002443

9. Leonid Volkov, 'Pervoye soobshcheniye', O vsyakoy vsyachine (blog), 28 September 2007, https://leonwolf.livejournal.com/2007/09/28/

10. Leonid Volkov, 'Kak ya byl plokhim nablyudatelem', O vsyakoy vsyachine (blog), 2 December 2007, https://leonwolf.livejournal.com/2007/12/02/

11. Leonid Volkov, 'Statistika', O vsyakoy vsyachine (blog), 27 February 2009, https://leonwolf.livejournal.com/2009/02/27/

12. 'Naval'nyy v Yekaterinburge: O prezidentskikh vyborakh, Royzmane i sataninskom gosudarstve', Politsovet, 25 February 2017, http://politsovet.ru/54595-navalnyy-v-ekaterinburge-o-prezidentskih-vyborah-royzmane-i-sataninskom-gosudarstve.html

13. Interview with an associate of Navalny from Yekaterinburg, 2017.

14. Jan Matti Dollbaum, 'Protest Trajectories in Electoral Authoritarianism: From Russia's "For Fair Elections" Movement to Alexei Navalny's Presidential Campaign', *Post-Soviet Affairs* 36, no. 3 (2020): 192–210.

15. 'Aleksey Naval'nyy i ego potentsial'nyye storonniki', Levada Center, 1 March 2021, https://www.levada.ru/2021/03/01/aleksej-navalnyj-i-ego-potentsialnye-storonniki/

16. Dollbaum, 'Protest Trajectories in Electoral Authoritarianism'.

17. In cooperation with OVD-Info, the independent online newspaper Meduza provides maps of participants and arrests at protest actions. For 26 March 2017, see 'Protestnaya karta Rossii', Meduza, 7 June 2017, https://meduza.io/feature/2017/06/07/protestnaya-karta-rossii; for 12 June 2017, see '12 iyunya na ulitsy vyshlo bol'she lyudey, chem 26 marta', Meduza, 13 June 2017, https://meduza.io/feature/2017/06/13/skolko-lyudey-protestovali-12-iyunya-i-skolko-zaderzhali

18. The survey was conducted with Elena Sirotkina and Andrei Semenov in January and February 2018. About 5,000 personal invitations were sent to subscribers of Navalny's official campaign groups in eight large cities—Moscow, St Petersburg, Vladivostok, Ivanovo, Tomsk, Barnaul,

Kazan, and Rostov. The sample was constructed to be representative for the age and gender distribution of the groups. For a more detailed description, see Jan Matti Dollbaum and Andrei Semenov, 'Navalny's Digital Dissidents: A New Data Set on a Russian Opposition Movement', *Problems of Post-Communism* (Forthcoming): 1–10. Published online in 2021: https://doi.org/10.1080/10758216.2021.1893123

19. Dollbaum, 'Protest Trajectories in Electoral Authoritarianism'.

20. 'Shtab Naval'nogo v Krasnodare: Kto eti lyudi i chem oni budut zanimat'sya', *RBK*, 13 March 2017, https://kuban.rbc.ru/krasnodar/1 3/03/2017/58c6434e9a7947a269ceec81

21. Natalia Forrat, 'Shock-Resistant Authoritarianism: Schoolteachers and Infrastructural State Capacity in Putin's Russia', *Comparative Politics* 50, no. 3 (2018): 417–49.

22. 'Leonida Volkova obvinili v prizyvakh podrostkov k uchastiyu v mitingakh: SK vozbudil delo', BBC News Russian, 28 January 2021, https://www.bbc.com/russian/news-55838513

23. Dollbaum and Semenov, 'Navalny's Digital Dissidents'.

24. Two surveys were used for comparison. One by the Levada Center conducted in late 2017, and another conducted by the Russian team of the World Values Survey. Eduard Ponarin, Anna Almakaeva and Natalia Soboleva, 'World Values Survey: Round Seven; Russia Datafile Version', Moscow: Higher School of Economics, 2017.

25. The median age in the Navalny survey is twenty-three. About two thirds of Navalny's core supporters have been through or are in higher education, compared with only about half in the general population.

26. About 44 per cent of respondents in the Navalny survey are in the highest three out of six categories on a scale of living standards. This contrasts with 57 per cent of internet-using residents of large urban centres in a 2017 Levada Center poll in the upper three categories.

27. Naturally, this is only a snapshot taken from one survey—albeit the only one that we know of. But, if Navalny becomes more known and popular, these differences on basic things like income, education—and possibly also gender—are likely to decrease rather than increase.

28. Georgiy Tadtayev, 'Roskomnadzor potreboval ot TikTok udalit' prizyvy k protestam', *RBK*, 20 January 2021, https://www.rbc.ru/politics/20/ 01/2021/600862309a7947b226f20083

29. 'Kazhdyy den' Naval'nyy', OVD-Info, 23 March 2018, https://ovdinfo.
    org/articles/2018/03/23/kazhdyy-den-navalnyy. In this analysis, OVD-
    Info documents thousands of repressive acts against supporters and
    activists of Navalny during his 2017–18 campaign.

30. Dollbaum, 'Protest Trajectories in Electoral Authoritarianism'.

31. For more details, see Dollbaum and Semenov, 'Navalny's Digital
    Dissidents'.

32. Ilya Budraitskis and Ilya Matveev, 'Putin's Majority?', *New Left Review*,
    Sidecar (blog), 9 February 2021; https://newleftreview.org/sidecar/
    posts/putins-majority

33. Navalny has publicly apologised for using a derogatory term about
    Georgians during the short war between Russia and Georgia in 2008.
    In recent interviews, associates have said that he has changed his views,
    but Navalny himself has not apologised for the things included in his
    NAROD videos of 2007. Masha Gessen, 'The Evolution of Alexey
    Navalny's Nationalism', *The New Yorker*, 15 February 2021, https://
    www.newyorker.com/news/our-columnists/the-evolution-of-alexey-
    navalnys-nationalism; Arkady Ostrovsky, '"I've mortally offended Putin
    by surviving": Why Alexei Navalny keeps fighting', *The Economist*,
    2 May 2021, https://www.economist.com/1843/2021/05/02/ive-mor-
    tally-offended-putin-by-surviving-why-alexei-navalny-keeps-fighting

34. 'Social desirability bias' is a well-known problem in survey research.
    For a summary, see Ivar Krumpal, 'Determinants of Social Desirability
    Bias in Sensitive Surveys: A Literature Review', *Quality & Quantity*
    47, no. 4 (2013): 2025–47.

35. The interviewee used the word *russkiy*—a term used to refer to Russian
    ethnicity rather than Russian citizenship, which is expressed with *ros-
    siyskiy*.

36. This interview was conducted by Irina Kozlova, research associate at
    the Russian Presidential Academy of National Economy and Public
    Administration under the President of the Russian Federation.

5. THE KREMLIN V. NAVALNY

1. Dmitriy Smirnov, 'Peskov ob"yasnil, pochemu Putin ne boitsya
   Naval'nogo', *Komsomol'skaya Pravda*, 19 January 2021, https://www.

kp.ru/daily/27228/4354766/; '"Nalichiye pretenziy k Naval'nomu ne imeyet otnosheniya k prezidentu Rossii"', Kommersant FM, 19 January 2021, https://www.kommersant.ru/doc/4653391

2. 'Tsentral'nyye stantsii metro Moskvy zakroyut v den' protestov 31 yan-varya', *Kommersant*, 29 January 2021, https://www.kommersant.ru/doc/4670680; 'SMI soobshchili ob obkhode kafe i barov v Moskve s pros'boy otklyuchit' Wi-Fi', *RBK*, 31 January 2021, https://www.rbc.ru/society/31/01/2021/6015c9ea9a7947382cdd73d7

3. Andrey Semenov, 'Pro-Navalny Protests are Breaking Records across Russia', Riddle, 16 April 2021, https://www.ridl.io/en/pro-navalny-protests-are-breaking-records-across-russia/

4. Aleksandr Litoy, Dmitriy Anisimov, and Grigoriy Durnovo, '"Dvortsovoye delo": kto eti lyudi i za chto ikh sudyat. Gid OVD-Info', OVD-Info, 15 February 2021, https://ovdinfo.org/navalny-protests

5. 'Kak vyyasnila "Meduza", po vnutrennim podschetam FSB, na yanvar-skiye mitingi vyshli 90 tysyach chelovek', Meduza, 9 March 2021, https://meduza.io/feature/2021/03/09/kak-vyyasnila-meduza-po-vnu-trennim-podschetam-fsb-na-yanvarskie-mitingi-vyshli-90-tysyach-chelovek

6. 'Putin rasskazal o lichnom uchastii v snyatii ogranicheniy na vyyezd Naval'nogo v FRG', *Izvestiya*, 22 October 2020, https://iz.ru/10773 64/2020-10-22/putin-rasskazal-o-lichnom-uchastii-v-sniatii-ogranichenii-na-vyezd-navalnogo-v-frg

7. Vladimir Putin, 'Address by President of the Russian Federation', Kremlin, 18 March 2014, http://en.kremlin.ru/events/president/news/20603. For a version of Putin's speech annotated with comments by various experts interpreting Putin's historical allusions, see 'Speech of Vladimir Putin', Dekoder, 18 March 2019, https://crimea.dekoder.org/speech

8. 'Putin Reveals Secrets of Russia's Crimea Takeover Plot', BBC News, 9 March 2015, https://www.bbc.com/news/world-europe-31796226

9. Samuel Greene and Graeme Robertson, *Putin v. the People: The Perilous Politics of a Divided Russia* (New Haven: Yale University Press, 2019).

10. Regina Smyth, Anton Sobolev, and Irina Soboleva, 'A Well-Organized Play: Symbolic Politics and the Effect of the Pro-Putin Rallies', *Problems of Post-Communism* 60, no. 2 (2013): 24–39.

11. 'Volodin podtverdil svoy tezis o tom, chto "net Putina—net Rossii"', TASS, 18 October 2017, https://tass.ru/politika/4658232

12. See, for instance, Mabel Berezin, 'Emotions and Political Identity: Mobilizing Affection for the Polity', in *Passionate Politics: Emotions and Social Movements*, ed. Jeff Goodwin and James Jasper (Chicago: University of Chicago Press, 2001), 83–98.

13. Greene and Robertson, *Putin v. the People*.

14. For an overview of the case, see 'Na Naval'nogo zaveli delo ob oskorblenii veterana iz-za rolika RT pro Konstitutsiyu: Sam pensioner postov oppozitsionera ne videl', Meduza, 18 June 2020, https://meduza.io/feature/2020/06/18/na-navalnogo-zaveli-delo-iz-za-posta-o-rolike-rt-pro-konstitutsiyu-oppozitsioner-yakoby-oskorbil-veterana-no-dazhe-ne-upominal-ego

15. Yevgeniy Zhukov, 'Naval'nomu pred"yavili obvineniye po delu o klevete na veterana voynu', Deutsche Welle, 22 July 2020, https://www.dw.com/ru/a-54268667

16. Alexei Navalny, '"Chayka"', Alexei Navalny (YouTube channel), 1 December 2015, https://youtu.be/eXYQbgvzxdM; Alexei Navalny, '"Chayka"', Navalny.com, 2015, https://chaika.navalny.com

17. Shaun Walker, 'The Luxury Hotel, the Family of the Top Moscow Prosecutor and Russia's Most Notorious Gang', *The Guardian*, 13 December 2015, https://www.theguardian.com/world/2015/dec/13/alexei-navalny-yuri-chaika

18. Alexei Navalny, 'Znakom'tes', synov'ya genprokurora—LSDU3 i YFYaU9', Navalny.com (blog), 9 June 2016, https://navalny.com/p/4905/

19. Ibid.

20. For an overview of the bill's passage through parliament, see 'O vnesenii izmeneniy v Federal'nyy zakon "O gosudarstvennoy okhrane" i otdel'nyye zakonodatel'nyye akty Rossiyskoy Federatsii', State Duma, 11 February 2017, https://sozd.duma.gov.ru/bill/99654–7

21. 'Gosduma odobrila rasshireniye polnomochiy FSO', *RBK*, 15 June 2017, https://www.rbc.ru/politics/15/06/2017/594105e89a79473d101832fb

22. Ben Noble, 'Authoritarian Amendments: Legislative Institutions as

Intraexecutive Constraints in Post-Soviet Russia,' *Comparative Political Studies* 53, no. 9 (2020): 1417–54; Ben Noble, 'Vagonchiki (Russia)', Global Informality Project, 2020, https://www.in-formality.com/wiki/index.php?title=Vagonchiki_(Russia)

23. Anastasiya Kornya and Ol'ga Churakova, 'Gosduma razreshila zasekrechivat' informatsiyu ob imushchestve i aktivakh krupnykh chinovnikov', *Vedomosti*, 15 June 2017, https://www.vedomosti.ru/politics/articles/2017/06/16/694626-zasekrechivat-imuschestve-chinovnikov

24. 'O vnesenii izmeneniy v otdel'nyye zakonodatel'nyye akty Rossiyskoy Federatsii v chasti obespecheniya konfidentsial'nosti svedeniy o zashchishchayemykh litsakh i ob osushchestvlenii operativno-rozysknoy deyatel'nosti', State Duma, 8 December 2020, https://sozd.duma.gov.ru/bill/1070431-7

25. Mariya Makutina, 'Siloviki poluchat shirokuyu neizvestnost'', *Kommersant*, 16 December 2020, https://www.kommersant.ru/doc/4615747

26. '"Ne tak-to prosto otravit' cheloveka 'Novichkom'": Rassledovatel' Khristo Grozev iz Bellingcat rasskazyvayet, kak on nashel vozmozhnykh otraviteley Naval'nogo', Meduza, 16 December 2020, https://meduza.io/feature/2020/12/16/ne-tak-to-prosto-otravit-cheloveka-novichkom; Ben Smith, 'How Investigative Journalism Flourished in Hostile Russia', *The New York Times*, 21 February 2021, https://www.nytimes.com/2021/02/21/business/media/probiv-investigative-reporting-russia.html

27. Yevgeniy Chernov, 'Pereletnyye litsa utekali iz Samary', *Kommersant*, 20 January 2021, https://www.kommersant.ru/doc/4653655; Ivan Tyazhlov, '"Magistral'" utekla v Sankt-Peterburge', *Kommersant*, 1 March 2021, https://www.kommersant.ru/doc/4710833

28. Mark Galeotti, 'Kremlin Turns on Russia's "Subversive Transparency"', *The Moscow Times*, 9 March 2021, https://www.themoscowtimes.com/2021/03/09/kremlin-turns-on-russias-subversive-transparency-a73178

29. 'O vnesenii izmeneniy v stat'i 183 i 320 Ugolovnogo kodeksa Rossiyskoy Federatsii', State Duma, 16 February 2021, https://sozd.duma.gov.ru/bill/1112804–7

30. Alexei Navalny, 'Kleptokraticheskoye puteshestviye: Tur po domam rossiyskikh milliarderov', Navalny.com (blog), 12 February 2016, https://navalny.com/p/4723/

31. See the documentary movie 'Kholivar: History of the Runet' by journalist Andrey Loshak. For a short clip including Putin's promise as remembered by investor Yegor Shuppe, see 'Fragment seriala "Kholivar" Andreya Loshaka ob istorii Runeta', Meduza (YouTube channel), 31 May 2019, https://www.youtube.com/watch?v=YfN_DLpjacU

32. Pavel Durov, Twitter post, 8 December 2011, https://twitter.com/durov/status/144775176742113281

33. Ingrid Lunden, 'Pavel Durov Resigns as Head of Russian Social Network VK.com, Ukraine Conflict was the Tipping Point', Tech Crunch, 1 April 2014, https://techcrunch.com/2014/04/01/founder-pavel-durov-says-hes-stepped-down-as-head-of-russias-top-social-network-vk-com/?_ga=2.29273212.1340845031.1617803886-738729247.1617803886

34. 'Telegram Retains Users after Russia's Ban amid Internet Chaos', *The Moscow Times*, 18 April 2018, https://www.themoscowtimes.com/2018/04/18/telegram-retains-users-after-russias-ban-amid-internet-chaos-a61204

35. 'Russia Lifts Ban on Telegram Messaging App after Failing to Block It', Reuters, 18 June 2020, https://www.reuters.com/article/us-russia-telegram-ban-idUSKBN23P2FT

36. Her real name is Anastasia Vashukevich. 'Rossiyskiye operatory nachali blokirovat' sayt Naval'nogo', BBC News Russian, 15 February 2018, https://www.bbc.com/russian/news-43072741

37. 'Roskomnadzor razblokiroval sayt Naval'nogo', BBC News Russian, 26 February 2018, https://www.bbc.com/russian/news-43083438

38. Andrei Nikitin, *Perm': Rodina rossiyskogo liberalizma* (Moscow: Moskovskaya shkola politicheskikh issledovaniy, 2004).

39. Formerly the philanthropic arm of the company, the Ford Foundation has been independent since 1974 and is one of the wealthiest private charitable foundations in the world.

40. Igor' Averkiyev, 'Kak rabotat' s vlast'yu: "Permskiye Pravila Povedeniya"', Stranitsy Averkiyeva, 10 November 2004, http://www.prpc.ru/averkiev/041110.shtml

41. Nikitin, *Perm'*.

42. 'Ochen' skoro vy (da, imenno vy) smozhete stat' "inostrannym agentom"—dazhe etogo ne zametiv. Chto?', Meduza, 4 December 2020, https://meduza.io/cards/ochen-skoro-vy-da-imenno-vy-smozhete-stat-inostrannym-agentom-dazhe-etogo-ne-zametiv-chto

43. 'Valentina Cherevatenko', Kavkazskiy Uzel, 27 October 2017, https://www.kavkaz-uzel.eu/articles/311673/

44. See https://fbk.info/, at the bottom of the page.

45. 'Nelogicheskoye odareniye: "Agora" i "Memorial" poluchili prezidentskiye granty', Grani.ru 19 June 2014, https://graniru.org/Society/ngo/m.230342.html

46. See, for example, Kirsti Stuvøy, '"The Foreign Within": State–Civil Society Relations in Russia', *Europe–Asia Studies* 72, no. 7 (2020): 1103–24, here 1108.

47. Aleksandra Zakhvatkina, '"Nuzhno vyyti iz etogo, ukrepivshis'": Lev Ponomarev—o likvidatsii dvizheniya "Za prava cheloveka"', Agentstvo Sotsial'noy Informatsii, 5 November 2019, https://www.asi.org.ru/news/2019/11/05/lev-ponomarev-2/

48. Marc Morjé Howard, *The Weakness of Civil Society in Post-Communist Europe* (Cambridge: Cambridge University Press, 2003). Also, see the debate on Yuri Levada's 'Homo Sovieticus' in Gulnaz Sharafutdinova, 'Was There a "Simple Soviet" Person? Debating the Politics and Sociology of "Homo Sovieticus"', *Slavic Review* 78, no. 1 (2019): 173–95.

49. See, for instance, Graeme Robertson, 'Protesting Putinism: The Election Protests of 2011–2012 in Broader Perspective', *Problems of Post-Communism* 60, no. 2 (2013): 11–23; or the works of Carine Clément, such as 'Unlikely Mobilisations: How Ordinary Russian People Become Involved in Collective Action', *European Journal of Cultural and Political Sociology* 2, nos. 3–4 (2015): 211–40.

50. Robertson, 'Protesting Putinism'.

51. Graeme Robertson, 'Managing Society: Protest, Civil Society, and Regime in Putin's Russia', *Slavic Review* 68, no. 3 (2009): 528–47.

52. Also, a study showed that the protests in December 2011 had, in the short term, a positive effect on people's trust in state institutions, especially among those who were critical of the authorities. One possible

explanation is that opposition-minded citizens had expected repression and were positively impressed when that did not occur. See Timothy Frye and Ekaterina Borisova, 'Elections, Protest, and Trust in Government: A Natural Experiment from Russia', *The Journal of Politics* 81, no. 3 (2019): 820–32.

53. 'Russia's Protestors on Trial: What You Need to Know about the Bolotnaya Case', Human Rights Watch, 18 December 2013, https://www.hrw.org/video-photos/interactive/2013/12/18/russias-protestors-trial-what-you-need-know-about-bolotnaya-case

54. Fabian Burkhardt and Jan Matti Dollbaum, 'Der Bolotnaja-Prozess', in Lexikon der Politischen Strafprozesse, ed. Kurt Groenewold, Alexander Ignor, and Arndt Koch, 2018, http://www.lexikon-der-politischen-strafprozesse.de/glossar/der-bolotnaja-prozess-2012/

55. Yegor Skovoroda, 'Tseremoniya zakrytiya', Russkaya Planeta, 24 February 2014, https://rusplt.ru/policy/bolotka-prigovor-8215.html

56. Burkhardt and Dollbaum, 'Der Bolotnaja-Prozess'.

57. The reason was that one of the administrative fines the verdict was based on had not come into effect at the time the case was opened—something that Dadin's lawyer had already pointed out at the trial.

58. Grigoriy Durnovo, '"Dadinskaya stat'ya": Chetyre goda spustya', OVD-Info, 1 February 2019, https://ovdinfo.org/articles/2019/02/01/dadinskaya-statya-chetyre-goda-spustya

59. Yelizaveta Fokht, 'Osuzhdennuyu po "dadinskoy stat'ye" Yuliyu Galyaminu lishili statusa deputata', BBC News Russian, 25 March 2021, https://www.bbc.com/russian/news-56528142

60. For OVD-Info's data on administrative cases, see 'Kak sudyat po stat'ye 20.2 KoAP: Statistika', OVD-Info, no date, https://data.ovdinfo.org/20_2/

61. For OVD-Info's data on individual protests, see 'Odinochnyye pikety: Dannyye', OVD-Info, no date, https://ovdinfo.org/data/odinochnye-pikety-dannye#1

62. Sergey Belanovsky and Anastasia Nikolskaya, 'Why Is Khabarovsk Backing Furgal?', Riddle, 21 July 2020, https://www.ridl.io/en/why-is-khabarovsk-backing-furgal/.

63. Mikhail Shubin, 'Kak podavlyali protesty v Khabarovske? Glavnoe',

OVD-Info, 28 December 2020, https://ovdinfo.org/articles/2020/12/28/kak-podavlyali-protesty-v-habarovske-glavnoe

64. Alexander Marrow, 'Russian Police Detain around 200 People, Including Leading Opposition Figures, at Moscow Meeting', Reuters, 13 March 2021, https://www.reuters.com/article/us-russia-politics-opposition-idUSKBN2B50AP

65. '"Otkrytaya Rossiya" nadoyela: Organizatsiyu, osnovannuyu Mikhailom Khodorkovskim, priznali nezhelatel'noy', *RBK*, 26 April 2017, https://www.rbc.ru/newspaper/2017/04/27/5900b60a9a7947c5e8ac8807

66. Dar'ya Korzhova, 'Miting na prospekte Sakharova sobral rekordnyye 50 000 chelovek', *Vedomosti*, 10 August 2019, https://www.vedomosti.ru/politics/articles/2019/08/10/808531-000

67. Taisiya Bekbulatova, Ivan Golunov, and Aleksandr Gorbachev, 'Byvshiy soratnik Alekseya Naval'nogo registriruyet Partiyu progressa: Naval'nyy uveren, chto u nego kradut partiyu—tak i est'', Meduza, 22 February 2018, https://meduza.io/feature/2018/02/22/byvshiy-soratnik-alekseya-navalnogo-registriruet-partiyu-progressa-navalnyy-uveren-chto-u-nego-kradut-partiyu-tak-i-est

68. 'Naval'nyy zapustil proyekt "Umnoye golosovaniye": On dolzhen ob"yedinit' oppozitsiyu, chtoby pobedit' "Edinuyu Rossiyu" v region-akh', *Novaya Gazeta*, 28 November 2018, https://novayagazeta.ru/news/2018/11/28/147156-navalnyy-zapustil-proekt-umnoe-golo-sovanie-on-dolzhen-ob-edinit-oppozitsiyu-chtoby-pobedit-edinuyu-rossiyu-v-regionah

69. Alexei Navalny, 'Umnoye golosovaniye: Otvety na voprosy i kritiku', Navalny.com (blog), 21 August 2019, https://navalny.com/p/6194/

70. Mikhail Turchenko and Grigorii Golosov, 'Smart Enough to Make a Difference? An Empirical Test of the Efficacy of Strategic Voting in Russia's Authoritarian Elections', *Post-Soviet Affairs* 37, no. 1 (2021): 65–79.

71. 'Mironov: "Umnoye golosovaniye" ne povliyalo na pobedu spravorossov na vyborakh v Mosgordumu', TASS, 9 September 2019, https://tass.ru/politika/6864618. Mironov forgot to mention, however, that among the party's candidates that Smart Voting brought into parliament was a so-called 'spoiler candidate', Aleksandr Solovyov. A Just Russia—

likely in collusion with authorities—placed him on the ballot presumably to confuse voters.

72. Yelena Mukhametshina and Maksim Ivanov, 'Gosduma otkryla sessiyu s obsuzhdeniya Alekseya Naval'nogo i vyborov v SShA', *Vedomosti*, 19 January 2021, https://www.vedomosti.ru/politics/articles/2021/01/19/854692-gosduma-otkrila

73. 'Elektoral'nyye reytingi partiy', Levada Center, 11 March 2021, https://www.levada.ru/2021/03/11/elektoralnye-rejtingi-partij-5/

74. '"Tsirk", "Umnyy golos" i "Polnyy vpered": Novaya strategiya partii vlasti v Moskve', Meduza, 26 March 2021, https://meduza.io/feature/2021/03/26/tsirk-umnyy-golos-i-polnyy-vpered-novaya-strategiya-partii-vlasti-v-moskve

6. NAVALNY AND THE FUTURE OF RUSSIA

1. Reuters, Twitter post, 3 February 2021, https://twitter.com/Reuters/status/1357036129594167296

2. 'Case of Navalnyye v. Russia: Judgment', European Court of Human Rights (ECtHR), 17 October 2017, http://hudoc.echr.coe.int/eng?i=001-177665

3. '"Zavedomo lozhnyy donos": Sut' dela "Iv Roshe", po kotoromu Aleksey Naval'nyy mozhet popast' za reshetku', Znak, 2 February 2021, https://www.znak.com/2021-02-02/sut_dela_iv_roshe_po_kotoromu_aleksey_navalnyy_mozhet_popast_za_reshetku

4. '"Vladimir the Poisoner": A Translation of Alexey Navalny's Speech in Court on February 2', Meduza, 2 February 2021, https://meduza.io/en/feature/2021/02/02/vladimir-the-poisoner

5. On appeal, Navalny's term was reduced to two years and six months. Max Seddon, 'Moscow Appeals Court Upholds Jailing of Putin Critic Navalny', *Financial Times*, 20 February 2021, https://www.ft.com/content/0765d2fb-abb7–4622–90b4–686e7475fa68

6. 'Father of Navalny Associate Remanded in Custody; Son Calls Charge "A New Level Of Villainy"', RFE/RL Russian Service, 7 April 2021, https://www.rferl.org/a/russia-zhdanov-father-custody-navalny-abuse-of-office/31191420.html

7. Data collected from OVD-Info, Mediazona, various press sources, and Twitter feeds of the local headquarters.

8. Sergey Romashenko, 'Protiv Lyubovi Sobol' vozbudili ugolovnoye delo', Deutsche Welle, 4 February 2021, https://www.dw.com/ru/protiv-sor-atnicy-navalnogo-sobol-vozbudili-ugolovnoe-delo/a-56452795; 'Protiv Sobol' vozbudili delo o narushenii neprikosnovennosti zhilishcha', *Kommersant*, 25 December 2020, https://www.kommersant.ru/doc/4628469

9. 'Father of Navalny Associate Remanded in Custody'.

10. He retweeted a picture with the date and time of the 23 January protests in Moscow. 'Glavnogo redaktora "Mediazony" Sergeya Smirnova arestovali na 25 sutok za retvit', Mediazona, 3 February 2021, https://zona.media/news/2021/02/03/smirnov

11. 'Delo o mitingakh i podrostkakh: Mera presecheniya zhurnalistam DOXA', Mediazona, 14 April 2021, https://zona.media/online/2021/04/14/doxa

12. 'Spisok zaderzhannykh v svyazi s sudom nad Alekseyem Naval'nym', OVD-Info, 2 February 2021, https://ovdinfo.org/news/2021/02/02/spisok-zaderzhannyh-v-svyazi-s-sudom-nad-alekseem-navalnym-2-fe-vralya-2021-goda; 'Real'nyy srok Naval'nomu: Protesty posle resheniya suda', Mediazona, 2 February 2021, https://zona.media/online/2021/02/02/aftercourt

13. Alexei Navalny, Instagram post, 15 March 2021, https://www.insta-gram.com/p/CMcVo3qFSvY/

14. Alexei Navalny, Instagram post, 29 March 2021, https://www.insta-gram.com/p/CM_6xtrF3s_/

15. Sergey Dolgov, 'Arestant vserossiyskogo masshtaba: Kak Naval'nyy vybivayet privilegii v pokrovskoy kolonii', Life News, 2 April 2021, https://life.ru/p/1388796

16. Aleksandr Borodikhin, Yelizaveta Pestova, and Dima Shvets, 'Nochnoy "Dozor": Pochemu Naval'nogo v kolonii budyat kazhdyy chas i chto takoye profilakticheskiy uchet', Mediazona, 25 March 2021, https://zona.media/article/2021/03/25/navalny-sklonen

17. Navalny, Instagram post, 15 March 2021.

18. Borodikhin, Pestova, and Shvets, 'Nochnoy "Dozor"'.

19. Alexei Navalny, 'Dva zayavleniya Alekseya Naval'nogo', Navalny.com (blog), 25 March 2021, https://navalny.com/p/6476/; Irek Murtazin, 'Medvedev razreshil', *Novaya Gazeta*, 20 April 2021, https://novayagazeta.ru/articles/2021/04/20/medvedev-razreshil

20. Alexei Navalny, 'Golodovka Sobol'', Navalny.com (blog), 16 August 2019, https://navalny.com/t/595/

21. Maria Butina had been charged and pleaded guilty to 'conspiracy to act as an agent of the Russian Federation within the United States'. 'Russian National Charged in Conspiracy to Act as an Agent of the Russian Federation within the United States', Office of Public Affairs of the Department of Justice, 16 July 2018, https://www.justice.gov/opa/pr/russian-national-charged-conspiracy-act-agent-russian-federation-within-united-states. After her release in 2019, she was deported to Russia. Jonny Tickle, 'Maria Butina, Once Jailed in US, Visits Navalny's Prison & Calls It "Exemplary", but Allies of Russian Opposition Figure Cry Foul', RT, 2 April 2021, https://www.rt.com/russia/519977-butina-prison-visit-navalny/

22. Yuliya Navalnaya, Instagram post, 13 April 2021, https://www.instagram.com/p/CNm-iqxlHjL/

23. Alexei Navalny, 'Kak vyglyadit propaganda nasiliya v "Novoy gazete" po mneniyu IK-2', Navalny.com (blog), 14 April 2021, https://navalny.com/p/6479/

24. Alexei Navalny, Instagram post, 7 April 2021, https://www.instagram.com/p/CNXy3DGFZx1/

25. Alexei Navalny, Instagram post, 23 April 2021, https://www.instagram.com/p/COAeBxIFNpL/

26. 'Prokuratura potrebovala priznat' FBK i "Shtaby Naval'nogo" ekstremistskimi organizatsiyami', *Novaya Gazeta*, 16 April 2021, https://novayagazeta.ru/articles/2021/04/16/prokuratura-potrebovala-priznat-fbk-i-shtaby-navalnogo-ekstremistskimi-organizatsiiami

27. Anastasiya Yasenitskaya, Dima Shvets, and Nikita Sologub, 'Tebya delayut ekstremistom: Chem grozit isk prokuratury FBK', Mediazona, 16 April 2021, https://zona.media/article/2021/04/16/fbk-extremism

28. 'Istochniki informatsii', Levada Center, 28 September 2020, https://www.levada.ru/2020/09/28/ggh/

29. Interview with Viktor, thirty-nine, from Yekaterinburg.

30. 'Uslovno Vash: Aleksey Naval'nyy i Yegor Zhukov', Ekho Moskvy (YouTube channel), 25 March 2020, https://www.youtube.com/watch?v=lnRIIqsuCp8

31. Yevgeniya Al'bats, '"Ya dumayu, vlast' v Rossii smenitsya ne v rezul'tate vyborov"', *The New Times*, 19 July 2011, https://newtimes.ru/articles/detail/38107/; Alexei Navalny, 'Ya, navernoye, dolzhen izvinit'sya', Navalny.com (blog), 5 May 2016, https://navalny.com/p/4860/

32. '"My stalkivalis' s situatsiyami, kogda situatsiya vykhodila za ramki zakona i privodila k raskachke gosudarstva": Putin ob aktsiyakh v podderzhku Naval'nogo', Mediazona, 25 January 2021, https://zona.media/news/2021/01/25/ptnnava

33. Benjamin Bidder and Christian Esch, 'Russian Opposition Leader Alexei Navalny on His Poisoning: "I Assert That Putin Was Behind the Crime"', *Der Spiegel*, 1 October 2020, https://www.spiegel.de/international/world/alexei-navalny-on-his-poisoning-i-assert-that-putin-was-behind-the-crime-a-ae5923d5–20f3-4117-80bd-39a99b5b86f4

34. Filip Noubel and Yevgeniya Plakhina, 'Alexey Navalny's Views on Migrants Run Counter to His Pro-Democracy Discourse', Global Voices, 9 February 2021, https://globalvoices.org/2021/02/09/alexey-navalnys-views-on-migrants-run-counter-to-his-pro-democracy-discourse/; Robert Coalson, 'Is Aleksei Navalny a Liberal or a Nationalist?', *The Atlantic*, 29 July 2013, https://www.theatlantic.com/international/archive/2013/07/is-aleksei-navalny-a-liberal-or-a-nationalist/278186/

35. Terrell Jermaine Starr, 'We Need to Have a Talk About Alexei Navalny', *The Washington Post*, 1 March 2021, https://www.washingtonpost.com/opinions/2021/03/01/we-need-have-talk-about-alexei-navalny

36. Françoise Daucé, *Être opposant dans la Russie de Vladimir Poutine* (Paris: Le bord de l'eau, 2016).

37. Alisa Volkova, '"Khvatit kormit' Kavkaz": Kak menyalsya natsionalizm Naval'nogo', Kavkaz.Realii, 1 February 2021, https://www.kavkazr.com/a/31075519.html

38. See, for instance, Bermet Talant, Twitter post, 24 February 2021, https://twitter.com/ser_ou_parecer/status/1364645136572022789

39. Sergey Smirnov, '"Byl samolet, i v nem ya pomer": Interv'yu Alekseya

Naval'nogo', *Mediazona*, 7 October 2020, https://zona.media/article/2020/10/06/navalny

40. Andrey Kozenko and Ol'ga Prosvirova, '"Moya likvidatsiya nichego ne izmenit": Interv'yu Alekseya Naval'nogo o ego vosstanovlenii i vozvrashchenii v Rossiyu', *BBC News Russian*, 6 October 2020, https://www.bbc.com/russian/features-54435835

41. Vladimir Ashurkov, Facebook post, 18 January 2021, https://www.facebook.com/vladimir.ashurkov/posts/3924279780956491

42. Alexei Navalny, 'Ogo', *Navalny* (blog), 26 April 2010, https://navalny.livejournal.com/453093.html

43. Bidder and Esch, 'Russian Opposition Leader Alexei Navalny on His Poisoning'.

44. Smirnov, '"Byl samolet, i v nem ya pomer"'.

45. Alexei Navalny, 'Spektakl' v teatre absurda', *Navalny* (blog), 7 December 2012, https://navalny.livejournal.com/755371.html

46. Alexei Navalny, 'Gollandchegi', *Navalny* (blog), 19 October 2011, https://navalny.livejournal.com/632543.html

47. Ibid.

48. Navalny, 'Spektakl' v teatre absurda'.

49. 'Vozvrashcheniye Alekseya Naval'nogo', Levada Center, 5 February 2021, https://www.levada.ru/2021/02/05/vozvrashhenie-alekseya-navalnogo/

50. 'Navalny's Poisoning', Levada Center, 1 February 2021, https://www.levada.ru/en/2021/02/01/navalny-s-poisoning/

51. '"Ya ne chuvstvuyu sebya odinokim": Dva poslednikh slova Naval'nogo za odin den"', *BBC News Russian*, 20 February 2021, https://www.bbc.com/russian/news-56137696

52. Surveys show that young people in Russia are more liberal than older generations, but not in all respects. Margarita Zavadskaya, 'Russia's GenZ: Progressive or Reactionary?', *Riddle*, 12 April 2021, https://www.ridl.io/en/russia-s-genz-progressive-or-reactionary/

53. '"Rossiya budet schastlivoy": Rech' Naval'nogo na apellyatsii', *Meduza* (YouTube channel), 20 February 2021, https://youtu.be/4yXPNieGgtA

54. Smirnov, '"Byl samolet, i v nem ya pomer"'.

EPILOGUE: 'THOSE WHO WANT TO FIGHT WAR MUST ONLY
            FIGHT DESPOTISM'

1. The law allows for a maximum sentence of fifteen years. 'Russian prosecutors call for Alexei Navalny to serve 13 years in prison', *The Guardian*,
   15 March 2022, https://www.theguardian.com/world/2022/mar/15/
   russian-prosecutors-call-for-alexei-navalny-to-serve-13-years-in-
   prison

2. 'In prison and on trial: Here's why Alexey Navalny is back in court and
   facing up to 15 more years behind bars', Meduza, 15 February 2022,
   https://meduza.io/en/feature/2022/02/16/in-prison-and-on-trial

3. '"This will lead to our country's collapse": Alexey Navalny's address to
   the Russian public as the state seeks new charges against him', Meduza,
   16 March 2022, https://meduza.io/en/feature/2022/03/16/this-will-
   lead-to-our-country-s-collapse

4. Ibid.

5. Alexei Navalny, Instagram post, 15 March 2022, https://www.insta-
   gram.com/p/CbIf-xcN4x6/

6. '"Bi-bi-si": ubityy v Buche Il'ya Naval'nyy okazalsya dal'nim rodstven-
   nikom politika Alekseya Naval'nogo', Meduza, 18 April 2022, https://
   meduza.io/news/2022/04/18/bi-bi-si-ubityy-v-buche-ilya-navalnyy-
   okazalsya-dalnim-rodstvennikom-politika-alekseya-navalnogo

7. Alexei Navalny, Twitter post, 19 April 2022, https://twitter.com/
   navalny/status/1516433250553679874

8. 'Ukraine war: Russian journalist Oksana Baulina killed in Kyiv shelling', BBC News, 23 March 2022, https://www.bbc.co.uk/news/world-
   europe-60855732; Alexei Navalny, Twitter post, 24 March 2022,
   https://twitter.com/navalny/status/1507009930582142976

9. '"This will lead to our country's collapse"'.

10. Alexei Navalny, 'Sud'ya po vyzovu: Kto stoit za fal'shivym delom
    Naval'nogo?', Navalny.com (blog), 15 March 2022, https://navalny.
    com/p/6618/

11. Navalny appealed his sentence, unsuccessfully. 'Naval'nyy: Apellyatsiya
    na prigovor po delu o moshennichestve, den' vtoroy', Mediazona,
    24 May 2022, https://zona.media/online/2022/05/24/naval-2

12. Alexei Navalny, Twitter post, 22 March 2022, https://twitter.com/
    navalny/status/1506247694804783113

13. Alexei Navalny, Instagram post, 30 September 2021, https://www.instagram.com/p/CUc2J77IZpE/

14. Alexei Navalny, Instagram post, 25 August 2021, https://www.instagram.com/p/CTASOJ8Ijik/

15. Alexei Navalny, Instagram post, 11 October 2021, https://www.instagram.com/p/CU4ffm2ow0K/

16. Alexei Navalny, Instagram post, 20 December 2021, https://www.instagram.com/p/CXtYBCIoSNR/

17. Alexei Navalny, Instagram post, 14 December 2021, https://www.instagram.com/p/CXdRvzloO2l/

18. Alexei Navalny, Instagram post, 10 January 2022, https://www.instagram.com/p/CYjdiM1IkEe/

19. Alexei Navalny, Instagram post, 9 July 2021, https://www.instagram.com/p/CRGwMqLtIWa/

20. Andrew Kramer, 'In First Interview From Jail, an Upbeat Navalny Discusses Prison Life', *The New York Times*, 25 August 2021 (updated 15 September 2021), https://www.nytimes.com/2021/08/25/world/europe/navalny-jail-prison.html

21. 'Read Excerpts From Navalny's Interview With The Times', *The New York Times*, 25 August 2021 (updated 20 October 2021), https://www.nytimes.com/2021/08/25/world/europe/navalny-interview-excerpts.html

22. Alexei Navalny, Instagram post, 26 March 2022, https://www.instagram.com/p/CbkDFtbNROw/

23. Simon Shuster, 'Exclusive: Alexei Navalny Urges Biden to Stand Up to Putin', *Time*, 19 January 2022, https://time.com/6140114/alexei-navalny-interview/

24. Vladislav Davidzon, 'The IT Whiz in Charge of Bringing Down Putin', Tablet, 11 January 2022, https://www.tabletmag.com/sections/news/articles/leonid-volkov

25. Interview with Vladimir Ashurkov, 9 May 2022.

26. Andrew Kramer and Aina Khan, 'Navalny, Putin's Imprisoned Foe, Wins E.U.'s Top Human Rights Award', *The New York Times*, 20 October 2021, https://www.nytimes.com/2021/10/20/world/europe/navalny-sakharov-prize-putin-russia.html; David Smith, '"All

I could do was film": the making of a shocking movie on Alexei Navalny', *The Guardian*, 23 April 2022, https://www.theguardian.com/film/2022/apr/23/alexei-navalny-documentary-film

27. Davidzon, 'The IT Whiz in Charge of Bringing Down Putin'.

28. According to Vladimir Ashurkov, the office consists of around 50 people—as of June 2022—with the number having increased markedly following the dissolving of Navalny's organisations in Russia in 2021. Interview with Vladimir Ashurkov, 17 June 2022.

29. '"Poka tochno ne yasno, kakim zverem my stanem. No tochno krasivym": "Meduza" publikuyet pis'mo Alekseya Naval'nogo, adresovannoye ego sotrudnikam i soratnikam', Meduza, 13 October 2021, https://meduza.io/feature/2021/10/13/poka-tochno-ne-yasno-kakim-zverem-my-stanem-no-tochno-krasivym

30. Davidzon, 'The IT Whiz in Charge of Bringing Down Putin'.

31. Sobol ended her campaign on 14 June 2021 after Navalny's organisations had been labelled extremist. Natal'ya Anisimova, 'Sobol' prekratila svoyu vybornuyu kampaniyu v Gosdumu', *RBK*, 14 June 2021, https://www.rbc.ru/politics/14/06/2021/60c762729a7947bacf5ae108

32. We discuss these and other details in Jan Matti Dollbaum, Morvan Lallouet, and Ben Noble, 'Alexei Navalny, "Smart Voting," and the 2021 Russian State Duma Elections', *Russian Analytical Digest*, no. 271, 4 October 2021, https://css.ethz.ch/content/dam/ethz/special-interest/gess/cis/center-for-securities-studies/pdfs/RAD271.pdf

33. 'Smart Voting', Levada Center, 12 October 2021, https://www.levada.ru/en/2021/10/12/smart-voting/

34. Felix Light, 'Russian Opposition Calls Foul After Ruling Party Landslide in Parliamentary Elections', *The Moscow Times*, 20 September 2021, https://www.themoscowtimes.com/2021/09/20/russian-opposition-calls-foul-after-ruling-party-landslide-in-parliamentary-elections-a75089

35. Andrey Zayakin, 'DEG protiv UG: Chto my ponyali pro elektronnoye golosovaniye v Rossii?', Fond Liberal'naya Missiya, 18 November 2021, https://liberal.ru/lm-ekspertiza/deg-protiv-ug-chto-my-ponyali-pro-elektronnoe-golosovanie-v-rossii

36. Leonid Volkov, 'Itogi Umnogo golosovaniya 2021 goda', Alexei Navalny

(YouTube channel), 23 September 2021, https://youtu.be/TPBfQH ISF9I

37. Alexei Navalny, Instagram post, 21 September 2021, https://www.instagram.com/p/CUFWtmZIMwP/

38. '"Poka tochno ne yasno, kakim zverem my stanem. No tochno krasivym"'.

39. Ben Noble and Nikolai Petrov, 'Russia elections may tighten Putin's grip on repression', Chatham House, 22 September 2021, https://www.chathamhouse.org/2021/09/russia-elections-may-tighten-putins-grip-repression

40. Sergei Guriev and Daniel Treisman, 'Informational Autocrats', *Journal of Economic Perspectives* 33, no. 4 (2019): 100–127.

41. Jan Matti Dollbaum, Morvan Lallouet, and Ben Noble, 'Alexei Navalny was poisoned one year ago. His fate tells us a lot about Putin's Russia', *The Washington Post*, 20 August 2021, https://www.washingtonpost.com/politics/2021/08/20/alexei-navalny-was-poisoned-one-year-ago-his-fate-tells-us-lot-about-putins-russia/

42. The website can be accessed at: https://www.gofundme.com/f/navalny-team

43. Ibid.

44. The channel can be accessed at: https://www.youtube.com/c/Популярнаяполитика

45. The website can be accessed at: https://www.gofundme.com/f/navalny-team

46. 'Sekret Shekherezady. Novaya yakhta Putina za 75 000 000 000 rubley', Navalny.com (blog), 21 March 2022, https://navalny.com/p/6620/

47. 'Dirizhyor putinskoy voyny', Navalny.com (blog), 12 April 2022, https://navalny.com/p/6621/

48. Catie Edmondson, 'Navalny's anti-corruption group urges Congress to place sanctions on 6,000 of Putin's midlevel cronies', *The New York Times*, 19 May 2022, https://www.nytimes.com/2022/05/19/world/putin-sanctions-aleksei-navalny.html. The list can be accessed at: https://acf.international/list-of-war-enablers

49. Interview with Sergei Guriev, 16 May 2022.

50. Ibid.

51. Ibid.

52. This section draws on interviews with associates of Navalny from Yekaterinburg in 2017 and in March 2022.

53. Evgeniya Kuznetsova and Elizaveta Lamova, 'Chto stalo s set'yu shtabov Naval'nogo posle priznaniya eye ekstremistskoy', *RBK*, 4 August 2021, https://www.rbc.ru/politics/04/08/2021/610414469a7947923d3 89e99

54. 'Navalny Associate Flees Russia Fearing Arrest', RFE/RL Russian Service, 24 November 2021, https://www.rferl.org/a/navalny-associ-ate-fatyanova-flees-russia/31576638.html; 'Another Navalny Associate Flees Russia, Fearing Arrest', Current Time, 26 November 2021, https://www.rferl.org/a/sergei-boiko-navalny-headquarters/31579861. html

55. Marianna Antonova, 'Soratnitsa Naval'nogo Liliya Chanysheva iz SIZO: "Moya sovest' chista"', Deutsche Welle, 11 February 2022, https:// www.dw.com/ru/soratnica-navalnogo-lilija-chanysheva-iz-sizo-moja-sovest-chista/a-60734412

56. Guy Faulconbridge, 'Russia fights back in information war with jail warning', Reuters, 4 March 2022, https://www.reuters.com/world/ europe/russia-introduce-jail-terms-spreading-fake-information-about-army-2022-03-04/

57. 'My priostanavlivayem rabotu: Zayavleniye redaktsii "Novoy gazety"', *Novaya Gazeta*, 28 March 2022, https://novayagazeta.ru/articles/ 2022/03/28/my-priostanavlivaem-rabotu

58. 'Rossiya—eto ne Putin. Ob"yavlyayem aktsiyu grazhdanskogo nepo-vinoveniya', Alexei Navalny (YouTube channel), 28 February 2022, https://www.youtube.com/watch?v=9tGB3v5ZntY

59. 'Activist Who Called For Protests Against War In Ukraine Detained In Moscow', RFE/RL Russian Service, 24 February 2022, https:// www.rferl.org/a/russia-activist-litvinovich-detained-ukraine/31720961. html

60. 'Russian Protests against the War with Ukraine. A Chronicle of Events', OVD-Info, 2 March 2022 (updated subsequently), https://ovd.news/ news/2022/03/02/russian-protests-against-war-ukraine-chronicle-events

61. Olexandra Vladimirova, 'Closed Shops, Zs, Green Ribbons: Russia's Post-Invasion Reality', *The Moscow Times*, 14 April 2022 (updated 1 July 2022), https://www.themoscowtimes.com/2022/04/14/closed-shops-zs-green-ribbons-russias-post-invasion-reality-a77344

62. The group refrained from posting pictures of the events on their Telegram channel—see Vesna, Telegram post, 2 April 2022, https://t.me/vesna_democrat/1364

63. Polling on—and during—the war should, however, be interpreted with extreme caution, including because of the distorting effect of 'social desirability' bias. Margarita Zavadskaya, 'On the harmfulness of Russian polls', Riddle, 4 May 2022, https://ridl.io/on-the-harmfulness-of-russian-polls/

64. OVD-Info LIVE, Telegram post, 12 March 2022, https://t.me/ovdinfolive/6037

65. 'Zaderzhaniye za belyy list bumagi', Ekho Kavkaza, 14 March 2022, https://www.ekhokavkaza.com/a/31752392.html

66. 'V Ivanovo na mestnogo zhitelya sostavili protokol za aktsiyu s romanom "1984"', News.ru, 14 April 2022, https://news.ru/society/bolshoj-brat-bdit-na-ivanovca-sostavili-protokol-za-akciyu-s-romanom-1984/

67. '"Antivoyennoye delo": gid OVD-Info', OVD-Info, 5 March 2022 (updated subsequently), https://ovd.news/news/2022/03/05/antivoennoe-delo-gid-ovd-info

68. See, for instance, the photos posted in the Telegram channel of the opposition group Vesna. The channel can be accessed at: https://t.me/vesna_democrat

69. Farida Rustamova, '"They're carefully enunciating the word clusterf*ck"', Faridaily (blog), 6 March 2022, https://faridaily.substack.com/p/theyre-carefully-enunciating-the

70. Andrey Pertsev, 'Vlasti ne ozhidali takikh zhestkikh sanktsiy—i teper' ne znayut, chto delat'. No uvol'nyat'sya chinovniki boyatsya: "Eto priravnivayetsya k begstvu, a za begstvo—rasstrelivayut"', Meduza, 9 March 2022, https://meduza.io/feature/2022/03/09/vlasti-ne-ozhidali-takikh-zhestkih-sanktsiy-i-teper-ne-znayut-chto-delat-no-uvolnyatsya-chinovniki-boyatsya-eto-priravnivaetsya-k-begstvu-a-za-begstvo-rasstrelivayut

71. Farida Rustamova, '"Now we're going to f*ck them all." What's happening in Russia's elites after a month of war', Faridaily (blog), 31 March 2022, https://faridaily.substack.com/p/now-were-going-to-fck-them-all-whats

72. Andrey Pertsev, '"Dovol'nykh pochti net": Kak utverzhdayut istochniki "Meduzy", za tri mesyatsa Putin nastroil protiv sebya i "partiyu voyny", i tekh, kto khochet mira. V Kremle nadeyutsya, chto "v oborimoy perspektive" on uydet,—i vybirayut preyemnika', Meduza, 24 May 2022, https://meduza.io/feature/2022/05/24/dovolnyh-pochti-net

73. Ben Noble, 'Rumours of a coup in Russia: What does this really say about the Putin regime?', Riddle, 17 May 2022, https://ridl.io/en/rumours-of-a-coup-in-russia-what-does-this-really-say-about-the-putin-regime/

74. Yevgeniy Stupin, Telegram post, 8 April 2022, https://t.me/evstupin/2899

75. Anton Kass, '"Razorvat' pupovinu s naval'nyatinoy": v KPRF ob"yavili spetsoperatsiyu—Zamestitel' Gennadiya Zyuganova potreboval isklyuchit' iz kompartii protivnikov deystviy VS RF na Ukraine', News.ru, 1 June 2022, https://news.ru/society/razorvat-pupovinu-s-navalnyatinoj-v-kprf-nazrela-specoperaciya/

76. Artem Ryabov and Andrey Prakh, 'Molodost' rezko ushla', *Kommersant*, 5 May 2022, https://www.kommersant.ru/doc/5340225

77. Kass, '"Razorvat' pupovinu s naval'nyatinoy"'.

78. 'Nazad v 1990-e. V TsB predskazali Rossii degradatsiyu', *The Moscow Times*, 22 April 2022, https://www.moscowtimes.ru/2022/04/22/nazad-v-1990e-v-tsb-predskazali-rossii-degradatsiyu-a19795

79. 'Prokuratura proveryayet zabastovku v Nizhnekamske', inkazan.ru, 5 March 2022, https://inkazan.ru/news/society/05-03-2022/prokuratura-proveryaet-zabastovku-v-nizhnekamske; Viktoriya Polyakova and Yekaterina Yasakova, 'Delivery Club oproverg zabastovku kur'yerov v Moskve iz-za snizheniya oplaty', *RBK*, 26 April 2022, https://www.rbc.ru/business/26/04/2022/626807c69a79471d795357d3

80. Shuster, 'Exclusive: Alexei Navalny Urges Biden to Stand Up to Putin'.

81. Alexei Navalny, Instagram post, 15 June 2022, https://www.instagram.com/p/Ce1EzKUtZvq/

82. Kira Yarmysh, Twitter post, 14 June 2022, https://twitter.com/Kira_Yarmysh/status/1536668006671073282

83. Mary Ilyushina, 'Navalny reportedly moved to high-security prison infamous for abuse', *The Washington Post*, 14 June 2022, https://www.washingtonpost.com/world/2022/06/14/navalny-russia-prison-melekhovo/; '"Pytochnyy konveyyer". Chto izvestno o kolonii IK-6, kuda otpravili Naval'nogo', RTVI, 14 June 2022, https://rtvi.com/news/pytochnyj-konvejer-chto-izvestno-o-kolonii-ik-6-kuda-otpravili-naval-nogo/

84. Alexei Navalny, Twitter post, 23 June 2022, https://twitter.com/navalny/status/1539884559248105472

85. Alexei Navalny, Twitter post, 1 July 2022, https://twitter.com/navalny/status/1542781100413620225

86. Ibid.

87. 'Russia's Navalny says he faces new criminal case, up to 15 more years in jail', Reuters, 31 May 2022, https://www.reuters.com/world/europe/jailed-kremlin-critic-navalny-says-new-criminal-case-opened-against-him-2022-05-31/

INDEX

INDEX

INDEX

INDEX

INDEX

INDEX

INDEX

INDEX

INDEX

INDEX

INDEX

INDEX